Beyond Christian Folk Religion

Beyond Christian Folk Religion

Re-grafting Into Our Roots (Romans 11:17–23)

EDWARD A. BECKSTROM

RESOURCE *Publications* • Eugene, Oregon

BEYOND CHRISTIAN FOLK RELIGION
Re-grafting into Our Roots (Romans 11:17–23)

Copyright © 2013 Edward A. Beckstrom. All rights reserved. Except for brief quotations in critical publications or reviews, no part of this book may be reproduced in any manner without prior written permission from the publisher. Write: Permissions. Wipf and Stock Publishers, 199 W. 8th Ave., Suite 3, Eugene, OR 97401.

All biblical quotations are taken from the New Revised Standard Version, copyright © 1989, Division of Christian Education of the National Council of Churches of Christ in the United States of America. Quotations from the Hebrew Scriptures are quoted exactly with the exception that the name of God, "Yahweh," has replaced the original "LORD" in the verses where it appears.

Resource Publications
An Imprint of Wipf and Stock Publishers
199 W. 8th Ave., Suite 3
Eugene, OR 97401

www.wipfandstock.com

ISBN 13: 978-1-62032-884-2

To all those who have become my biblical mentors and inspiration over the years, from my seminary professors, United States Air Force Chaplains who supervised over or served with me, and to the many scholars in the last forty years whose research, scholarship, and writing have inspired me and sent me in further quests of biblical understanding and Christianity's roots (Rom. 11:17–23).

CONTENTS

Abbreviations | ix
Introduction—Inquiring Minds | xi

Part One Christian Folk Religion: What is it, do I have it, and what's next?
  1 Christian Folk Religion | 3
  2 The Hellenization of the Christian Church | 31
  3 Yahweh, God of Israel | 51

Part Two Moving Beyond Christian Folk Religion
  4 The Baptizer | 81
  5 The Son of Man | 97
  6 The Kingdom | 119
  7 A New Reality, New Rules | 139
  8 Opponents of Jesus | 160
  9 Quiet Piety | 185
  10 Power and Glory | 206
  11 A Few Parting Observations | 225

Bibliography | 237
Ancient Document Index | 241
Subject Index | 251

ABBREVIATIONS

AD	Anno Domini, "The Year of Our Lord"
a.k.a.	Also known as
Apoc	*Apocrypha*
BAR	*Biblical Archaeology Review*
BAS	*Biblical Archaeology Society*
BC	Before Christ
BTB	*Biblical Theology Bulletin*
ca.	Circa, "about"
CD	*Cairo Damascus Document*
DJD	*Discoveries in the Judean Desert*
DSS	*Dead Sea Scrolls*
DSSE	*The Complete Dead Sea Scrolls in English*
EB	*Encyclopaedia Britannica*
EDB	*Eerdmans Dictionary of the Bible*
EDEJ	*The Eerdmans Dictionary of Early Judaism*
Gr.	Greek
HB	*Hebrew Bible*
Heb.	Hebrew
HS	*Hebrew Scriptures*
JW	*Jewish War*
KJV	*King James Version*
NRSV	*New Revised Standard Version*

NT	*New Testament*
NTS	*New Testament Studies*
OT	*Old Testament*
SBL	*Society of Biblical Literature*
TB	*Tyndale Bulletin*
V.	Verse
Vv.	Verses

Introduction

Inquiring Minds

I RECENTLY SAW A sign in front of an automobile repair shop that caught my attention. The sign read, "Do you think of God as your steering wheel or as your spare tire?" Yes, it's clever, but there's a lot of meat in that question and it gave me some pause for thought. Does God indeed steer your path through life, or is he an accessary you can use only when you need him? I fear that most of us fall into the second category. He's useful to have around in an emergency, and then our cry can be, "Why did this have to happen to me?" Unfortunately, for even many regular church goers, Sunday morning is good time to remember the spiritual side of life, but we're all too happy to end the weekend and get back to the routine of life. Life must go on. And we busy ourselves with all the activities that involve us. The Sunday routine is our cushion we lean on when we need him.

I'm not exactly sure when, as a boy, I went beyond that stage, but I believe it occurred sometime in my early twenties. And so this book began to be written more than fifty years ago, although not one word was put on paper until the spring of 2012. It began because of a myriad of questions which flooded my mind so many years ago: questions my parents couldn't answer; questions my pastors, college professors, and seminary professors couldn't, or wouldn't answer. I began searching for answers in academic books, Biblical dictionaries, commentaries, and religious articles in magazines and scholarly journals. And the questions were not even raised, much less answered, at least not that I could find.

Inquiring Minds

I didn't think my questions were off the wall, or unique, either. I couldn't imagine others were not asking the same questions. For me it seemed as though there was a disconnect between the Old and New Testaments. The stories of the Old Testament never seemed to connect with the stories of the New Testament. The Old Testament simply ended, with no clear conclusion. I was told the last of the prophets was Ezra, who was from the fifth century BC, then there was a gap of about four hundred years, and the New Testament began with the birth of Jesus. The story of Israel was left hanging, and a totally different story began. I was sure that I was not alone sensing that. Just a few years ago I was teaching an adult Sunday school class when one of my students was a man who was never afraid to ask questions many other people think but wouldn't dare ask. He was a devout member of the congregation to which my wife and I belong, and he was an avid volunteer in all aspects of the congregation's life and ministry. In one class he asked, "Why does the God of the Old Testament always seem angry, vindictive, and mean, while the God of the New Testament is said to be a God of love?" Exactly—that's a common perception. In fact it's a question I asked myself repeatedly over the years. Recently I heard a modern Christian song with this line in it, "Jesus saves us from the Father's wrath." No, my adult Sunday school student was far from alone in his question and it again raised the similar question that had troubled me most of my life.

At seemingly every checkout counter in supermarkets across the United States there are racks of pulp tabloids which hawk supposed scandals of whomever the celebrities are who are in the current news, or are the hot topics of the day. The motto of one of the best known of these rags is "Inquiring minds want to know." Although I have never read any of these scandal sheets, I would probably classify myself as being an inquiring mind. All my life I have sought answers to whatever question should come to mind, no matter how trivial, complex, mundane, or difficult. Over the years my inquiring nature has served me well, but at times it has proven frustrating. The questions concerning the apparent disconnect between the Old and New Testaments became a major concern of mine in the early 1960s when I was attending Pacific Lutheran Theological Seminary in Berkeley, California. Though I had asked several seminary professors about it, I received no satisfactory answers. Then one day, in looking at books in the seminary bookstore, one book caught my attention. It was a book entitled *Paul: The Theology of the Apostle in the Light of Jewish Religious History* by the German scholar H. J. Schoeps. In this early work,

Inquiring Minds

first published in German in 1959, with its English version published in 1961, Schoeps seemed to me to be the first to address this very issue. In it, Schoeps challenges the Apostle Paul on his understanding of Judaism. This, even though Paul in Philippians 3:5–6 claims that he is, through and through, Hebrew and of the faith of Judaism: he says that he "was circumcised on the eighth day, a member of the people of Israel, of the tribe of Benjamin, a Hebrew born of Hebrews; as to the law, a Pharisee; as to zeal, a persecutor of the church; as to righteousness under the law, blameless." Despite Paul's claim, Schoeps charges that Paul has a tendency to ethicize Judaism, to understand it "as a moral law, disconnected and isolated from the controlling reality of the covenant." Schoeps goes on to say that "the Old Testament idea of Torah is best explained as instruction embracing both law and doctrine." The problem according to Schoeps, is that in the Septuagint (LXX), a Greek translation of the Hebrew text, the Hebrew word Torah is replaced with the Greek word *nomos* which simply means, "Law", and omits the teaching of doctrine. According to Schoeps, this results in a shift of emphasis toward legalism. And the Torah then implies a moral way of life *prescribed* by God[1] rather than one that is pleasing to God. This change in usage was not original with Paul, as Schoeps readily admits, but it began when the Hebrew Scriptures were translated into Greek in the third century BC in Alexandria, Egypt as the version known as the Septuagint (or LXX), so named for the seventy-two scholars who did the translation. In that edition Torah (law and doctrine) was replaced with *nomos* (Law). The Greek translation of the Old Testament is addressed by Schoeps as the Hellenizing of Judaism. He thus concludes "that the source of many Pauline misunderstandings with regard to the evaluation of the law and covenant is to be sought in the legalistic distortion of the perspective for which Hellenistic Judaism was responsible."[2]

At last there was a source which approached one of my main questions, yet it was one lone voice, as far as I knew. I wondered why. It also raised in my mind the issue of the conflict between Paul and the Jerusalem Church which is reflected in several of Paul's letters, particularly Galatians and 1 Corinthians (Gal 2:3, 12; 6:12–13; 1 Cor 7:18; cf. Acts 15:24). According to Galatians there was a faction from the Jerusalem Church who was visiting Paul's churches telling the Gentiles that they must become Jews and

---

1. Schoeps, *Paul*, 29.
2. Ibid.

be circumcised before they can become followers of Jesus. Galatians was written primarily to refute this undermining of his authority and teaching:

> I am astonished that you are so quickly deserting the one who called you in the grace of Christ and are turning to a different gospel– not that there is another gospel, but there are some who are confusing you and want to pervert the gospel of Christ. But even if we or an angel from heaven should proclaim to you a gospel contrary to what we proclaimed to you, let that one be accursed! As we have said before, so now I repeat, if anyone proclaims to you a gospel contrary to what you received, let that one be accursed! (Gal 1:6–9)

When one question flares up it seems to call into question many other issues. After all "inquiring minds want to know." Over the years many of the other questions coming to my mind were also either never addressed at all, or were answered in ways that made little or no sense to me. I wondered why so many of Jesus' parables seemed to be in the form of riddles such as the parable of the "dishonest manager" in Luke 16:1–9 where Jesus says that

> the master commended the dishonest manager because he had acted shrewdly; for the children of this age are more shrewd in dealing with their own generation than are the children of light. And I tell you, make friends for yourselves by means of dishonest wealth so that when it is gone, they may welcome you into the eternal homes. (Vv. 8–9)

Though Jesus explains the parable in verses 10–13 its explanation is convoluted by logic contrary to the way most of us think. I wondered why—inquiring minds . . .

I wondered why, in the parable of the rich man and the beggar Lazarus in Luke 16:19–31, which follows on the heels of the parable of the dishonest manager, the rich man simply "died and was buried" and then confined to Hades, while the beggar, who also died, "was carried away by the angels to be with Abraham." The rich man's only sin seems to be that he was rich: "dressed in purple and fine linen and who feasted sumptuously every day," and the beggar's primary virtue lay in the fact that he was poor, "covered with sores, who longed to satisfy his hunger with what fell from the rich man's table." And this theme fits well with Luke's version of the Beatitudes:

> Blessed are you who are poor,
> for yours is the kingdom of God.

Inquiring Minds

> Blessed are you who are hungry now,
> for you will be filled.
> Blessed are you who weep now,
> for you will laugh.
> Blessed are you when people hate you, and when they exclude you, revile you, and defame you on account of the Son of Man. Rejoice in that day and leap for joy, for surely your reward is great in heaven; for that is what their ancestors did to the prophets.
> But woe to you who are rich,
> for you have received your consolation.
> Woe to you who are full now,
> for you will be hungry.
> Woe to you who are laughing now,
> for you will mourn and weep.
> Woe to you when all speak well of you, for that is what their ancestors did to the false prophets. (Luke 6:20–26)

It seems that the only people who receive God's blessings are the miserable, the mistreated and the abused, while the affluent, the happy and the popular are accursed and apparently doomed. Thus it is better to be miserable than it is to be happy and contented. Why? Inquiring minds . . .

There are so many difficult sayings of Jesus often simply ignored by Christians, while there is a plethora of passages loved and repeated over and over again. Perhaps the most quoted is John 3:16, of course. Who hasn't seen a sporting event when someone in the stands holds up a large banner simply citing the scripture verse? How many times have you heard repeated Jesus' saying, "I am the way, the truth and the life. No one comes to the Father except through me" (John 14:6)? Or this familiar passage, "I am the resurrection and the life. Those who believe in me, even though they die, will live, and everyone who lives and believes in me will never die" (John 11:25, 26)? These and similar passages are beloved by Christians everywhere, and are comforting words. But what about the difficult words of John the Baptizer who called the most religious and the most righteous of Israel a "brood of vipers" and then asked them, "Who warned you to flee from the wrath to come?" (Matt 3:7), and the same words flowed from Jesus when again he spoke to the religious and righteous, "You brood of vipers! How can you speak of good things, when you are evil?" (Matt 12:34). Or again when Jesus pronounced woes against the religious standard bearers of the day, the scribes and the Pharisees, who "sit on Moses' seat," yet who "tie up heavy burdens, hard to bear, and lay them on the shoulders of others; but they themselves are unwilling to lift a finger to move them"

(Matt 23:2–4). He then went into more scorn when he told them "you lock people out of the kingdom of heaven" (Matt 23:13), and called them "blind guides", and "blind fools" (vv. 16–17), and "hypocrites" (vv. 13, 23, 25, 29). Christians will often say (or think) he is talking to them (the ancient scribes and Pharisees), not necessarily to us. We're not the ones who tie up heavy burdens, or who "lock people out of the kingdom of heaven." After all, we call people into the kingdom of heaven. "Believe in Jesus and you will be saved," we say, or we ask them, "Do you take Jesus as your personal savior?" We're not blind guides, or hypocrites. He was only talking about them. In a matter of minutes we have swept away a sizeable portion of Jesus' ministry and teaching, and dismissed it as being irrelevant to us. What has brought us to such a state? Inquiring minds . . .

I think a part of the answer is the word "comfort." We want words of comfort. It is also what we think the gospels are all about: "the good news of Jesus Christ, the Son of God" (Mark 1:1). We mistake that as meaning we can omit the bad news when it sounds like that to us, and assume it is aimed at other people. We filter out the uncomfortable from the comfortable until we arrive at "the peace of God which surpasses all understanding" (Phil 4:7). And that's "good news." I have often found the most profound teachings of Jesus precisely in some of his hardest sayings and have challenged Christians to take these sayings to heart, and I have occasionally been accused of not preaching "good news." If that's true, then how could Mark have said of his gospel that it is "the good news of Jesus Christ, the Son of God?" The hard sayings of Jesus also appear in Mark: "If any want to become my followers, let them deny themselves and take up their cross and follow me" (8:34). Speaking to the religious and righteous, Jesus said, "Isaiah prophesied rightly about you hypocrites, as it is written,

> This person's honors me with their lips,
> but their hearts are far from me;
> in vain do they worship me,
> teaching human precepts as doctrines." (Mark 7:6 –7)

The "good news" of Jesus Christ is the entirety of all the gospels, the letters, the history of Acts, and the apocalypse of Revelation. This is the whole message of the New Testament scriptures. Yet many of us would like to pick and choose "this bit" and "that bit" and omit or ignore the rest. In 1965 Canadian columnist Pierre Berton addressed this very issue in his little book *The Comfortable Pew: A Critical Look at Christianity and the Religious Establishment in the New Age*. At one time he was actively part of a mainline church, from which he voluntarily withdrew, because he was dismayed at the practice of "churchianity" as he saw it. Because of his reputation as an author and commentator (he was the dean of Canadian columnists for most of his life), the Anglican Church in Canada asked him to write an article that would outline his reasons. His reasons went far beyond article status and ended up in this book. In it he carefully describes the comfort level people feel in the pew, and he saw that as direct opposition to some of the primary messages of Jesus, such as the admonition that each person who wants to become a follower of his must "deny themselves and take up their cross and follow me" (Matt 16:24; Mark 8:34; Luke 9:23). This is uncomfortable advice to set before a congregation who only wants to hear of "the peace of God which surpasses all understanding" (Phil 4:7) or that "the one who believes and is baptized will be saved" (Mark 16:16). Denying ourself, and picking up a cross are hard pills to swallow, and in application are certainly uncomfortable.

All of these questions, and still more, were constant companions of mine even through an active career as a minister, including a life's calling as a United States Air Force Chaplain, where I learned that I was not alone seeking answers to these questions. They were often on the lips of congregants of many of the denominations I served in the military setting.

It proved the truth of a saying a group of us jokingly coined toward the end of our seminary training, "Seminary gave us all the answers to the questions people never ask." But then, where were the answers to be found? Is it in my personal talks with seminary professors? They didn't seem to have the answers I was asking. During my fourth and final year of seminary studies I wrote the rough draft of an unassigned thesis I wanted to explore on my own. It raised the primary question which plagued me the most, what led to the conflict between Paul and some members of the Jerusalem Church? And particularly, why did the Jerusalem Church and its primarily Jewish voice become silent and end up lost to the Gentile Christian church? My rough draft was called *The Judaizers: Paul's Nemesis*. It was about 80 pages long, typed single spaced, with virtually no margins, and in a typewriter's elite type, its smallest type, which is about an eight-point font. I raised my question in the paper and gave it to Dr. Eric Wahlstrom, my New Testament professor, and a renowned Lutheran scholar, and asked him if he would read it. He agreed, read it, liked it, and said it raised some very important and poignant questions, but he had no answers. He simply did not know! Yet, inquiring minds . . .

Inquiring Minds

After I retired from active ministry in 1996 I had more time to bring myself up to date on the advancement of biblical studies since my academic years. I began to do this in the late 1990s. Rather quickly I discovered that in the early 1970s several scholars had begun to pursue the very questions I had raised in seminary twenty years earlier. The studies began in 1973 with the book *Jesus the Jew: A Historian's Reading of the Gospels*, by Geza Vermes. It sent shock waves through the biblical academic communities when it first appeared because for the first time scholars had to rethink the Judaism of Jesus, and consequently the Judaism of the first century in general. It was so popular reprints were issued in 1983, 1994, and 2001. He also expanded his first volume with two later books on the same subject: The *Religion of Jesus the Jew*, in 1993, and *Jesus in His Jewish Context* in 2003. Just four years after Jesus the Jew was published, E.P Sander's groundbreaking study of first century Judaism appeared in 1977: *Paul and Palestinian Judaism: A Comparison of Patterns of Religion*. What is so unique about his study is that he was the first Christian scholar who went deeply into the study of first century Judaism using almost entirely original Jewish rabbinic literature including the *Mishnah*, the *Tosefta*, the *Mekilta*, the *Mekilta of Rabbi Simeon ben Yohai*, the *Sifra, Sifre Numbers, Sifre Zuta, Sifre Deuteronomy, Midrash Tannaim, Babylonian Talmud, Palestinian Talmud, Midrash Rabbah, Tanhuma, Aboth D Rabbi Nathan*, and several other *Midrashim*. These are all listed here just to show how extensive his research had been. Such a thorough study had never been done by Christian scholars. While some scholars have questioned Sanders' methodology, his main theses have never been seriously challenged. While a detailed explanation of his findings is beyond the scope of this book (his study is 627 pages long), it is important to understand that it sheds new light on the religion of Jesus' faith, and has caused scholars to reexamine the writings of Paul and question the common interpretations of his letters. Paul was a self-proclaimed Pharisee and presumably well versed in the Judaism of his day, yet many Pauline scholars in the past have interpreted him in such a way that it gives the impression that Paul's understanding of his own Jewish faith is a distortion of the Judaism of his own day. For instance, the common view in many books on Paul, and also among ministers who preach and teach about Paul in their churches, is that Paul taught in his letters that Christ frees them from the legalistic demands of the Jewish law. An impression often given is that Judaism, as a legalistic system, was based on a merit system, which then opened the way to salvation. The common misconception Christians have is that the more of the individual law requirements—there are 613—that a person kept, the better standing that person had with God. If a person's merits were more than their demerits, they would be saved. But if the demerits outnumbered the merits they would not be saved. Sanders response to this is that

> Although the Rabbis emphasize that the commandments carry rewards (or punishment for non-fulfillment), they also warn against fulfilling the commandments in order to earn payment. Rather, one should perform the required commandments without ulterior motive and because they are in themselves good ('for their own sake') or from love of God ('for the sake of Heaven').[3]

A couple of pages later Sanders takes the thought a little farther:

> Although the Rabbis believed that God, being just and faithful, rewarded man for service and punished him for transgression, they did not think that one should serve God either from desire to gain a reward or from fear of punishment, but only from love of God.[4]

Often the misconceptions among Christian scholars have been brought on by not understanding the concept of a covenantal relation with God, which is central to an understanding of Israel's faith. Summarizing this relationship, Sanders explains:

> God has chosen Israel and Israel has accepted the election. In his role as King, God gave Israel commandments which they are to obey as best they can. Obedience is rewarded and disobedience punished. In case of failure to obey, however, man has recourse to divinely ordained means of atonement, in all of which repentance is required. As long as he maintains his desire to stay in the covenant, he has a share in God's covenantal promises, including life in the world to come. The intention and effort to be obedient constitute the condition for remaining in the covenant, but they do not earn it.[5]

He then goes on to say that

---

3. Sanders, *Paul and Palestinian Judaism*, 120.
4. Ibid., 122.
5. Ibid., 180.

> Their legalism falls within a larger context of gracious election and assured salvation. In discussing disobedience and obedience, punishment and reward, they were not dealing with how man is saved, but with how man should act and how God will act within the framework of the covenant. Within that framework, they were determined to understand and obey God's commands as best they could, but they did not think that they earned their place in the covenant by the number of mitsvot [commandments] fulfilled. Nor did they think that the transgression of more commandments than were fulfilled would damn them.[6]

A decidedly important concept in Jewish faith that must be understood by Christians as it is directly opposed to common Christian belief, is that salvation is not an individual achievement, but is corporate and collective. However, a careful examination will show that it is also a central teaching of the New Testament (i.e., Rom 11:26). Relying on the studies of G.F. Moore in the first volume of Moore's three volume series *Judaism in the First Three Centuries of the Christian Era: The Age of the Tannaim* (1927– 3), Sanders goes on to say,

> Religion as a personal relation between God and man he held to be the primary characteristic of Rabbinic Judaism, and he considered that herein lays its most significant advance beyond the older religion of Israel. Moore recognized, to be sure, that the personal relationship with God was maintained in the fellowship of the religious community . . . But even more than the fact that the Rabbis could speak of both collective and individual reward and punishment, the pattern of religion which we have been discussing demonstrates how individual and collective religion were combined. We note that the individual's place in God's plan was accomplished by his being a member of the group. Thus we find virtually no individual quest for salvation in Rabbinic literature. The question is whether or not one is an Israelite in good standing. On the other hand, simple heredity did not ensure salvation. That came to all those Israelites who were faithful.[7]

To sum up, Sanders' study of the Judaism of Jesus' day, rather than being a legalistic religion of merits and demerits based on harsh laws which bound Jews to a life of slavery to the laws under the close scrutiny of a wrathful God, they understood God in the same way Paul taught his

6. Ibid., 181.
7. Ibid., 237–38.

congregations, that God is loving, merciful, kind, forgiving, and by his choosing Israel to be his people he also poured out his grace upon them as a collective people. The primary requirements he made of them, are the same requirements Paul taught his churches, faithfulness, love, repentance. Following the success of his major study, linking it to a new perspective in understanding Paul, Sanders followed it with *Jesus and Judaism* in 1985 which won him the 1990 Louisville Grawemayer Award in Religion.

Following Sanders, many other scholars began to study similar themes, i.e., Ben F. Meyer's *The Aims of Jesus*, first published in 1979, and then reprinted with an Introduction by N.T. Wright, in 2002. But among the most thorough studies in the last twenty years is the massive three volume series by Wright himself. As an Anglican scholar, N.T. Wright, published his three volume series under the general title *Christian Origins and the Question of God*: Vol. 1, *The New Testament and the People of God* in 1993; Vol. 2, *Jesus and the Victory of God*, in 1996; and Vol. 3, *The Resurrection of the Son of God*, in 2003.

It is to these scholars particularly, and also to many more listed in the bibliography, that I extend my deepest gratitude for helping me in my quest which has dogged me throughout most of my life. It has also taught me that this quest has enriched my life because God is my steering wheel, and not just my spare tire, and thus I have been kept on the right road because inquiring minds want to know.

When I was a little boy and would ask my dear mother questions about God, or about Jesus, or about religion in general, if she did not know the answer she would tell me, "Eddie, there are just some things we must accept on faith." While that's true to some extent, there are answers available to many of our questions. Yes, faith plays a major role in my life, but so does revelation. My faith tells me that through the centuries God has been busy over those centuries revealing his majesty and loving kindness to us as we are able to understand it. How that revelation takes place is determined within each and every one of us. It is often determined by how open or closed our minds are to new insight, or whether we're content to just hear that "old time religion" from the pulpit, or in the bible study class over and over again, or perhaps in an inspirational book that reaches our preset comfort level. I, for one, am uncomfortable at any preset level. I want to grow and develop, and as a minister I feel obliged to expand that comfort level so I can help others expand theirs as well. We would not seek out a medical doctor to be our physician who practices medicine as it was known fifty years ago. That would be reckless endangerment to our health. Why should we not turn to ministers and teachers who are up-to-date on the latest in biblical studies and theology? Today I rejoice that I have not lived by that answer my mother gave me to just accept things on faith, I simply have to know. Apparently there are others who have had to know as well; hopefully you're one of them.

PART ONE

Christian Folk Religion
What is it, do I have it, and what's next?

1

Christian Folk Religion

THERE IS A LAND to which we cannot travel. There is also a culture we cannot visit, and a language very few people in the world can read or understand. If we were able to travel to this land or visit this culture we would be completely out of our element. It is a land where its people are almost entirely illiterate. It is estimated that probably no more than 1% of its citizens can read or write and only a small portion of its inhabitants control almost all of its wealth and power. The bulk of its citizens are poor, or invalids, who slave on the property owned by the elite of society, yet live in squalor and on the edge of starvation. The land is dotted with small villages, many of which have populations of 150–200 people. The rulers of this land, who have almost all of its political power, are not citizens of the land, but occupiers, and who occupy it with an iron fist. Their seat of power is located 2983 kilometers (1,850 miles) away, which takes about 25 days journey by sea and land. Very few of its citizens speak the language of the occupiers, and most of the occupiers do not speak the language of the citizens. So the *lingua franca* of commerce and the mildly educated citizens of the land is a third language.

The daily culture of this land is abhorrent to the vast majority of modern western Europeans and Americans. Women and the underclasses have no status in the courts, or even in the religion of the land. Men, women and children with infirmities are excluded from participating in any public or religious activity. Disabled citizens are believed to be disabled because they have reaped the wrath of God, paying for their own sins or the sins of their parents, grandparents, great-grandparents or even great-great-grandparents. They have no rights, no social standing, and cannot even enter the temple to worship. Yet this citizenry has had the longest uninterrupted religious faith in the history of the world. It was into this land that a young man by the name of Yeshua bar Yosep gained some prominence, as he and his followers began to challenge many of the customs of the day, became a champion of the underclasses, and questioned religious assumptions made by the clergy and power brokers. Eventually, at the age of 36, he was arrested, tried and convicted of crimes against the citizenry, the religious establishment, and the foreign occupiers, and executed as a heretic and royal pretender. While reports circulated that his lifeless body had been snatched, as it was missing, his supporters maintained that actually he had been raised from the dead. The bulk of the people, whether citizen or occupier, discounted such nonsense, but the reports continued and though in 40 years the land and country were destroyed by the occupiers, eventually (300 years later) the small band of Yeshua's followers had grown into such a formidable number they overtook the occupiers and became the only legal religion of the western world.

Of course, this little understood land, culture, and environment was the ancient land of Israel as it was in the first century, when Jesus lived. Its citizens were faithful Jews who believed they were the People of God, the God of their ancestors, Abraham, Isaac, and Jacob who lived some 2000 years before. Yeshua bar Yosep was actually the Aramaic name of Jesus. Jesus is a Greek translation of Yeshua. If it had been translated directly into English his name would have been Joshua. He was also called the "son of Joseph" ("bar Yosep" in Aramaic) in Luke 3:23, 4:22; John 1:45; 6:42; cf. Matt 13:55, but he was more commonly known as Jesus of Nazareth, or Jesus the Galilean (the northern region of Israel where Jesus grew up). Thus "Jesus," the English equivalent of the Greek word, *Jesous*, is the name by which he is known throughout the world, although there are a growing number of Jews, who today believe Jesus was truly the Messiah of the Jews, and call him by his Aramaic name, Yeshua. These Jewish believers do not consider themselves Jewish Christians, but rather Messianics, or Messianic Jews. This title identifies them as ethnic Jews who believe Jesus *is* the Jewish Messiah, yet they remain ethnically and religiously Jewish and keep its way of life and worship. They also observe traditional Jewish Festivals (Passover, Yom Kippur, Rosh Hashanah, etc.), and are led by rabbis, rather than pastors. Some of them continue to keep the laws of Torah, but may be selective about certain Torah restrictions, such as eating only kosher foods. Some Messianics are kosher, and some are not. It is just a matter of preference. This, today, is very similar to the faith of the Jerusalem church 2000 years ago. Messianics hold dear the Hebrew Scriptures and study and follow the New Testament as well. Messianic Judaism is a rapidly growing phenomenon throughout the world. It is estimated that today there are approximately 250,000 Messianics in the United States. The Messianics should not be confused with the group "Jews for Jesus," which is a conservative evangelical group of Christian Jews who are intensely evangelistic in their lives and ministry.

It is important in this study that we recognize some distinctions in terminology. Jesus' name is not Jesus Christ. Christ is a title, which, in Greek, *Christos*, means anointed, and is equivalent to the Hebrew word for Messiah, *Mashiyach*. Though in his letters the Apostle Paul commonly calls him Jesus Christ or Christ Jesus, he is properly referring to him as Jesus the Messiah, or the Messiah, Jesus. Paul in his Greek letters calls him by the equivalent Greek terms, *Jesous Christos*, or *Christos Jesous*, but these are translations of the Hebrew terms into Greek. The term Jesus Christ as commonly used today, or Christ, is one of the hallmarks of what I call Christian folk religion. It is religious talk which is comfortable in our own culture, but bears little relationship to the people, the language, the culture, and the faith of the ancients among whom Jesus was the Christ, the anointed Messiah of the Jews, who was promised, expected, prayed for, and hoped for in their sacred scriptures. It was this Messiah through whom Yahweh, the God of their ancestors, established and inaugurated the kingdom of God. It was God's reign "on earth, as it is in heaven" that Jesus taught his disciples to pray for (Matt 5:10 and par.). It is also this Messiah who is called Savior, Lord, the Lamb of God, the Son of God, the Son of Man, and the Good Shepherd.

THE LANGUAGE OF THE BIBLE

The language of the people of Israel was Aramaic which had become the common language of the Near East from the time of the Babylonian exile in the sixth century BC. Although the original language of Israel was Hebrew, Aramaic was spoken in ordinary speech by the common populace, and Hebrew became the language primarily of religion because the Hebrew Scriptures were all composed in Hebrew except for a few

Part One: Christian Folk Religion

chapters in Daniel (2:4b–7:28). Chapters 1:1—2:4a and 8—12 of Daniel are in Hebrew. The Roman occupiers spoke Latin, and the *lingua franca* of the day was Greek, which was introduced by Alexander the Great, King of Macedonia, in the fourth century BC when he conquered the Near East. Thus, there were four languages in usage in Israel in Jesus' day: (1) Aramaic (which Jesus spoke), (2) Hebrew, used in the synagogue, prayer, and in the study of the scriptures. Jesus knew Hebrew as well as Aramaic because he read from the scriptures in synagogues, although whether he interpreted the scriptures in Hebrew in the synagogues, or reverted to Aramaic, is not known. (3) The New Testament was written in Greek because most of the people of the Roman world would understand that language as well as Latin, and perhaps Aramaic or Hebrew. And fourth, of course, there was Latin, the language of the Romans. There is an early report at the end of the first century that the Gospel of Matthew was originally written in Hebrew, but no evidence of this exists, and there is some debate as to whether the report of its original version being in Hebrew really means Hebrew or Aramaic. Both languages are very similar and Aramaic uses the Hebrew alphabet, and the report of Matthew being composed originally in Hebrew was made by a man with a Greek name, Papias, who may not have known the difference between the two languages.

As I have said above, the common language of Jesus, however, was Aramaic. There are a few Aramaic words in the gospels, but only one complete phrase in Aramaic, and that is one of Jesus' most memorable sayings, as he cried it out from the cross: *Eloi, Eloi, lema sabachthani*, a quote from Psalm 22:1, translated "My God, my God, why have you forsaken me?" (Mark 15:34). It is the only complete phrase spoken by Jesus and preserved in his original language. All the other sayings of Jesus are translations into the Greek, which may be more correctly considered paraphrases of what he said, as they were remembered by witnesses to his teaching, preaching, and healing. This may account for some of the differences of the wording many of his sayings have in the various gospels, where parallel sayings are recorded. Our first is a simple example given to illustrate these differences. It occurs in the story of Jesus feeding the multitude in Matt 14:13–21, Mark 6:30–44, Luke 9:10–17, and John 6:1–13. Focusing only on the sayings of Jesus in the story, Matt 14:16–21, reads, "Jesus said to them, 'They need not go away; you give them something to eat.'" Mark 6:37: "But he answered them, 'You give them something to eat.'" Luke 9:13: "But he said to them, 'You give them something to eat.'"

John 6:5: "When he looked up and saw a large crowd coming toward him, Jesus said to Philip, 'Where are we to buy bread for these people to eat?'" Note the close similarities between Matthew, Mark, and Luke, but also note the major change in John's account, which the evangelist explains like this in the following verse: "He said this to test him [Philip], for he himself knew what he was going to do." With conflicts such as this, we are often confronted by ambiguities and riddles, which we will address later in this study, but dealing with it now would be premature. Perhaps we should focus on one of the major turning points in Jesus' ministry, when he asks his disciples a pivotal question. The question is asked almost midway in each of the synoptic gospels, Matthew 16:13–20; Mark 8:27–33; and Luke 9:18–22. At Caesarea Philippi, in northern Palestine, Jesus inquires of his disciples: (Matt 16:13–20) "'who do people say that the Son of Man is?' And they said, 'Some say John the Baptist, but others Elijah, and still others Jeremiah or one of the prophets.' He said to them, 'But who do you say I am?' Simon Peter answered, 'You are the Messiah, the Son of the living God.'" Compare this with Mark 8:27–30: "He asked his disciples, 'Who do people say that I am?' And they answered him, 'John the Baptist; and others Elijah; and still others, one of the prophets.' He asked them, 'But who do you say that I am?' Peter answered him, 'You are the Messiah.'" And finally, Luke 9:18–20: "He asked them, 'Who do the crowds say that I am?' They answered, 'John the Baptist; but others Elijah; and still others, that one of the ancient prophets has arisen.' He said to them, 'But who do you say that I am?' Peter answered, 'The Messiah of God.'" While these changes in wording may seem slight, there is one very significant change. It is the difference between Matthew's version and the other two. Jesus' question in Matthew is entirely different from Mark and Luke. In it Jesus asks "Who do people say that *the Son of Man* is?", but in Mark and Luke it is "Who do people (or "the crowds" in Luke) say that *I* am?" In chapter 5, when we discuss "Son of Man," it will be clear why this distinction is so important. While, yes, Jesus calls himself "the Son of Man," its meaning is far more than a circumlocution identifying himself, but a discussion of this will have to remain until we get to chapter 5. With these variances it is impossible to know which of these dialogues come closest to the original Aramaic exchange. It is easy to see the dilemma the modern interpreter faces.

Part One: Christian Folk Religion

WHY CHRISTIAN FOLK RELIGION AROSE

If the description of ancient Israel, or of Jesus, or of God, as I spoke of it above, sounds a little foreign to you it is because we have become so accustomed to the language of Christian folk religion we have often forgotten the real story behind the story the gospels are telling us. It is therefore important that we understand exactly what Christian folk religion is and why it is so common. Therefore it is time to define, and describe, what I mean when I speak of Christian folk religion, but before we get that far, it's important to understand what is meant by Folk Culture and Folklore because they are part of our everyday lives, no matter what age we live in, or what land, or what religion we profess.

Folk Culture

One scholar defined Folk culture as "a culture practiced by a small, homogeneous rural group." But this definition is too narrow. It localizes and isolates various cultures from each other. Actually it is a culture that practices traditions native to that culture, and stories passed among the common folk of that culture. It often includes such things as stories (i.e., *Grimms Fairy Tales* from Germany), songs (i.e., *Barbara Allen*, from England), mythology (i.e., *Big Foot*, from the United States, *Leprechauns*, from Ireland), legends (i.e., *The Legend of Sleepy Hollow*, from the United States), and superstitions (i.e., "a broken mirror brings seven years of bad luck," from the United States). It is part of a broader spectrum of practices often referred to as folklore—a termed coined in 1846 by Englishman W.J. Thoms to identify the customs of uncultured classes, but has been extended to include popular arts and crafts of the common folk. In the vernacular it is, we might add, that which makes our particular existence comfortable. It is what we are used to, whether as members of some organization, or region of the country, or ethnic group, or nationality. In the southern United States, for instance, there are certain practices which may not be observed in other parts of the country. One observance is the respect shown when a funeral procession passes by on the highway. It is customary for persons walking along the sidewalk, or roadway, to stop and turn to the procession with their hand over their heart. And oncoming traffic on the other side of the street will often stop in respect for the dead. This not necessarily practiced in other parts of the country. It is part of the folk culture.

Christian Folk Religion

Folk culture is not usually mandated by law, but rather by custom. It can consist of types of music, oral stories and history, popular beliefs, and traditions of a particular culture or subculture. Robert A. Georges and Michael Owens Jones, in their book *Folkloristics: An Introduction*, have identified four areas of study within folklore: artifacts, describable and transmissible entity (oral tradition), culture, and ritual behaviors.[1]

"Artifacts," as Georges and Jones describe them, are objects used within the folk culture, such as flags (national flags, organizational flags, sports flags, banners, etc.), images (pictures, drawings, sculptures), dolls (voodoo dolls, effigies, etc.), and numerous religious artifacts. Religious artifacts can include sacramental vessels, candles, processional crosses or crucifixes, the Star of David, processional Bibles, the Catholic ark which holds the sacred host, clergy vestments, choir robes, chancel paraments, prayer books, hymn books, liturgical books, menorahs, baptismal fonts, pulpits, lecterns, and many more. Personal artifacts often include jewelry identifying a person's faith, or a Bible which the person carries. A religious symbol on a car can be a cross, Star of David, or the simple outline of a fish. Contrary to popular belief the fish is not a symbol representing Jesus telling the fishermen Peter and Andrew, "Follow me, and I'll make you fish for people." This is a common and understandable error. Actually the symbol of the fish was one of the earliest Christian symbols used by early Christians during times of persecution when they wanted to announce a clandestine location for a Christian worship service and the persecutors wouldn't understand its significance. They would scratch it into a stone block of the house (today we'd consider this graffiti), or building, where the clandestine worship service was to be held. The fish symbol stood for the Greek word for fish: *ichthus*. This word is an acronym of the first letters of the Greek words for Jesus (*I*esous), Christ (*C*hristos), God's (*T*heos), Son (*U*ios), Savior (*S*oter), "Jesus Christ, Son of God, Savior." It was certainly a proud symbol to display. These artifacts often clearly identify the folk culture from which a person comes.

As we are particularly focusing on religious culture, the religious artifacts mentioned above have not only symbolic meaning, but also intensely emotional connections to the members of a particular culture. In the United States, religious flags, such as the Christian flag, the Jewish religious flag (not the flag of Israel), may, during a religious service, be displayed in a more prominent position that even the Stars and Stripes,

---

1. *Op cit*, 313.

Part One: Christian Folk Religion

but following the service must once again be placed into subservient position to the American flag which is to be placed or flown higher, or to the right of the religious flag, or on a staff placed forward of the other flag. The national flag of Israel is actually designed to remind its citizens of the *Tillit*, the blue and white striped Jewish prayer shawl. The flag is designed with the Star of David in the center on a broad white strip bordered on the top and the bottom with narrower blue stripes. It is thus loaded with religious symbolism, and is both a cultic, as well as national folk artifact.

The second area of study, "oral tradition," plays a major role in religious folk culture. Almost all religious stories and scriptures start out as oral tradition. It is believed that the earliest stories in the Bible were circulated orally for centuries before being committed to writing. This is particularly true of The Old Testament, which is more properly called The Hebrew Scriptures. The term used by the Jews for the Hebrew Bible is *Tanakh*, an acronym for the Masoretic Text's three subdivisions of *Torah* ("Teaching," the first five books of the Bible), *Nevi'im* ("Prophets"), and *Ketuvim* ("Writings"), thus *TaNaKh*. The earliest stories of the Hebrew Bible, particularly the stories of Abraham and the conquest of Canaan, Moses and the exodus, the tribal judges, and the early monarchy of Saul, David and Solomon, are believed to have been told and retold orally from generation to generation until they began to be written down sometime between the eleventh and ninth centuries BC. David, the king by whom all future kings would be compared, lived, it is believed, in about the eleventh century BC. This gives some indication of the span of time when oral tradition was the primary, or perhaps only, record telling the story of Israel and its patriarchs. I remember reading many years ago a statement by William Foxwell Albright, who is sometimes called the "Father of modern Biblical Archaeology," in his book *From the Stone Age to Christianity*, saying that oral transmission of stories were less likely to be changed than they are after they're committed to writing. This is because these stories are transmitted verbatim from one generation to the next to preserve their heritage. To keep the story in its original form they were sometimes sung, or recited in particular meter. Anthropological studies have shown this to be true even today of primitive societies which do not yet have a written language. Once the stories are written down, they can be subject to minor changes by scribes who either miscopy the text, or adjust the language, or sometimes miss seeing some of the words. This has been noted in religious manuscripts found in caves along the northwest shores of the Dead Sea in 1947- 1956, now known as the "Dead

Sea Scrolls." Scrolls, or fragments of scrolls, have been found of every book of the Hebrew Bible except the book of Esther. These manuscripts were copied between about 200 BC and AD 60. We know this because the community which produced these scrolls came into existence about 150 BC and fled the area in AD 68 when Israel was being destroyed by the Romans in the First Jewish Revolt of AD 63–73. Those for whom the scrolls were a sacred library, as they fled the area, deposited their precious library in caves above and in and around the center of their community, known as Qumran. The biblical scrolls and fragments are a full one thousand years older than any previously known text from the Bible. Since their discovery, scholars have poured over the scrolls or fragments (hundreds of thousands of fragments from 970 identified scrolls) letter by letter and compared them with biblical texts copied about AD 895. They have discovered whole verses which had been omitted from the later texts of the Bible and thus not commonly included in our translations of scripture. Words, or phrases, had been changed (or omitted) over the centuries since the earlier scrolls were copied. The later texts sometimes had words crossed out, and changed, or even notes written in the margins. Sometimes words written in the margin of an earlier document, a scribe would later integrate into the text itself as though it was part of the original biblical book, or whatever the document happened to be. We may come to believe that the inserted phrase or verses are part of the original biblical book, when it was simply a comment made by an earlier scribe in the margin. When studying a biblical passage today, we might do the same thing to remind us of a thought we had while studying it. In contrast, the Dead Sea Scrolls have revealed whole passages omitted from our text which were inadvertently missed by a scribe as his eyes passed from one line to another inadvertently. A verse from one of the psalms, which scholars had known for years was missing, has been found in the Dead Sea Scrolls. The reason they knew the verse was missing was because in its Hebrew form the first word of each verse forms an acronym reading down, and the acronym forms a phrase signifying the theme of the psalm. So the text of the Bible has undergone many changes since its story has been told in writing rather than oral. The oral stories might have been more accurate. It is believed that there was less likelihood of the stories being changed when they were told by great-grandparents, to grandparents, to parents and finally to children. All were told orally, perhaps in rhythmic rhyme, or to the folkloric tune of the people.

Part One: Christian Folk Religion

> I love to tell the story of unseen things above,
> Of Jesus and his glory, of Jesus and his love.
> I love to tell the story, because I know it's true;
> It satisfies my longings as nothing else would do.
> I love to tell the story;
> Twill be my theme in glory
> To tell the old, old story
> Of Jesus and his love.

And even today we still love the folk songs of our youth, at least I hope so.

The third area of the study of folklore, the "cultural area," is its cultural impact on our lives. It is that aspect of our lives we often find most comforting and with which we identify ourselves. It is our tradition. Often we speak of "our faith" when perhaps we should speak of our "tradition." The denomination to which we belong, or non-denomination we claim, is not correctly called our "faith." As Christians we are not of the Roman Catholic faith, or the Protestant faith, we are Protestant or Catholic by tradition, because we accept that tradition, or we reject the other tradition. This tradition is usually based on belief, but belief and faith are not synonymous terms. Belief is how we think, and what we are convinced to be true, but faith is how we act on what we believe.

The classic definition of faith is that found in Hebrews 11:1: "Now faith is the assurance of things hoped for, the conviction of things not seen." The operative words of this verse are "assurance" and "conviction." Although both words are nouns, each is a form of a verb (assure and convict). These are not passive words, they demand action. To have faith we must act with the full confidence that what we believe is absolutely true, whether it makes any reasonable sense or not. One of the most powerful examples of faith is given in the story of the exodus, when, under the leadership of Moses, the children of Israel were fleeing the Egyptian Pharaoh (probably Rameses II) and his armies in the thirteenth century BC. It is found in Exodus 14:5–15. Picture this: imagine that you are with the Israelites who have just fled Egypt, but the Pharaoh and his chariots are in hot pursuit. Suddenly a great sea looms in front of you. Pharaoh's mighty army flanks you on the right, and on the left, and hems you in from behind. You are trapped! It is no wonder that your whole tribe begins to complain to Moses. "Was it because there were no graves in Egypt that you have taken us away to die in the wilderness? What have you done to us, bringing us out of Egypt? Is this not the very thing we told you in

Egypt, 'Let us alone and let us serve the Egyptians'? For it would have been better for us to serve the Egyptians than to die in the wilderness" (vv. 11–12). And your leader Moses turns to God and relays your frustrations and fears back to him. God listens to Moses' fears and the terror of his people, but then God barks back at Moses, "Why do you cry out to me? Tell the Israelites to go forward!" It is the call to faith! "Go forward!" It is the only option. And when you take that first step into the waters of the sea, you have taken the leap of faith, and the waters part and you are on dry ground. Is that story a myth? Is it a legend? No, it's your heritage. It is a story Jews have heard a thousand times, especially once every year at the celebratory Passover meal, when the youngest in the family asks, "Papa, what is so special about this meal?" And he tells the story of the exodus yet again. It is, again, one of the folk tales, whether told in rhyme, or plain story, or song:

> I love to tell the story, because I know it's true,
> It satisfies my longing, as nothing else can do.

And that's what folk tales do, they satisfy our longing to know about our heritage and give us hope for the future.

The fourth area of folklore is "behavior," and this invariably means rituals. Rituals often run our lives. They are part of our culture and make us who we are. They identify our values and style of life. When we break from traditional rituals we can experience feeling guilty because we are not doing what our nature tells us is the right thing to do! Nevertheless, it is part of our folk culture. When the American flag passes by, or the Pledge of Allegiance is said, Americans traditionally stand, remove their hats, and put their hands across their hearts, or if they are military and in uniform, they snap to attention, and salute. We walk our dogs often down the same paths, sidewalks and streets, at the same time of the day, day in and day out. We have traditional times when we eat our meals, and the same places where we eat certain meals, whether at the kitchen table, or dining room table, or in our laps as we watch television. Sometimes our rituals arise from habits we have formed. They go from the simple way we tie our shoes (just try to tie your shoes using your hands in a different way and you'll find out how difficult it is), to the rituals we go through as we enter our automobile before we turn on the engine.

Persons from different cultures have different comfort zones around them. A comfort zone determines how near or far away it is comfortable for us to stand or sit by strangers or casual friends. For those of us

Part One: Christian Folk Religion

who descend from northern Europeans, we have a comfort zone of about one arm's length from our body. This "comfort zone" totally surrounds us. When two people get into a heated argument, they tend to invade each other's comfort zone. Thus the expression (often yelled in anger), "Get out of my face!" Drill sergeants and Tactical Instructors leading military basic training classes deliberately speak harshly to recruits, and stand with their faces 3–4 inches from the recruit's face just to intimidate him or her. It's just a part of teaching discipline through intimidation. In theaters or other gatherings of people we don't know or know well, we feel most comfortable leaving at least one vacant seat between us and another person. People from cultures other than our own will have different comfort zone distances. People from the southern countries in Europe or Latin America, have much closer comfort zones, often about the distance from a shoulder to an elbow. Travelers who are traveling for the first time in those countries often mistake a simple conversation they see between two people as arguing. They will see two men—say in Italy—standing very close ("in each other's face") speaking loudly, arms and hands flaying about, and then suddenly the men will both break out in laughter. The American thought they were arguing. The Italians may just have been sharing a good joke, or funny story! They simply have a different cultural expression and "comfort zone."

At sporting events we can witness all sorts of strange behavior by fans, even if we don't participate in those behaviors. Macho young men often appear in freezing cold weather at a football game, wearing no shirt, but with their bodies decorated in their team's colors. When their team scores a touchdown, college students will raise other students above their heads, where they do pushups, to celebrate. Crazy! And some people suffer from phobias so terrifying that they are careful not to step on a crack in the sidewalk, for fear they might, "break my mother's back." Remember the show on television about the "defective detective," Monk, and his obsessive compulsive disorder? Or some people become petrified at the thought of having to fly in an airplane. A young airman friend of mine didn't have a phobia of flying, but just didn't like it. Once I joked with him and said, "Well, you'll only go when your number's up." He retorted back, "I'm not worried about *my* number being up, but what if the pilot's number is up?" I was speechless.

But there is perhaps no area of life where rituals dominate more than in religious life. Rituals can be very simple, such as a family holding hands while praying before meals, or even just bowing our heads and folding our hands. Depending on your tradition, you might be making the sign of the cross at various times during a worship service, or bowing, or genuflexing before the altar or cross. It can be raising your hands and head toward heaven during songs of praise or thanksgiving. It can be kneeling in prayer, or as in some cultures, lying prostrate before God. If you have ever been to the Holy Land you've undoubtedly visited the Western Wall ("Wailing Wall"—an unfortunate misnaming) in Jerusalem, and seen the ultra-orthodox Jews bobbing repeatedly before the wall as they read from the Hebrew Bible, and repeat the daily *Shema* prayer, "Hear, O Israel: Yahweh is our God, Yahweh alone!" (Deut 6:4). No matter what our religious tradition is, it is filled with rituals that direct our religious lives. Religious rituals are so ingrained that there is an old saying which is perhaps truer than we'd like to believe, "The seven last words of the church are 'But we've always done it that way!'" We have often taken it for granted that how we act, what we do, and our lifestyle, is the right one, and perhaps the model of the true Christian. We often believe that any major variant from that form of living is not right and needs to be corrected. Once I was having a conversation with a Catholic priest when he told me a story I have never forgotten. He told me of a little girl who faithfully came to his church and attended Sunday School every Sunday, and then would stay for the Mass afterward. One day one of his Sunday School teachers came to him and said, "Father, some of our teachers are concerned about Susie." That wasn't the little girl's name, but we'll call her that. The teacher continued, "She's become somewhat of a distraction to the other children in the Sunday School class. She comes with a dirty face and disheveled clothes and her hair is matted, often dirty and never combed. Something ought to be said to her parents, we think she might be neglected at home." What the priest then said to the well-meaning teacher came as a shock to me at the time. He said to her, "Let me tell you about little Susie. Her parents are not well off, but they both work hard to keep a roof over their heads and food on the table, but they have a problem. They're both alcoholics and on Saturday evenings they binge drink and fall into their beds drunk. They've tried to keep Susie from coming to church, but she wants to come, so she gets up herself, dresses as best she can, and sneaks out of the house so she can come to Sunday School and Mass. If you would like to, you can arrange to meet Susie at church a few minutes before Sunday School and help her wash her face and straighten out her dress a bit, and perhaps brush her hair for her, but if you say one word to her that makes her feel she doesn't look good enough for your class, or makes her think that in any way she's not welcome in this church just as she is, I will hold a private Novena prayer service for the damnation of your soul!" The well-meaning Sunday School teacher had personal standards as to what is proper decorum. She completely missed Jesus' teaching, "Let the little children come to me, and do not stop them; for it is to such as these that the kingdom of heaven belongs. And he laid his hands on them and went on his way." (Matt 19:14–15)

Christian Folk Religion

Thus far we have covered some of the folk rituals which may be part of our religious heritage, but presently I want to examine some of the very common aspects of the Christian faith that are prevalent in our beliefs and practices. Certain rituals, artifacts, oral traditions, and cultural elements often go hand-in-hand with this, and may certainly vary with your particular tradition. But there are common beliefs that most of us share. It is time we turn to them. What I will be describing is particularly true of Western Christianity, and Eastern Orthodoxy may, or may not share all of them.

For Christians the sacred tradition is contained in the Bible, which consists of the Old and New Testaments. The New Testament in all Christian Bibles consists of 27 books. The Old Testament (Hebrew Scriptures) varies in its content depending on whether your Bible is a Protestant Bible or Catholic Bible. The Protestant Bible's Old Testament traditionally contains 39 books, but may also include in a separate section, the 11 books of The Apocrypha, and some Deuterocanonical books such as 1 and 2 Esdras (sometimes named 1and 2 Ezra), the Letter of Jeremiah, Prayer of Azariah, 3 and 4 Maccabees, and Prayer of Manasseh. The Roman Catholic Bible's Old Testament follows the books which were translated into Greek in Alexandria Egypt between 300 and 200 BC known as the Septuagint, or LXX. Septuagint means "seventy," so named for the approximate number of scholars who were involved in translating the Hebrew into Greek, thus the use of the Roman numeral used as a kind of shorthand. The reason for the Greek translation of the LXX was the fact that increasingly Hebrew was becoming a dead language for most Jews, and Hebrew was only used in local worship or the study of the sacred scriptures. The fear was that the common people would no longer be able to read the sacred books, and thus there appeared to be the need for a Greek version as the commonly understood language was becoming Greek. Many of the quotations of the

Christian Folk Religion

scriptures cited in the New Testament are from the LXX, not the Hebrew text. The Catholic Old Testament follows this Greek translation and has 46 books because the Apocrypha is an integral part of it. Although the Apocrypha traditionally has 11 books, some of the Apocryphal books are actually additions to the books of Esther and Daniel, and integrated with those books. Thus the Catholic Old Testament has 46 books rather than 50.[2] It should be explained why the LXX varies from the Hebrew Bible. The canon of the Hebrew Bible was not finalized until after the destruction of the temple in Jerusalem in AD 70. With its destruction Judaism had to be completely restructured because the Jewish way of living centered so completely on their only temple, which was in Jerusalem. It was believed to be where the presence of God dwelt and was the symbol of God in their midst. With its destruction the sacrifices ceased, the high priest, the chief priests, temple priests, and the Sadducees who controlled the temple were no more. Therefore, following the loss of the temple, a movement began which is known as the "Rabbinic movement." The former teachers of Judaism, the Pharisees, slowly became known as Rabbis, which actually means "teacher." They became the leaders of the new face of Judaism, and it was decided that the study of the Hebrew Bible would take the place of sacrifices and temple rituals. But what exactly could be called scripture had not ever been decided. Thus in the late first or early second century the Rabbis met to decided what books would be included in the Hebrew Bible, and what would be excluded. One of the criteria for inclusion was that the book must have been composed in Hebrew originally and not in Greek, thus retaining the purity of the use of Hebrew as the language of God's inspiration. Some of the books, while enormously popular among the Hebrews, were only known in Greek, and were thus not included. The most popular, but excluded, of these Greek only books are Sirach (a.k.a. Ben Sirach or Ecclesiasticus), Wisdom of Solomon, and 1st and 2nd Maccabees. All of these are part of the Septuagint, but not of the traditional Hebrew Bible. It is now believed, however, that at least Sirach was composed originally in Hebrew.

The Hebrew Bible, used within Judaism today, is composed of the same books included in the Protestant Old Testament but numbered differently and placed in a different order. In order to avoid confusion I prefer the term Hebrew Scriptures, rather Hebrew Bible, for the Old Testament. Only the Jewish Bible will be called Hebrew Bible. But from here on out I will use the Hebrew Scriptures instead of Old Testament

2. I will be using the term "Hebrew Scriptures" when referring to the "Old Testament" (see below).

when referring to the 39 books of the Protestant Bible, which record the story of Israel before John the Baptizer and Jesus. However, I think it is important that I explain how the Jewish Hebrew Bible is arranged. As already mentioned, it is often referred to as *Tanakh* (Torah, Prophets, and Writings).

THE CANON OF THE HEBREW BIBLE

Torah (Teaching)	*Nevi'im* (Prophets)	*Ketuvim* (Writing)
1. Genesis	A. Former Prophets	A. Poetical books
2. Exodus	1. Joshua	1. Psalms
3. Leviticus	2. Judges	2. Proverbs
4. Numbers	3. Samuel (1 & 2)	3. Job
5. Deuteronomy	4. Kings (1 & 2)	B. Five Rolls
	B. Latter Prophets	1. Song of Songs
	1. Isaiah	2. Ruth
	2. Jeremiah	3. Lamentations
	3. Ezekiel	4. Ecclesiastes
	4. The Twelve	5. Esther
	(12 Minor Prophets, 1 book)	C. Historical books
		1. Daniel
		2. Ezra/Nehemiah
		3. Chronicles (1 &2)

Thus the Hebrew Bible contains twenty-four books in a different order, but with the same canonical text as the Hebrew Scriptures included in the Protestant Bible.

YOUR FAITH STORY

When you think of your faith story, there undoubtedly comes to mind certain images and thoughts which direct the way you express that faith. These images and thoughts probably stem from a particular tradition, whether it is a family tradition or a religious tradition, which helps you relate your faith story to you. It can largely depend on an overall understanding of a broad sweep of your life's values. Many people consider their values to be conservative, and others, moderate, and still others liberal. In religion, as well as in politics, a person whose values are at one end of the spectrum, are considered to be opposed to those whose values are at the other end of the spectrum. So it becomes liberal, versus conservative, or vice versa. Those who consider themselves moderate often believe themselves to be middle-of-the-road which can lean people one way or another as a particular idea appeals to them. In American society there seems to be a major divide between those who consider themselves conservatives and those who consider themselves liberals. Unfortunately, one side often demonizes the other, which is not, I believe, what God either envisioned or intends. This split between conservatism and liberalism is especially prevalent in the United States. While in the United Kingdom there is also a strong divide, it is confined more to political issues than religious issues.

In the United States it divides both state and church. In the scenario I am going to suggest to you I am hoping it will not fit into either side of the argument. However, there will be terms I will refer to which describe different types of religious practice, and understanding of worship. These are more the result of our folkstyle than the truth, falsehood, or value of our faith. They are simply differences, just as there are differences in ethnicity, culture, economical status, and lifestyle. Some of these differences you will know, and are probably part of your church's practice, or a practice with which you feel most comfortable, even if you are not a member of a particular denomination, or any form of organized religion. Here are some of the divisions which separate one group from another: "liturgical worship" (a formal, pre-designed worship format) vs. "non-liturgical"; "creedal" (ascribing to the ancient creeds of the church, i.e., the Apostles Creed, the Nicene Creed, the Athanasian Creed) vs. "non-creedal," which may have its own statement of faith or creed though not ascribing to the wording of the ancient creeds; an "episcopal" form of church government (not meaning the denomination, although the Episcopal Church has an episcopal hierarchy of priest, bishop, archbishop etc., as does Catholicism, Anglicanism, Lutheranism, etc.) vs. "congregational" structure (where there is no regional or national hierarchy setting rules for the congregation, rather the congregation is basically autonomous); and then "sacramental," where certain church rites are considered especially sacred or sacramental (such as the Lord's Supper/Communion/Eucharist, and Baptism, Marriage, etc.) v. "non-sacramental," where such rites are important, but perhaps more symbolic. There are other categories or subcategories, but we do not need to get into them here. Doctrines and dogmas have been the arguing point between the various denominational factions for centuries. It is interesting that the longest and most passionate pleading ever made by Jesus, was made on the night of his betrayal as he begged his Father that his disciples "may be one, as we are one" (John

Part One: Christian Folk Religion

17:11). Yet, almost from the moment of his death, the divisions began: do Gentiles need to become Jews first? "Yes," some in the Jerusalem church said. "No," Paul told his churches. And early in the young history of the church, Paul also cried out, "Each of you says, I belong to Paul, or I belong to Apollos, or I belong to Cephas [Peter], or I belong to Christ. Has Christ been divided? Was Paul crucified for you? Or were you baptized in the name of Paul?" (1 Cor 1:12–13).

We're not here to either divide, or conquer, but rather to reflect, what is the Christian faith? If you see yourself in the scenario I am about to present to you, it is no judgment on your faith or my own. It is simply the scenario I have heard my whole life: in my early years, repeated in my seminary training, and heard over and over again from Christians in all denominations and in many various cultures. I love the Christian story, but much of it comes from tradition more than biblical teaching. I am hoping that in this brief study that follows we can recognize what we already know and then move beyond to explore facets of faith we may never have been exposed to before.

All Christian Scriptures, regardless of denomination, are divided into two sections, the old and the new. The old is generally considered exactly that, old, perhaps ancient history, no longer totally relevant, and most certainly out of date. In many Protestant traditions, and especially in my own, the division between the old and the new is described as "law" (old) and "gospel" (new). Although it is rarely seen among the American clergy, it is still seen occasionally in Europe, where some Protestant ministers wear two white tabs that hang below their clerical collar in the shape of an upside down "v" signifying the division between law and gospel. One tab represents "law," the old, and the other tab, "gospel," the new. The implication is that "law" is bad, but "gospel" is good. "Law" is legalistic, the old; "gospel"—the good-news of Jesus Christ—the new.

In a large segment of modern Christianity it is believed that the Old Testament's main message points toward the coming of Jesus Christ. It is believed that is the message of the prophets, and the psalms. As early as the third chapter of the Bible, the prediction of the coming of Jesus is believed to be in the story of the snake who leads Adam and Eve into temptation to sin. Doesn't God in Gen 3:5 say to the snake?

> I will put enmity between you and the woman,
> and between your offspring and hers;
> he will strike your head,
> and you will strike his heel.

Many Christians believe that in this early story of the snake in Paradise, the snake is actually Satan. Many also believe this to be a clear predictor that although it will be Satan who will cause the crucifixion of Christ, it will be Christ, who through his crucifixion and resurrection will crush the power of the devil. This is pure folk religion. Students who have a thorough knowledge of the Bible know that the word devil never appears in scripture until the New Testament. Four passages in the Hebrew Scriptures do use the word in the plural, "devils" (Lev 17:7; Deut 32:17; 2 Chr 11:15; Ps 106:37), but these verses are about pagan gods or goddesses, not a personified opponent of Yahweh, the God of Abraham, Isaac, and Jacob. The idea that the snake is Satan or the devil is a misunderstanding of the culture, from which the story comes.

The expectation of Jesus is even seen in the story of the construction of the tabernacle after Moses led the children of Israel out of Egypt. The tabernacle was a temporary, nomadic temple, a tent, really, which was carried to Canaan by the Israelites as they sojourned for a generation in the Sinai desert after fleeing slavery in Egypt. It too is often thought of as a kind of prophecy of the coming of the Messiah. In such thinking the tabernacle was a type of Jesus Christ, who would bring the presence of God into the midst of the people of God. Thus, it is believed by many, that it also foretold the coming of Jesus. Once settled in Canaan, and the monarchy developed, King Solomon, the son of King David, replaced the tabernacle with the permanent temple. The temple, built on top of the mountain in Jerusalem called Temple Mount was believed to be where God's presence dwelt in the inner sanctuary, the Holy of Holies.

It was also during the traveling through the Sinai desert that God called Moses to the top of Mt. Sinai, where he gave Moses and the Israelites, his holy law. The law is summarized in the Ten Commandments listing the dos and don'ts of what God's people must do to keep God's favor, and what they must refrain from doing to avoid God's wrath. The people must not worship other gods or idols. They must keep the Sabbath as a holy day. They must honor their parents, refrain from murder, adultery, theft, lying, or coveting a neighbor's possession, or his family. But the whole law of which the Ten Commandments are just a summary is spelled out in careful detail, especially in the book of Leviticus, often called The Holiness Code. There are 613 individual laws which specify what you can and cannot eat, who you can and cannot come in contact with, what actions are acceptable to God and which are abhorrent to him. They are so explicit they are impossible to live up to. In fact, Christian faith says that they expose the underside of human nature, and show us our sinfulness. They set up a wall between the life our sinful nature wants to lead, and our ability to receive God's mercy and tender care.

Even all the daily sacrifices in the Jerusalem temple were not enough to appease God's wrath for the sin his law exposed in us. God told the prophet Amos (5:21–24) as much:

> I hate, I despise your festivals,
> and take no delight in your solemn assemblies.
> Even though you offer me your burnt offerings and grain offerings,
> I will not accept them;
> and the offerings of well-being of your fatted animals
> I will not look upon.
> Take away from me the noise of your songs,
> I will not listen to the melody of your harps.
> But let justice roll down like waters,
> and righteousness like an ever-flowing stream.

It seems there is no escape from the law. It has us trapped in our sin. God demands justice and our righteousness. And it was even Paul, in the New Testament, who said in Romans (7:7–11):

> If it had not been for the law, I would not have known sin. I would not have known what it is to covet if the law had not said, "You shall not covet." But sin, seizing an opportunity in the commandment, produced in me all kinds of covetousness. Apart from the law sin lies dead. I was once alive apart from the law, but when the commandment came, sin revived and I died, and the very commandment that promised life proved to be death to me. For sin, seizing an opportunity in the commandment, deceived me and through it killed me.

Thus, according to Paul, the law becomes the agent of death, because it separates us from what God demands of us. Ultimately it condemns us. Therefore, we must have some way to escape this condemnation, and that can only be a Savior. Such a Savior is the hope and expectation of the people of Israel, spoken of in the Hebrew Scriptures. It is what Job (19:25–27), who has lost everything: his family, his house, his health, confidently expects:

> I know that my Redeemer lives,
> and that at the last he will stand upon the earth;
> and after my skin has been thus destroyed,
> then in my flesh I shall see God,

> whom I shall see on my side,
> and my eyes shall behold, and not another.
> My heart faints within me!

Who cannot read these words without singing them to the great hymn in Handel's oratorio, "Messiah?" It signals the great expectation of the prophets Jeremiah, Isaiah, Ezekiel. Ultimately the great hope of Israel is announced by Isaiah (7:14–15):

> The Lord himself will give you a sign. Look, the young woman [a Virgin—KJV] is with child and shall bear a son, and shall name him Immanuel [i.e., God is with us]. He shall eat curds and honey by the time he knows how to refuse the evil and choose the good.

The prophet Micah (5:2–4) even tells where this will happen:

> But you, O Bethlehem of Ephrathah,
> who are one of the little clans of Judah,
> from you shall come forth for me one who is to rule Israel,
> whose origin is from of old,
> from ancient days.
> Therefore he shall give them up until the time
> when she who is in labor has brought forth;
> then the rest of his kindred shall return to the people of Israel.
> And he shall stand and feed his flock in the strength of Yahweh,
> in the majesty of the name of Yahweh his God.
> And they shall live secure, for now he shall be great to the ends
> of the earth;
> and he shall be the one of peace.

And then again in Isaiah (11:1–5):

> A shoot shall come out from the stump of Jesse,
> and a branch shall grow out of his roots.
> The spirit of Yahweh shall rest on him,
> the spirit of wisdom and understanding,
> the spirit of counsel and might,
> the spirit of knowledge and the fear of Yahweh.
> He shall not judge by what his eyes see,
> or decide by what his ears hear;
> but with righteousness he shall judge the poor,
> and decide with equity for the meek of the earth;
> he shall strike the earth with the rod of his mouth,
> and with the breath of his lips he shall kill the wicked.

Part One: Christian Folk Religion

> Righteousness shall be the belt around his waist,
> and faithfulness the belt around his loins.

Such was the expectation of Israel and the prophecy of their prophets. It seems that the prophecy of Israel ended with the prophets Ezra and Nehemiah somewhere around 400 BC following the return of exiles from Babylon in the late sixth century.

The Bible then turns to the Good News of the New Testament. It begins with announcement in both the gospels of Matthew and Luke, telling of the birth of Jesus, in Bethlehem, the city of the birth of Jesus' ancestor, King David, the greatest king Israel ever had. Jesus' birth is accompanied by the arrival of astrologers from the East who follow a star announcing the birth of The King of the Jews, and bring him gifts of gold, frankincense, and myrrh. His birth is announced by angels, and attended by shepherds (told in Luke's account).

Eventually the family moves to Nazareth, where Jesus grows up and learns carpentry, the trade of his supposed father, Joseph. Little else is heard about the early years of Jesus' life except, as told in Luke, when he travels with his parents, relatives, and friends to Jerusalem and its temple at the age of twelve, perhaps for his Bar Mitzvah, the rite of entry into manhood.

Then, when Jesus is about thirty years old, a cousin of Jesus, known as John the Baptist, (whom I refer to as John the Baptizer, a description of what he does, rather than a title) appears on the scene after spending considerable time in the wilderness, and comes baptizing people for the forgiveness of sins, and announcing to all of Israel the words of the prophet Isaiah (40:3–5):

> The voice of one crying out in the wilderness:
> Prepare the way of the Lord,
> make his paths straight.
> Every valley shall be filled,
> and every mountain shall be made low,
> and the crooked shall be made straight,
> and the rough ways made smooth;
> and all flesh shall see the salvation of God.

We teach this message in Sunday School, perhaps not exactly as I've laid it out here, but something very close to this version. And we've heard our ministers preach this story over and over again. And we've sung George Bennard's great song, written in 1913, a thousand times:

> On a hill far away stood an old rugged cross,
> The emblem of suffering and shame.
> And I love that old cross where the dearest and best,
> For a world of lost sinners was slain.
> So I'll cherish that old rugged cross,
> Till my trophies at last I lay down;
> I will cling to that old rugged cross,
> And exchange it someday for a crown.

And now, we wait for Jesus to return for a second time. This time he says he will come on the clouds of heaven, in power and great glory and this will spell the beginning of the end of the world and the institution of everlasting paradise.

Does this in anyway describe what you believe? In summary, the core beliefs are:

1. Jesus' coming was prophesied by the great prophets before him.
2. He was born of the Virgin Mary in Bethlehem.
3. He was baptized by John the Baptist in the river Jordan.
4. He was tempted by the devil.
5. He was the Son of God and the Son of Man, both divine and human at the same time.
6. He preached and taught about the kingdom of God and the kingdom of heaven.
7. He said that those who believed in him would be saved, and go to heaven.
8. He healed the sick, the lame, the blind, he drove out demons, and he raised the dead.
9. He violated the standard religious practices of the day.
10. He was betrayed, mocked, abused, crucified and died.
11. He was raised on the third day and was seen by women near the empty tomb, by disciples walking along the road to Emmaus, by his disciples in the Upper Room, and many others.
12. Fifty days later, on the day of Pentecost, he sent the Holy Spirit, who filled the lives and hopes of thousands of people and thus began the great movement of the church of Jesus Christ, in Jerusalem, and then spread around the known world.

Part One: Christian Folk Religion

13. Sometime later, Jesus also appeared to a young Pharisee by the name of Saul, who was then converted to Christianity, changed his name to Paul, and planted churches throughout Asia Minor (Turkey), Greece, and onto the doorsteps of Rome itself.

14. This same Jesus will come again, in the Second Coming, on clouds of heaven, with power and glory and will destroy the devil and all wickedness in a terrifying war which will result in the end of the world, and then a new heaven and a new earth will be created, where the true believers will dwell in the presence of God Almighty, and the Lamb of God (Jesus) for all eternity.

The record of the faith above is recorded in what we call The Holy Bible, which is the absolute authority for its truth. It is God's Holy Word. For many people, that means that God inspired its writing, or perhaps even dictated its words. And also for many people The Holy Bible contains no contradictions, no errors, and is verbatim from God's will.

SOME CLOSING OBSERVATIONS

What I have just skimmed through describes the core of Christian belief as probably the majority of people have heard it, grown to love it, and can almost repeat it by heart. It doesn't matter from which denomination you come, or what your religious practices might be, the message is essentially the same. It has been forged across the centuries, by ministers and theologians through all the countries of the western world. It is certainly the message with which we feel most comfortable. In fact it is a comforting message, and indeed Good News.

There have been times in the past, however, when it has been distorted and where it has created deep scars and sorrow, persecution, death, and destruction. It has been forced on populations on the pain of death, such as during the Crusades of the Middle-Ages, and the Inquisitions also of the Middle-Ages. In America it spawned witch hunts in Salem, Massachusetts, and in Germany the Holocaust where six million Jews were slaughtered charging that they were "Christ killers." Today professed Christians demonize whole populations of people of the Muslim faith for being terrorists, anti-American, etc. This faith in Jesus Christ is not good news to all people. Jesus, who said that we should love our neighbors as we love ourselves, has often been lost in our passion to believe that we and we alone, are right. That we and we alone, have the truth.

Christian Folk Religion

That somehow God, and his Son, Jesus, are on our side, and ultimately we will win the war over wickedness. Many years ago it was the author and humorist Mark Twain, who in his too infrequently read novella, *The Mysterious Stranger* (the "mysterious stranger" just happens to be the devil in disguise), has the devil list the accomplishments of Christianity and points out that it was the Christians who invented gunpowder and who have perfected the instruments by which we can effectively slaughter other members of the human race. That's not good news. How have those of us who proclaim our faith in the Prince of Peace reached such a state? The Prince of Peace arose in a culture where there was a sense of tolerance, not brutality and injustice. In the early years of Israel, it is true, they were an awful force to be reckoned with. An early description of Israel's God says, "Yahweh is a warrior" (Exod 15:3). The stories of the conquest of Canaan are often brutal and unforgiving. In those stories, ancient Israel was often commanded to annihilate entire populations of captured cities along with anything that remains alive (Deut 20:17–18). According to Numbers 21:2–3:

> Then Israel made a vow to Yahweh and said, "If you will indeed give this people into our hands, then we will utterly destroy their towns." Yahweh listened to the voice of Israel, and handed over the Canaanites and they utterly destroyed them and their towns; so the place was called Hormah [i.e., destruction].

The Hebrew word for annihilate or utterly destroy is *charem* or *herem*, which was a war of total destruction where a captured territory was purified of all evil so that it could be dedicated to Yahweh. Some have defined the word *herem* as "holy war," although such an extreme term may be going too far. This concept is very similar to the Muslim belief in *Jehad*, a concept for which we demonize almost all the people of one of the largest faiths in the world. One scholar has said that *herem* applied only occasionally to loot, and not to idolatrous objects; but in its application to enemies, it involved extermination, and thus the verb acquired its secondary sense of "to destroy." He goes on to argue that the concept of *herem* or *haharim* should not always be taken to imply holy war, but rather "devoted to Yahweh." In his conclusion he maintains that

> where the word herem/haharim is used with its full religious force (and always, in its nominal form), it means uncompromising consecration without possibility of recall or redemption. It was not applied to idolatrous objects, but to things which could

27

have been taken as plunder or people who could have been enslaved. It was not the normal procedure of war, although the verb could be used in a secondary sense to denote overwhelming destruction of the enemy. The application of herem did not make a war holy; but it did introduce a special theological dimension which forbade taking booty, or prisoners, or both, according to the instructions given in the particular case.³

Although the practice was brutal by today's standards and seen as inhumane, it was considered a dedication to the divine power and splendor of Yahweh. However, by the first century AD, Israel was known, not as a pacifist state, but particularly tolerant of others and their religious faith. The largest court in the temple complex in Jerusalem was called "The Court of the Gentiles," where peoples of all nations were allowed to worship whatever god(s) they bowed down too, as long as they brought no profane item into the temple compound. Thus, pagan Romans could worship their gods there in silence, as long as they did not impede the worship of Yahweh, or compel the Jews to do so as well.

Jesus was especially accepting of those whose faith lay outside Jewish Yahwism. One time a Roman soldier, a centurion, came to him and asked him to come and heal a servant of his. The centurion knew that for Jesus to enter the house of a Gentile, under the laws of Jewish purification, he would be rendered impure, and he would have to submit to purification rites. Respecting that Jewish law, he told Jesus he need not enter his house to cure the man, but only speak the word, and "my servant will be healed" (Matt 8:8). When Jesus heard that he was amazed and said to those who followed him, "Truly I tell you, in no one in Israel have I found such faith." A little later in Matthew another story is told of a Canaanite woman who shouted after Jesus, "Have mercy on me, Lord, Son of David; my daughter is tormented by a demon." The disciples pled with him to send her away, and Jesus said to her, "I was sent only to the lost sheep of the house of Israel," but she pled all the more, "Lord, help me," and he again replied, "It is not fair to take the children's food and throw it to the dogs." To this seemingly cruel retort, the poor lady answered, "Yes, Lord, yet even the dogs eat the crumbs that fall from their master's table," to which Jesus answered, "'Woman, great is your faith! Let it be done for you as you wish.' And her daughter was healed instantly" (Matt 15:22–28). For Jesus, even those of a totally foreign religion, were praised for the

---

3 Lilley, "Understanding the Herem." *TB*, 176.

quality of their faith, even if it was not focused on Jesus' Father God, Yahweh, but was a pagan faith. On another occasion, as he was speaking to his disciples, he gave one of his most famous teaching messages:

> I am the good shepherd. I know my own and my own know me, just as the Father knows me and I know the Father. And I lay down my life for the sheep. I have other sheep that do not belong to this fold. I must bring them also, and they will listen to my voice. So there will be one flock, one shepherd. For this reason the Father loves me, because I lay down my life in order to take it up again. (John 10:14–17)

What are we to make of this? It is clear that Jesus is speaking of multiple sheepfolds, ("I have other sheep that do not belong to this fold"). It is for them, also, that he says he lays down his life. How is it they will listen to his voice, if they are victims of Christian violence because they do not yet listen to his voice? But violence has often been the recourse of Christianity, to spread The Good News. Scandinavia was conquered that way by St. Olaf Haraldson in the eleventh century, and Christianized. The Norwegian coat of arms depicts an axe, held by a lion, which symbolizes how St. Olaf brought Christianity to its pagan Vikings.

As we will see throughout this study, Jesus was intent not on conquering the world, but ushering in a new world order. That world order would include what the angels sang at his birth, "On earth peace, goodwill among people" (Luke 2:14). It was a world order that would change human behavior, where love would be the standard by which all people would be judged, and hatred would dissipate. Jesus called it the kingdom of God, or the kingdom of heaven (this latter term appears mostly in Matthew).

Such a new world order had also been spoken of by the prophets before him. Isaiah foresaw a day when:

> there shall be endless peace for the throne of David and his kingdom. He will establish and uphold it with justice and with righteousness
> from this time onward and forevermore.
> The zeal of Yahweh will do this. (9:6–7)

And again, a day when

> The wolf shall live with the lamb,
> the leopard shall lie down with the kid,
> the calf and the lion and the fatling together,
> and a child shall lead them . . .

Part One: Christian Folk Religion

> They will not hurt or destroy on all my holy mountain;
> for the earth will be full of the knowledge of Yahweh
> as the waters cover the sea. (11:6–9)

We eagerly wait for the time when the world that Jesus has promised will finally arrive, and which the prophets expected before him, but today that seems to be far in the future. I know that there are many who believe we are living in the end time, but Christians have always believed that, even the Apostle Paul in the first letter we have from his hand, 1 Thessalonians, which was written perhaps in AD 52. In 4:13–18 he tells his church in Thessalonica about the second coming of Jesus, and as he describes it he boldly declares, "Then we who are alive, who are left, will be caught up in the clouds together with them to meet the Lord in the air" (v. 17). By the time he wrote 2 Thessalonians, perhaps a year later, Paul was no longer as confident that Christ's return was immanent:

> As to the coming of our Lord Jesus Christ and our being gathered together to him, we beg you, brothers and sisters, not to be quickly shaken in mind or alarmed, either by spirit or by word or letter, as though from us, to the effect that the day of the Lord is already here. (2 Thess 2:1–2)

2

The Hellenization of the Christian Church

OUR WORLD IS DECIDEDLY different from the world we encounter in any part of the Bible. Jesus died on April 7, AD 30. That date has been calculated on the basis of the fact that Jesus died on the Friday before the start of the festival of Passover. Passover was a moveable feast and it only fell on the Sabbath every few years. We know that Pontius Pilate was Prefect of Judea until AD 36, when he was removed from office by Rome for being too brutal. The only year in which the beginning of Passover occurred on the Sabbath during what we know of as Jesus' ministry, is the year 30, and modern computers place that date, according to today's calendars, on April 7.

The first church to be established following the crucifixion was the church in Jerusalem, of which James, Jesus' brother, became the leader following the leadership of Peter. Apparently he became a convert to the Jesus movement (known at the time as "The Way") sometime following the resurrection. The Jerusalem church considered itself a Jewish fellowship whose members believed that the prophesied Messiah had indeed come in the person of Jesus. The members of the Jerusalem church kept all of the Jewish laws, festivals, and cultural traditions most Jews tried to keep. They attended the temple regularly, and also met together for a common meal on a regular basis. In a recent article, Geza Vermes says that

> in addition to their attachment to the Law of Moses, including worship in the Temple, the religious practice of the first Jewish

Part One: Christian Folk Religion

> Christians also included the "breaking of the bread" (Acts 2:46). This breaking of the bread was not a purely symbolic cultic act but a real meal. It had the double purpose of feeding the participants and symbolically uniting them with one another as well with their Master Jesus.[1]

The first century historian Josephus said that James was so ardent in his worship that his knees were callused and looked like "camel's knees." The church began as truly Jewish. The church then began to spread to the north into Syria and south into Egypt. There are even reports that it spread eastward, even as far as India, but the main direction was north and south, and the biblical accounts of Acts and the letters of Paul take us to the north into Syria and thence westward across Asia Minor and eventually into Rome.

According to Acts, Paul began his traveling ministry from the church in Syrian Antioch, on the northeastern shores of the Mediterranean Sea. In essence he was a traveling missionary from that church, and received its blessing. The church there became famous as the first time the word "Christian" was used to describe its members (Acts 11:26). The accounts in Acts make it clear that it was a church which was at least bi-ethnic. It had both Jews and Gentiles in its congregation. Paul being a Roman citizen, as well as a Jewish Pharisee, it was a happy mix of both the Jewish and Gentile cultures.

As a Pharisee Paul was fluent in Hebrew, but also being a child of the Diaspora, from the important seaport town of Tarsus, he also carried Roman citizen status. Rome did not grant citizenry lightly to those not from the city of Rome itself. A person or a member of his family had to have served honorably in the Roman army for an enlistment of at least 25 years, or come from a town which had received special recognition for its contributions to the empire. Because Paul declares proudly that he is a Pharisee, the son of Pharisees (Acts 15:6; Phil 3:5), it is unlikely that anyone in his family served in the Roman army, and thus it is assumed that his hometown of Tarsus, being at the time an important seaport, must have given extraordinary support to Rome's military, to be awarded citizenry to its citizens:

> In 66 BCE [BC] Tarsus became the capital of the new Roman province of Cilicia . . . During the chaos of the civil war, in 47 CE [AD] Tarsus placed itself on the side of the emperor, which at first

---

1. "Jewish to Gentile," *BAR*, Nov/Dec 2012, 54–55.

The Hellenization of the Christian Church

made great difficulties for the city but then earned it the favor and patronage of Anthony and Augustus . . . Tarsus was considered a center of Stoic philosophy . . . According to Strabo, "the inhabitants [of Tarsus] exhibited such great zeal for philosophy and education in general that in this regard they surpassed even Athens, Alexandria and every other place." . . . Tarsus can thus in every respect be considered a metropolitan center of Hellenistic culture . . . In the imperial period, the rights of a citizen could be obtained in Tarsus for five hundred drachmas; the apostle's ancestor could have purchased it and Paul could have inherited it.[2]

Paul was an ideal candidate to expand the church westward through Asia Minor, Greece, and beyond. He therefore launched the three missionary journeys mentioned in Acts, from his home church in Antioch. As the church began its move from Semitic/Near Eastern Oriental culture into a new culture, it moved into an environment totally foreign to Semitic thought patterns and the system of logic by which the Near East perceives reality. Even today travelers across Turkey (Asia Minor) will notice a difference in cultures from East to West. Eastern Turkey is decidedly more influenced by Near Eastern thought than Western Turkey, which is much more European in culture. The dividing line between the two is subtle and indistinct, but Galatia, which is a region almost midway between Eastern and Western Turkey seems to lean more toward Western cultural influences. Ancyra (modern day Ankara, the capital of Turkey) was the ancient capital of Galatia. This region begins to show more marked European influences than regions to its East, which are more Near Eastern.

Paul did a wonderful thing in his letters by carefully translating the Jesus movement's Jewish message into language a non-Jewish audience could understand. He did this not only by his use of Greek as the language of choice for his writings, but also by his selection of Greek words to represent very Jewish concepts. One of the most common words Paul substitutes for its Jewish counterpart is the Greek word *nomos*, which literally means, Law; its Jewish equivalent is *Torah*, which, as we've seen, really means "teaching," or "instruction," and the law is only part of that teaching, occurring mainly in Exodus and Leviticus. This becomes important to understand, if we are to grasp Paul's use of the term. Our understanding that law is legalistic, and becomes a burden, may be correct as far as it goes, but in Paul's usage *nomos* (Law) might have a broader meaning when taken in context. This has been dramatically shown in a

---

2. Schnelle, *Apostle Paul*, 58–60. The quote from Strabo is from Georg. 14.5.13.

Part One: Christian Folk Religion

groundbreaking book written by Methodist author, E.P. Sanders (1977) in *Paul and Palestinian Judaism*. Its publication was the first time that a comprehensive study had been done by a Christian scholar of first century Judaism, and related it to Paul's writings. This massive book is academic in the extreme and beyond the scope of this study. Its full bibliographical description is given in the Bibliography for those who want to venture through its pages. It is well worth the time and effort however, and it will change much of your understanding of Paul. It has done so for a significant number of scholars and students of the Bible which have developed a movement known as "New Perspectives on Paul." N.T. Wright, a former Anglican Bishop, and one of the most widely respected biblical scholars in the world today, is a leading proponent of the "New Perspectives on Paul" movement. A link to copious numbers of books, articles, blogs, etc. can be found on the internet at http://www.thepaulpage.com. Suffice it to say that the modern concept that Paul believes Judaism is, at best, legalistic, and that he believes Jews thought that meticulously following the minutia of the law's requirements would earn merits given by God and would lead to salvation, is wrong. Only the most conservative, and legalistic, Jews believed that. Not even the Pharisaic majority. They believed that salvation came through living a covenantal life, where they already experience God's mercy, grace, and forgiveness for whatever failings they may have. That is the same mercy, grace, and forgiveness Paul, a Pharisee, told his Gentile readers was now being given to them through the suffering, death and resurrection of the Jewish Messiah, Jesus. But even during Paul's writing career, some of his churches were plagued by conflicting understandings of the Christian message, especially in congregations composed of both Gentiles and Jews. Perhaps none of his letters express this more clearly than his letter to the Galatians, addressed to the churches of central Asia Minor, in the region of Galatia. In it he tells the Gentile members not to be fooled into believing that they must first become Jewish before they can become Christians. In an uncharacteristic burst of anger, after a brief introduction of greeting, in Galatians 1:6–8 he launches into this tirade:

> I am astonished that you are so quickly deserting the one who called you in the grace of Christ and are turning to a different gospel not that there is another gospel, but there are some who are confusing you and want to pervert the gospel of Christ. But even if we or an angel from heaven should proclaim to you a gospel contrary to what we proclaimed to you, let that one be accursed!

The Hellenization of the Christian Church

There can be no stronger language than to say that even if and angel from heaven should teach them something different than what Paul taught them, that messenger should be cursed! He then spends the bulk of his short letter telling them that Gentiles do not need to become Jews first and undergo the rite of circumcision, which was the mark of Judaism. What he is telling them is that through Christ they are now receiving the same mercy, grace and forgiveness God has always shown the People of God, Israel.

The second letter which addresses the division between Jewish members and Gentile members is the important letter to the Romans, perhaps the most eloquent letter he wrote. The church at Rome was not a church founded by him, but it was a church he planned to visit, and he used his letter to the church to introduce himself and summarize his teachings. It is in Romans 5:1 that Paul introduced his readers to "justification by faith." One of the issues in the church at Rome was a debate going on between its Jewish members and its Gentile members. It is now believed, however, that the vast majority of the members of the Roman church were Gentiles, not Jews. The question was: who has priority in God's eyes, Jewish Christians or Gentile Christians? The Jewish Christians were apparently asserting that because they are children of the covenants made between God and Abraham, and between God and Moses, that certainly their heritage gave them priority. But the Gentile Christians did not agree. The majority of the Jews had rejected Jesus as Messiah they reasoned, and the grace and mercy of God had turned to the Gentiles, and thus they had priority before God. It was a silly thing to debate, but it shocked Paul that there should be such squabbling. He had already addressed something similar in Galatians 3:28, where he said that there is no longer Jew or Greek, slave or free, male and female, for all of you are one in Christ Jesus. And he affirmed the same thing in Colossians 3:11. Now he had to say it once more, but this time he spelled the issue out in more detail. In chapters 9–11 of Romans, Paul explains that yes, Jews are the children of the covenant, and therefore have priority in the eyes of God, and yes, they have, in large part rejected the Messiahship of Jesus, and thus God has turned to the Gentiles, but they are still the children of the covenant even if, "as regards the gospel, they are enemies of God for your sake; but as regards election they are beloved, for the sake of their ancestors; for the gifts and the calling of God are irrevocable" 11:28–29. For Paul, the message is clear. Has God turned his back and rejected his covenant people? "By no means!" Paul cries out in 11:1–2: "God has not rejected his people he foreknew." Yes, the Jew always has priority in God's eyes because of the eternal covenant he made with them. In every passage where Paul mentions Jew and Greek in the same sentence, it is always in that order, Jew then Greek, the order of priority, it is one sure indication of the culture out of which Paul came, where in Jewish culture, status was always indicated by where people sat or reclined while eating, or the order of the listing of status as we see here, where Jew is at the head of the line.

But then, a few verses later Paul warns against anyone getting a swelled head over priority. He says that the rejection of Israel allowed for God's grace to be given to the Gentiles (v. 15). The Gentiles have actually been grafted onto the root stock, which is Israel. The grafted branches, replace the native branches broken off because of their rejection, and in their place a wild olive shoot (the Gentiles) has now been grafted in their place to share the rich root of the olive tree. Then he gives the Gentiles a clear warning: "do not boast over the branches. If you do boast, remember that it is not you that support the root [i.e., the Gentiles do not support the root], but the root that supports you" (11:18). This section of Paul's letter has been too long neglected by the predominantly Gentile Christian church.

This brief sketch outlines a church which had become divided into two principle factions, Jew and Gentile. Vermes describes the similarities and dissimilarities between the two:

> They both agreed on some essentials and ardently expected the impending second coming of Christ, the resurrection of the dead and the inauguration of the Kingdom of God. Paul himself insisted that it would happen in his own lifetime (1 Thess 4:15–17). In other respects, however, they saw things differently. The original Judeo-Christian baptism (a rite of purification) and the breaking of the bread (a solemn communal meal) were transformed in the gentile church under the influence of Paul. Baptism developed into a mystical participation in the death, burial and resurrection of Jesus. The communal meal became a sacramental reiteration of the Last Supper. The perceived differences soon led to animosity and to an increasing anti-Jewish animus in the gentile church.[3]

This split within the church can best be seen in two of the most important Christian documents written following the destruction of Jerusalem and its temple during the "Great Revolt" (a.k.a. "First Jewish Revolt" or *Jewish War*) of 66–73. The two ancient books are *The Didache*

---

3. Vermes, "Jewish to Gentile," 57.

The Hellenization of the Christian Church

("the Teaching"), and the anonymously written *Letter of Barnabas*. *The Didache* was written in the last half of the first century by an anonymous author(s) and includes an ethical way of life for members of the Jesus movement. It begins by saying, "The teaching of the Lord through the twelve apostles to the Gentiles. There are two paths, one of life and one of death, and the difference between the two is great" (*Did* 1:1)[4]. The author then goes on to give a catalogue of proper behavior for one who travels the "path of life." It is strongly influenced by Jesus' Sermon on the Mount in Matthew 5–7. It is believed that *The Didache* is the first to call the communal meal "the thanksgiving" (literally "Eucharist"). But the book includes a stern warning:

> And so, welcome anyone who comes and teaches you everything mentioned above. But if the teacher should himself turn away and teach something different, undermining these things, do not listen to him. But if his teaching brings righteousness and the knowledge of the Lord, then welcome him as the Lord. But act towards the apostles and prophets as the gospel decrees. Let every apostle who comes to you be welcomed as the Lord. (*Did* 11:1–4)[5]

The second book, representing a totally Gentile frame of reference is *The Letter of Barnabas*. Although it is named as though it was written by Barnabas, the traveling companion of Paul, Barnabas was long dead by the time it was written, which is believed to be about AD 120. Already by this early date the letter has decidedly anti-Jewish overtones, but the early Gentile church so prized it that the fourth century codex Sinaiticus included it as being among the books of the New Testament, although it was dropped from the canon in later codices. The first specifically anti-Jewish sentiment begins in chapter 4:

> Watch yourselves now and do not become like some people piling up your sins, saying the covenant is both theirs and ours. For it is ours. But they permanently lost it . . . when Moses had just received it . . . When they turned back to idols they lost it. For the Lord says this: "Moses, go down quickly, because your people, who you led from the land of Egypt, has broken the law". Moses understood and cast the two tablets from his hands. And their covenant was smashed—that the covenant of

---

4 Ehrman, *Lost Scriptures*, 212.
5. Ibid., 215.

Part One: Christian Folk Religion

> his beloved, Jesus, might be sealed in our hearts, in the hope brought by faith in him. (*Barn* 4:6–8)[6]

Notice now the distinction between "ours" (Gentile's) and "theirs" (Jews'). The covenant is now the sole possession of the Gentiles, while the Jew's are "piling up your sins saying the covenant is both theirs and ours." A little later, at the end of chapter 7, he boldly proclaims, "We have ourselves been perfected so as to become heirs of the Lord's covenant." In the very next chapter he makes the first known accusation against the Jews charging them with killing Christ, the same charge made by the Nazis which led to the holocaust.

When the temple was still in existence, the Jews regularly offered a red heifer as a sacrifice to God according to the law in Numbers 19:2–10. In chapter 8 of Barnabas the author says the heifer was a symbol for Christ. "The calf is Jesus," he says, "The sinful men who make the offering are those who offered him up for slaughter. Then they are no longer men and the glory of sinners is no more" (v. 2). With that sentiment growing within Gentile Christianity, the severance of the "wild olive shoot" (the Gentile church) from the "rich root" (the Jewish church) (Rom 11:17) was complete, the very thing Paul warned against. "It is not you that support the root, but the root that supports you," Paul cries out in verse 18. The severance became official in 180 when Irenaeus wrote his book *Against Heresies* which decreed that the Jewish Christian church, by then called "Ebionites," was heretical.

There is a movement within Judaism that identifies itself as Messianic Jews, or simply Messianics. Messianic Jews are practicing Jews who believe that Jesus (whom they refer to by his Hebrew name "Yeshua") was indeed the Messiah of the Jews, and treasure the canon of the New Testament just as much as Christians, but do not regard themselves as Christian, because they believe the term Christian applies to the Gentile church. Messianics may, or may not, observe the laws of the Holiness Code of Leviticus 17–26, but they do celebrate the majority of Jewish holidays of Passover, Day of Atonement, etc. Normally, however, they do not celebrate Christian holidays like Christmas or Easter. They do celebrate Yeshua's birth during the festival of Hanukkah, however, and they celebrate his crucifixion and resurrection during the feast of Passover. Messianics therefore celebrate their belief in the Messiah, Yeshua/Jesus, far differently than is common in the Christian community, which

---

6. Ibid., 222.

The Hellenization of the Christian Church

is more strongly influenced by Greek culture and philosophy. Thus the term Christian, to their way of thinking, is more correctly applied to the Gentile form of belief than the Jewish.

During the summer of 2011 my wife and I led a group of members from our church in Montgomery, Alabama on a trip to the Holy Land. Next to the Sea of Galilee is a museum which houses a first century boat that was found in the late 1980s. The museum is run by a group of Messianics, and in their gift shop, when I made a purchase there, a bookmark was placed in the sack with my purchase. On the bookmark was this quotation from Paul's letter to the Romans, "The root supports you! (Rom 11:18)." I have never been able to get that out of my head since, because it's absolutely true. Christianity had been grafted onto the Jewish rootstock, the native stock of God's everlasting covenant. We are not, as some people proclaim, the New Israel. We are not Israel at all. We are not the children of the covenant. We are a "wild olive shoot," to use Paul's terminology. Then Paul warns us that:

> You will say, "Branches were broken off so that I might be grafted in." That is true. They were broken off because of their unbelief, but you stand only through faith. So do not become proud, but stand in awe. For if God did not spare the natural branches, perhaps he will not spare you. Note then the kindness and the severity of God: severity toward those who have fallen, but God's kindness toward you, provided you continue in his kindness; otherwise you also will be cut off. (Rom 11:19–22)

He then explains a mystery most Christians haven't even known existed, and this is it:

> A hardening has come upon a part of Israel, until the full number of the Gentiles has come in. And so all Israel will be saved; as it is written,
>
> > "Out of Zion will come the Deliverer;
> > he will banish ungodliness from Jacob."
>
> "And this is my covenant with them, when I take away their sins". (Rom 11:25–27)

When Paul says: "A hardening has come upon a part of Israel," he does not specify *why* that "hardening" happened. Apparently it was not of Israel's doing because in 11:11 he indicates the "hardening" was part of God's master plan. Its purpose was to bring salvation to the Gentiles. It was God showing his grace toward us! The "hardening has come upon a

Part One: Christian Folk Religion

part of Israel, *until the full number of the Gentiles has come in*" (v. 25, the emphasis is mine). Today, as explained above, the Messianic movement is rapidly growing. It is believed there are as many and a quarter of a million Messianics in America which celebrate their faith in Yeshua/Jesus in synagogues across the nation.

Within Israel itself there are people of great faith who practice Judaism faithfully, and there are Jews who claim to be secular Jews (i.e. non-practicing) who also, when you listen to them carefully, have deep abiding faith, but do not practice kosher laws, nor keep the traditional festivals, and may attend the synagogue irregularly, if at all, and then there are totally non-believing Jews who may not believe in God at all (atheists), or simply don't know if God exists (agnostics), just as there are such folks in our communities. Does the hardening refer to their rejection of Jesus as Messiah? I sincerely dispute that thought. If Jesus could praise the faith of a pagan Roman centurion, and the faith of a pagan Canaanite, wouldn't he praise the Jew of faith even more, regardless of whether that person believed he was the Messiah or not? The hardening, I believe, refers to people of Israel who have lost their faith. They have given up on God. The Messiah has not come for them, or so they believe. They have suffered persecution and even the near extermination of their people. They perhaps feel that they've had enough of God. This, I believe is the part of Israel Paul is referring to. In any event, this hardening is only temporary until the full number of Gentiles has come in, when "all Israel will be saved" (Rom 11:26). According to Paul we Christians are not the New Israel, as I've often heard from pulpits and preachers and Sunday School teachers. We are grafted onto the root stock (Rom 11:17–23), which is Israel.

But here is the main point. As the church moved westward and become more and more Gentile, it also became culturally more Western than anything Judaism had ever known. This was not Paul's fault as some have claimed. In fact, as his letters show, he tried to keep this from happening. But happen it did. So I think it is time to explore (in summary however) what it means to be Hellenized (i.e., think and act like Greeks).

First of all, remember that the Greco-Roman world was a pagan world and each of the two influencing cultures of Greece and Rome had its own pantheon of gods. The combined cultures also were dominated by primarily Greek philosophy, theology, mythology, and way of life. These factors influenced everything the people within these cultures believed, lived, and worshiped. Gentiles who embraced the worship of Jesus were being asked by those who established churches within that culture to abandon their way of life, and their way of thinking. It was not enough to simply believe that Jesus was the embodiment of a God who was the reality for a people who lived in a world totally different from their own. As Paul quickly learned, that transformation was far more difficult than simply believing. Paul's Corinthian correspondence shows his frustration having to deal with members of the churches there who dined on "food sacrificed to idols" (1 Cor 8:4, 10:19–21). There remained strong pagan influences and tendencies which held powerful sway in their way they lived their lives including how they interpreted their understanding of Jesus and the gospel message, even as taught by the church's founders, whether the Apostle Paul or others.

The Western world has kept to the sense of reality, which is based on the pagan Greek philosophy of truth (remember when Pontius Pilate asked Jesus, "What is truth?" (John 18:38)? This philosophy was the product of several Greek philosophers. Plato and his followers in the fourth-century BC stressed the importance of transcending the physical world, which is a perceived reality, and is more an illusion than real. It therefore becomes a goal to escape this "illusion"—which can be corrupt or evil—as quickly as possible and move toward the purely spiritual world, or ideal world, which is, in truth, the "real world." Plato was followed by his student Aristotle, who taught that truth tends to be empirical, scientific, or according to common sense—"seeing is believing." Following Plato and Aristotle was Epicurus (340?–270 BC) who taught that happiness is the highest good. The goal for the Epicurean, therefore, was to experience endless bliss. One more major influence was a Greek school of philosophy founded by the philosopher Zeno in about 308 BC, known as "Stoicism." The Stoic school emphasized that its adherents stoically (i.e., calmly) accept all occurrences emanating from the gods' will, or the natural order of things. Although there are many Greek philosophies, this is enough for now. If you think carefully, you will be able to detect these thoughts in some of the beliefs we have outlined in the previous chapter.

There is at least one other major difference between the reality we Westerners cling to which must be mentioned as it plays a major role in our interpretation of scripture. Only people who think in terms of linear reality are a product of Greco-Roman cultural—and pagan—influences. We see things in straight lines. Look in any history book that has a "time line," often at the bottom of its pages, and you will see what I mean. It shows the "chronology" of events from a certain starting date to a certain ending date. Many books on Jesus have such a chronology of his life

Part One: Christian Folk Religion

illustrated on a time line. The synoptic gospels of Matthew, Mark, and Luke appear to follow such a time line of his life starting from his birth (Matthew and Luke), or the beginning of his ministry (Mark), and end with his crucifixion, death, and resurrection, yet that's not of the end of their story. Each of them point forward toward the future. Matthew ends with the commission to make disciples of the whole world; the long ending of Mark closes by saying that the disciples dispersed proclaiming the good news everywhere; and Luke says that they went back to Jerusalem with "great joy" blessing God "continually in the temple. This is cyclical thinking. It is a "never ending" story. The same this is true in John's gospel, although it is entirely different from the other three. There is no straight line chronology of Jesus' life. John seems to jump all over the place in Jesus' life and ministry compared to the synoptics. John has Jesus cleansing the temple in Jerusalem almost at the beginning of Jesus' ministry (John 2:13–22), while the synoptics each have him cleanse the temple just five days before his crucifixion. John has Jesus going to Jerusalem three different times during his ministry, while the synoptics only have him there once during his ministry, and that is the last week of his life. Luke in 9:52, about midway into his ministry, specifically says that Jesus "set his face to go to Jerusalem," and a little later in 13:33, he laments over the fact that Jerusalem is his ultimate destination by saying, "I must be on my way, because it is impossible for a prophet to be killed outside of Jerusalem." If you try to write a "life of Jesus" based on John's gospel, you will find it almost impossible. Instead of constructing a "life of Jesus," John constructs blocks or "themes" of Jesus' ministry. It is a very valid format, but you must remember that John has only one intended purpose, and that is that "these things are written so that you may come to believe that Jesus is the Messiah, the Son of God, and that through believing you may have life in his name" (20:31). That is his purpose. He is not outlining or summarizing Jesus' life, but interpreting Jesus' teachings to reach that purpose for the gospel, and he does so in blocks or various themes. At the close of John's gospel he laments that he could not write more when he says, "There are also many other things that Jesus did, if every one of them were written down, I suppose that the world itself could not contain the books that could be written" (21:25).

John's gospel, especially, and the other gospels as well, illustrate a nonlinear understanding of reality, which is common among most other people in the world. That reality is cyclical. It originated in Eastern thought and is common among Jews, Arabs, people from India, and

The Hellenization of the Christian Church

the Far East (all oriental peoples), and is also known to exist in all of native-American culture—the American Indian, the Mayan, Inca, Arctic and Antarctic cultures. In a cyclical understanding of reality, all of life runs in cycles. There is no positive beginning, and no positive ending. The only true geometric figure is the circle, followed by the oval. All the ancient peoples worshiped, lived, and believed that life is a series of cycles. Artists know that a straight line does not exist in nature. There is never a beginning or ending to anything. From the atom to the vast universe itself everything is spinning around something else. The idea of something beginning somewhere and ending somewhere else is the invention of Greco-Roman (pagan) thought, philosophy and theology, and has been incorporated into our interpretation of the Bible down to our present day. In Jewish thinking, the only true beginning begins with God, which is why John begins his gospel right there, "In the beginning was the Word, and the Word was with God, and the Word was God. He was in the beginning with God" (John 1:1–2). And the only true ending is also only God's, as the author of Revelation wants us to understand so clearly that he reminds us of it three[7] times, almost from the start of his book, "'I am the Alpha and the Omega,' says the Lord God, who was and who is to come, the Almighty" (1:8). It is again repeated in 21:6, "I am the Alpha and the Omega, the beginning and the end." If his readers still don't get this he repeats it one last time in 22:13, "I am the Alpha and the Omega, *the first and the last* (my emphasis), the beginning and the end." This final reminder is important because he spells it out in the phrase telling us that *he* "is the first and last." Everything begins and ends with him. He is the eternal creator God. Time and space are both creations of his. The author of Revelation wanted us to know this because his book is not about "the end of the world," as is so often thought, but rather about the earth's *renewal* by God. In fact, in all the Hebrew Scriptures, in the New Testament, and in Rabbinic Literature until late in the second century, there is no mention of the term "end of the world" where it signifies a time in history when the world comes to an end.

Take another look at John's gospel, and look at the last story of the gospel (21:20–23). It's a story about Peter asking the risen Jesus about the future of "the disciple whom Jesus loved." Jesus simply answers Peter by saying, "If it is my will that he remain until I come, what is that to you? Follow me!" That's the main point. John's gospel really never ends. It is a

---

7. The KJV also includes a 4th occurrence of the saying in 1:11, but most ancient manuscripts do not support that reading.

cycle, coming back to "Follow me!" Again it repeats the calling of Jesus' first disciples in John 1:35–42.

When God created the world, according to Genesis, he pronounced his creation "very good" (1:31). Try as we might, through human sin, or human folly, we cannot corrupt the "good" of God's creation. He rules that creation and if, at some time, the earth becomes so corrupt that his creation must be destroyed, God has failed, and *he does not fail!* He renews, redeems, and cradles his creation. *He* is the "Alpha and Omega, the first and the last." And this is why the world did not end on December 21, 2012, when Westerners believed the Mayan calendar ended. The Mayan calendar never ends; it just begins a new cycle—like flipping our calendar over at the end of December to the New Year and the "beginning" of a new cycle. For the Mayans, just like our year, the world simply started a new cycle. This cyclical understanding of time and space is a major departure from Western thought, which brings us right back to those pagan Greek philosophers which have influenced our thinking about our world, the time and space in which *we* live, and the way we interpret our Bibles.

Brian Knowles, in his article "The Hebrew Mind vs. The Western Mind," compares the way Westerners understand reality, and the way Hebrews understand it. A few of his most important observations[8] are that:

First, the Westerner believes a split separates the natural from the supernatural world, while the Eastern mind perceives the supernatural in everything. A common saying in Western culture is that "*seeing* is believing." What we can experience with our senses is "fact," but anything else is open to question. This is not so in ancient Hebrew thought. The existence of God is never questioned, it is taken for granted. Psalms 14:1 and 53:1 both echo each other by starting out proclaiming "Fools say in their hearts, 'There is no God.'" And then the two Psalms go on to describe such people as "corrupt" and "abominable" that do no "good." Atheism and agnosticism were unthinkable. The only question in the mind of the ancients was "which god is our God?" The eventual answer to that among the Hebrews was that Yahweh was their God who called them and led them out of slavery in Egypt. That realization, however, did not necessarily preclude the existence of other gods. Even Herod's temple complex in Jerusalem contained a huge courtyard called "The Court of the Gentiles" where Gentiles could worship their god(s) if they wished. They were not, however, allowed to enter the more sacred areas of the temple grounds

---

8. Knowles, 3.

The Hellenization of the Christian Church

where only Jews were permitted. Signs were posted at regular intervals along the stone balustrade warning non-Jews not to venture beyond that point on pain of death. One such sign found in 1870—inscribed in Greek—reads: "No foreigner may enter within the balustrade and enclosure that surround the Temple. Anyone apprehended shall have himself to blame for his consequent death."[9] Everyone, it was believed had his/her god(s). As was common throughout the ancient world worshipers could attend any temple to worship their own god(s) although, perhaps, not in the sacred precincts, but the question of the existence of god(s) was not an issue as it so often is in Western culture.

The Eastern/Oriental mind sees the supernatural in everything. There is no nation or people who do not worship something. As we will see in chapter 4 the oldest archaeology site in the world, discovered in 1995 and still under excavation, is one of the most important finds in history. The discovery, announced to the world in February 2010, is 11,600 year old Göbekli Tepe, which was built as a group of twenty circular worship sites before there were villages, or agriculture, or perhaps even family units. The supernatural has been assumed to be the natural "reality," seemingly forever. The American Indian, for example, believed that animals each have their own spirits, and they gave thanks to the buffalo they hunted for providing them with food and clothing. Just a cursory reading of the Bible reveals the belief that everything is the work of God, and that the supernatural pervades all of earth's activity.

Second, as already mentioned, the Westerner has a linear logic, while the Easterner perceives a cyclical logic or "block" logic. It can be argued that perhaps the only perfect geometric shape is the circle because it is the one shape which dominates the entire universe. In the atom, protons circle the neutrons. In the solar system moons circle the planets and the planets circle the sun. In the galaxies the stars circle the intense centers, and galaxies circle each other. While the old adage says that the shortest distance between two points is a straight line the shortest distance between two points on the earth (essentially a ball) is a curved line. Theoretically if a person drew a straight line long enough, say along the equator, the line would again meet itself, forming a circle. In oriental thought everything is cyclical. The American Indians, North, Central, and South, each pattern their lives on cycles, or circles. The Central American Mayan Indians' calendar is cyclical. That's why the world

---

9. Shanks, *Temple Mount*, 67–68.

Part One: Christian Folk Religion

did not end on December 21, 2012 when the Mayan calendar ended. It simply started the cycle all over again. For the North American Indians the circle was everything: life itself was cyclical, as it is for all cultures which descend from Eastern thought. The Native-Americans dwelt in round teepees, wigwams, or wikiups; their dances are always in circles, and their dress always depicts the images of spirits which surround them. The Hindus of India believe in reincarnation, carrying on the cycle of one life to the next. The Hebrew always believed that life never really ends, but only goes from the realm of visibility on earth to another realm beyond the sight of most humans. The one thing the Hebrews prayed for most, however, was not to be separated from God in death, which they envisioned as going down "to the pit," or to the realm "of the dead" (Job 33:24; Ps 28:1; 30:3; 88:4; 143:7; Prov 1:12; Isa 51:14; Eze 26:20, etc.).

Three times in the book of Revelation[10] God says, "I am the Alpha and Omega, the beginning and the end" (1:8; 21:6; 22:13). He alone has a "beginning" and an "end," and he is eternal. In him the beginning and the end meet. Again, it is a cycle.

Third, Westerners believe strongly in human individualism, while Eastern thought sees the importance of being part of the group, such as the family, whether nuclear or extended. The extended family has all but been lost in Western culture, especially North Western culture, but is vitally important in all the Eastern countries. Traditionally Eastern societies were most often tribal societies, each with their hierarchy of status. This was especially true among the Hebrews and they were justly proud of being God's children or chosen people. Paul, especially, emphasized that there is a "People of God," to which the Israelites belong, and to which Gentiles have been called to membership. It is to the "People of God," collectively, that salvation has been promised. Thus, individual salvation is the construct of the Western mind and not the biblical promise. One *must* be a member of the People of God to receive salvation.

Fourth, Westerners place great value on the equality of persons, while Eastern logic believes that value is derived from one's place in hierarchies. Later in this study we'll see how often Jesus speaks of status as it determines where one sits at dinner, etc. Even his disciples are ranked according to their status, the highest status belongs to Peter, James, and John. They are constantly mentioned first in all the gospels and are closest to him at the Last Supper (Matt 26:20–25 and parallels).

---

10. The KJV also quotes it a fourth time (in Rev 1:11), but it is omitted from the most ancient mss.

Murphy-O'Connor states that "in the culture of the Near East, no one condescends to visit a social inferior."[11]

Fifth, in our culture, we believe that nature is ruled by human power and understood by applying laws of science. In Hebraic thought, however, God rules everything, and relationship with him determines the future.

Sixth, in Western thought we perceive reality as often being static: facts are facts, "that's just the way it is," whereas Eastern culture understands everything as active, always tied with what we do. This difference in cultures presents many problems in our interpretation of scripture. For example: we think that what we "believe" is tied to our thoughts about what is real, or not real. In Jesus' commission to his disciples in Mark 16:16 he tells them, "The one who believes and is baptized will be saved; but the one who does not believe will be condemned" (cf. John 3:16–18; 6:35–36; etc.), and most Christians perceive this to mean that if you accept Christ as your savior you will receive salvation. But Jesus, throughout his ministry, called on people to "follow me," and repeated that phrase eighteen times. Belief, for the ancient Easterner, was not simply what a person thought about something, but how it caused a person to act. "If any want to become my followers, let them deny themselves and take up their cross and follow me," Jesus said in Matthew 16:24 and its parallels. This commands much more that "right thoughts" about Jesus. It springs directly from his culture.

The first major influence from Hellenization in Western Christianity is seen in understanding of salvation (the third observation above). In Greek thought, salvation was primarily understood to be the escape from this inferior material world[12] (Plato's philosophy) and a return to the transcendent, all-encompassing spiritual existence. Thus, our Western Christian emphasis on returning to God's realm when we die, where we will experience heavenly bliss forever, leaving behind this evil world of existence. Christians commonly believe in Jesus because he's our Savior and he is our assurance of entrance into heaven. This is classic Platonic thought. The material world is an inferior reality and it is our desire to escape it. Individually we seek, through our faith in Jesus to enter into a new spiritual existence. Epicurean philosophy has taught us to seek happiness, rather than responsibility. Believe in Jesus and you go to heaven, where you enjoy an eternity of happiness, endless bliss.

---

11. 2008, 129.

12 This is exactly the opposite from biblical thought.

Part One: Christian Folk Religion

There is no such concept in the history of Judaism, or in Jesus' teachings, if you believe that Jesus is truly the Jewish Messiah. Jews believed that their main task was to live moral, righteous lives before God. They also believed that it was their responsibility to see that their families, and/or neighbors, do likewise. They were to seek justice, live peaceably, care for the underclasses of society (the poor, the physically disabled, and all the disadvantaged). They seldomly spoke about what happens to them after death. The one thing, however, that terrified them most was being separated from God, especially at death. They often prayed that they would not be dragged into the pit (Ps 9:15; 30:3; 40:2; 55:23; 88:4; 143:7, etc.), which was always a euphemism for being separated from God. They were more concerned about this separation, than they were about their own salvation. But they understood God would save them through the covenant; that he would protect them and remain with them as long as they tried to live lives pleasing to God, which yes, included following his pattern for life, the Holiness Code. If they continued to lead Godly lives they knew that somehow God would hold them in his care. It did not so much matter to them how he would do this, their faith just knew that he would. As covenant people it was the promise of the covenant and, as such, the whole people would be saved corporately. Thus Paul says that "all Israel will be saved." This is clearly the message of Jesus in his parable of the rich man, and the beggar Lazarus. Both died, but the rich man was consigned to torment, while the beggar lay in Abraham's bosom (Luke 16:19–31). Western Christianity has often used this parable as an illustration of heaven and hell, but it is a classic Jewish lesson in righteous living. The rich man is in torment, not because of any wickedness on his part, but simply because he lived in luxury while the poor beggar suffered. In the parable Abraham tells the rich man, "Child, remember that during your lifetime you received your good things, and Lazarus in like manner evil things; but now he is comforted here, and you are in agony" (v. 25). This is a pictorial depiction of Jesus' teaching elsewhere when he told his disciples, "It will be hard for a rich person to enter the kingdom of heaven. Again I tell you, it is easier for a camel to go through the eye of a needle than for someone who is rich to enter the kingdom of God" (Matt 19:23–24; Mark 10:24–25). In classic Judaism, as seen in these statements by Jesus, salvation is predicated on one's responsibility in life to care for those who in life are the victims of social injustice, or wicked indifference. In the parable, Abraham's bosom is not a metaphor for eternal bliss in heaven, but a pictorial representation of the covenant

The Hellenization of the Christian Church

people, who were descendants of Abraham. They are in God's keeping. They are sheltered and protected by God. And it is collective. All those, who belong to the People of God, are sheltered by this covenant. That sheltering continues following death. They need not, therefore, live in fear of losing that sheltering as long as they live responsible lives based on the two fundamental precepts of God's law, "'You shall love the Lord your God with all your heart, and with all your soul, and with all your mind.' This is the greatest and first commandment. And a second is like it: 'You shall love your neighbor as yourself.' On these two commandments hang all the law and the prophets" (Matt 22:37–40; Mark 12:29–31). But along with this is a sheer warning that belief in God, or belief in Jesus, is not enough. Such belief must be accompanied by a life where a person accepts responsibility for those less fortunate who are powerless in a powerful world. Is this a form of social gospel? No, it is covenantal gospel where those of us who are in the covenant, and want to remain there, care for all those who are in God's care (Matt 5:43–48). Those who are automatically included in God's covenant are the classes Jesus calls "blessed" in the Beatitudes with which he begins his Sermon on the Mount, (Matt 5:1–11; cf. the "Sermon on the Plain" in Luke 6:20–26): "the poor," "those who mourn," the meek," "those who hunger and thirst for righteousness," "the merciful," "the pure in heart," "the peacemakers," "those who are persecuted for righteousness sake," "you when people revile you and persecute you and utter all kinds of evil against you falsely on my account." This is a collective list of those who are specially kept within God's care and are the "blessed." The list can be divided into two categories: those who are victims of oppression or social status (the poor, meet, those seeking justice, persecuted), and those who show mercy and care for those who are the victims (the merciful, the pure in heart, the peacemakers). In Jewish theology, it was the salvation of the covenant people as a whole, not the individual, which drove them to live lives of faithfulness and mercy toward those who cannot experience mercy in a world filled with indifference and cruelty. This Jewish understanding of what it means to be a covenant people can be summarized best in the words of E.P. Sanders, in Paul *and Palestinian Judaism*. The Jews of Jesus' day believed:

> that Israel stands in a special relationship to God as a result of God's election of them. God acted on their behalf, and they accepted his rule. It pleased God to give his people commandments, and the fulfilling of them is the characteristic religious act of the Israelite: it is his way of responding to the God who

chose and redeemed him. In attempting to give a rationale for the election, the Rabbis appealed to the free grace of God and sometimes to the concept of merit. God's rule entails obedience, and it also brings benefits and suffering upon his people, but even the suffering is beneficial. In any case, the Israelite is to fulfill what he was commanded; he does not question that God is fulfilling his role as king, judge, and redeemer.[13]

---

13. *Op cit.*, 106.

3

Yahweh, God of Israel

IN 1894, AT THE age of 56, the wilderness enthusiast and environmentalist, John Muir, in writing about the Sierra Nevada Mountains of California, which he called the "Range of Light," wrote this about the creation of one of the world's most spectacular mountain ranges:

> It is hard without long and loving study to realize the magnitude of the work done on these mountains during the last glacial period by glaciers, which are only streams of closely compacted snow-crystals . . . The pre-glacial condition of the range was comparatively simple: one vast wave of stone in which a thousand mountains, domes, cañons, ridges, etc., lay concealed. And in the development of these Nature ["God"][1] chose for a tool not the earthquake or lightning to rend and split asunder, not the stormy torrent or eroding rain, but the tender snow-flowers noiselessly falling through unnumbered centuries, the offspring of the sun and sea. Laboring harmoniously in united strength they crushed and ground and wore away the rocks in their march, making vast beds of soil, and at the same time developed and fashioned the landscapes into the delightful variety of hill and dale and lordly mountain that mortals call beauty . . .
>
> Contemplating the works of these flowers of the sky, one may easily fancy them endowed with life: messengers sent down to work in the mountain mines on errands of divine love. Silently flying through the darkened air, swirling, glinting, to their

---

1 Muir almost consistently used the term "Nature" for "God as creator."

Part One: Christian Folk Religion

appointed places, they seem to have taken counsel together, saying, "Come, we are feeble; let us help one another. We are many, and together we will be strong. Marching in close, deep ranks, let us roll away the stones from these mountain sepulchers, and set the landscape free. Let us uncover these clustering domes. Here let us carve a lake basin; there a Yosemite Valley; here, a channel for a river with fluted steps and brows for the plunge of songful cataracts. Yonder let us spread broad sheets of soil, that man and beast may be fed; and here pile trains of boulders for pines and giant Sequoias. Here make ground for a meadow; there a garden and grove, making it smooth and fine for small daisies and violets and beds of healthy bryanthus, spicing it well with crystals, garnet feldspar, and zircon." Thus and so on it has oftentimes seemed to me sang and planned and labored the hearty snow-flower crusaders; and nothing that I can write can possibly exaggerate the grandeur and beauty of their work. Like morning mist they have vanished in sunshine, all save the few small companies that still linger on the coolest mountainsides, and, as residual glaciers, are still busily at work completing the last of the lake basins, the last beds of soil, and the sculpture of some of the highest peaks.[2]

"God saw everything that he had made, and indeed, it was very good." (Gen 1:31)

THE ANCIENTS OF THE ANCIENT

About nine miles northeast of the town of Sanliurfa in eastern Turkey is a hill named Göbekli Tepe (pronounced Guh-behk-LEE TE-peh). The name of the hill means Potbelly Hill. On its top is one of the oldest archaeological ruins ever discovered. Carbon 14 testing has shown that the site was established approximately 11,600 years ago, or almost 10,000 BC. That's 7,400 years older than the Great Pyramid on the Giza Plateau in Egypt, and 7,700 years older than Stonehenge in England. The site was first looked at by Istanbul University and the University of Chicago in 1964, but at that time it was thought the hill contained a Byzantine cemetery and was not considered to be a major archeological find until 1994 when German archaeologist Klaus Schmidt visited the hill and believed the ruins were far older than the Byzantine period. Excavations began the following year and have been going on ever since.

2. Muir, *The Mountains of California*, 13–15.

Yahweh, God of Israel

On April 22, 2008 the discovery was made known to the world in an article by Nicholas Birch in the English journal *The Guardian* titled "7,000 Years Older than Stonehenge: the Site that Stunned Archaeologists." Two years later my wife and I were with a small Grand Circle Tours group traveling throughout southeastern Turkey when one couple asked if we could visit the site. Although in May 2010 the dig was not yet open to the general public, and because our group had only 15 members, special permission was granted by the archaeological team, headed by Schmidt, to make the visit. Our small bus climbed the gravel road up the hill and parked in the parking area where we were met by one of the archeological team members who served as our guide at the site. We then walked to the top of the hill and were stunned by what we saw. We could see several huge circles (only 4 of the estimated 20 found by ground penetrating radar have been excavated so far) measuring from 30 feet to almost 100 feet. The circles are surrounded by rectangular stone walls 6 feet high. What was unique about these circles was what was inside. Megalithic hewn pillars 9 to 18 feet tall are inside the circles. Two of the tallest pillars in each circle are in the circle's center. It is believed the pillars supported a roof, which peaked in the center.

Jean and I had visited Stonehenge years before, but we had seen nothing resembling this. The megalithic pillars were hewn out of limestone (quarried from bedrock pits about 330 feet from the top of the hill). Each column is shaped in the form of a "T." This gives them a humanoid appearance without a head. Many of the columns are decorated with relief carvings which are of an amazing quality. Some are three-dimensional on the sides or corners of the pillars and some are bas reliefs carved into the face of the column. Some of the reliefs depict powerful animals, such as bulls, lions, boars, donkeys, foxes, and gazelles. Others show creepy and crawly snakes and other reptiles, insects, spiders, scorpions. And some are of birds, particularly vultures. It is believed that what we were witnessing was the very first temple ever found. This seems to be confirmed by the existence of one pillar which appears to depict the body of a priest (albeit with no head) who is wearing a loincloth, a belt, a tunic with a V shaped neck opening, and what appear to be fingers of both left and right hands coming around the corners of the pillar. The images of vultures seem to indicate that the site may also have been a necropolis where humans may have been lain on above ground piers or platforms and been decomposed by vultures. Human bones have been found on the site along with bones of many animals, perhaps all were sacrifices. These structures were built

Part One: Christian Folk Religion

5,500 years before the cities of Mesopotamia, which is the region in the Near East where the archaeological site is located. It is in the very northern tip of Mesopotamia. Only about 30–40 miles southeast of the sight is the village of Haran, where Abraham lived for forty years (Gen 11:31). These circles and megaliths were built before the beginning of agriculture and the breeding of animals, which is believed to have begun about one thousand years later. In *the Guardian* article Birch reports that the archaeologist Schmidt said, "I think here we are face to face with the earliest representation of gods. They have no eyes, no mouths, no faces. But they have arms and they have hands. They are makers. In my opinion, the people who carved them were asking themselves the biggest questions of all. What is this universe? Why are we here?[3] "And perhaps that was the prime motive behind such a primitive ancient people building a temple complex before there were villages, or agriculture or social organization. They had an idea, a conception, of something beyond themselves which they could not understand, but which they believed might be able to protect them from the unknown.

We have no idea what or how they were worshiping, but it is fairly certain that this was a worship site. These megalithic pillars had to have been muscled up the steep hill from where they were quarried by perhaps as many as 500 men. And there they built the very first known stone structure in the world, to be found almost 12,000 years later. And it was a temple, or group of twenty temples, structures dedicated to the deities, or deity.

The meaning of the relief carvings is baffling. It could be that the animals and insects were the object of their worship. The flora and fauna of Asia Minor was much plusher than it is today and could support such an array of animals and scary critters. Perhaps the worshipers were asking them to do no harm. Or perhaps some unseen deities were being asked to protect the people from the dangers that lurked all around them. We can only speculate about what it was all for. But of this we can be sure: the need to worship apparently was the driving force to build elaborate structures even before societies began to be formed among the hunter gatherers of the ancients. And so it has continued down through history. As Myer rightly observes, "Without exception the great religions of antiquity ascribed the all-encompassing world of custom no less than the world of nature to the gods."[4]

3. Op cit., *The Guardian*.
4. Meyer, 93.

The stories of the pantheons of gods is well known from the religions of the ancient societies of Egypt, Babylonia, Assyria, Mesopotamia, Greece, and Rome, and from the great monotheistic religions of Israel, Christianity and Islam. Today deistic faith is the predominant faith of nearly all cultures and societies. True atheists and agnostics are a small, though often highly vocal, minority. During World War II there was the saying that "there are no atheists in foxholes."

So it is that we seem to have always searched the heavens for the answer to Klaus Schmidt's question, "What is this universe? Why are we here?"

Einstein once defined God as "the illimitable superior spirit who reveals himself in the slight details we are able to perceive with our frail and feeble minds."[5] We've been trying to perceive that revelation throughout our whole history. Sometimes we've been pretty good at it, but at other times we've been pretty sloppy. Then there's the statement that came from the French philosopher, Voltaire (1694–1778), who famously said, "If God did not exist, it would be necessary to invent him."[6] There's probably more truth in that than we'd like to think. A close examination of many of the sayings about God sound like people have invented him. Another French philosopher, Blaise Pascal (1623–1662), said, "The heart has its reasons of which reason knows nothing."[7] Yet when we try to define God, it is primarily by reason, rather than the heart. Perhaps that is why there have been so many missteps along the way.

GOD IN THE MORE RECENT MIND

In 1956 an autobiography of the boxer Rocky Graziano, was made into a movie. The book and movie were called *Somebody Up There Likes Me*. God, the Divine and the Almighty, in the space of five little words, has been reduced to "Somebody up there." In common parlance he is also the "Man upstairs," and sometimes even, "the Big Guy." In 1977, God even appeared in the guise of George Burns in the comic movie, *Oh God*. Irreverent sounding, though often amusing, terms and depictions such as these are part of our relaxed cultural world. We have grown up with them

---

5. Harris, 17.

6. Ibid., 2.

7. www.brainyquote.com/quotes/authors/b/blaise_pascal.html#QS7xPC6OfrTSMA6V.99

Part One: Christian Folk Religion

and think of them simply as folksy talk about God. God is our buddy, our friend, and our companion. He is also: "the Lord willing," "God bless you," and other casual sayings.

What we don't realize, or even acknowledge, is that in the Bible they are not folksy at all, but blasphemous epithets strictly prohibited by the Ten Commandments, "You shall not take the name of the Lord your God in vain." It is interesting that in the original Hebrew of the Hebrew Bible, the passage would correctly be translated, "You shall not take the name of Yahweh, your God, in vain." The Hebrew word for Lord is *Adonai*, which is a sovereign title for God, not the name he gave to Moses when speaking to him out of the burning bush. The story in Exodus 3:13–14 reads, "Moses said to God [Heb. *elohim*], 'If I come to the Israelites and say to them, "The God of your ancestors has sent me to you, and they ask me, 'What is his name?' what shall I say to them?" God said to Moses, 'Yahweh.'" Yahweh has always been recognized as the sacred name of God, but it is so sacred it was never pronounced by the common people for fear that at that moment they might have an impure thought and break the commandment which tells them not to take his name in vain. The Hebrew alphabet does not have vowels, so no vowels appear in the Hebrew Scriptures, and no vowels appear in the name of God, "Yahweh." In the Hebrew Scriptures it is simply four consonants, YHWH. Vowels are indicated, however, by small coded symbols above or below the consonant which has a vowel sound following it. This "vowel pointing" as it has sometimes been called, was invented between the seventh and eleventh centuries by a society of Hebrew scholars, known as the Masoretes, because Hebrew was becoming an extinct language and as it was only used in religious training, common people were forgetting how to properly pronounce its words. Thus the vowels needed to be indicated. The Masoretes worked actively from ca. 600–950 and their "pointed" versions of the Hebrew text became known as the "Masoretic Text" or MT. Today the MT considered as the most authoritative text by scholars appears in the Leningrad Codex[8] copied ca. 1008/1009 and is the version of the Hebrew Bible upon which modern translations are based. One word, however, never had any vowel pointing, and that was the name of God. The only person who was ever supposed to pronounce God's name, was the high priest of the temple, and that was just once a year, on the Day of Atonement (*Yom Kippur*), when he would enter the Holy of Holies and

---

8. "Masoretic Text" EDB, 868.

Yahweh, God of Israel

pray to God in his sacred name for the forgiveness of all of Israel's sins of the past year. Thus, in the Hebrew Scriptures, when God's name appears, it is only four consonants, YHWH, never to be pronounced. Some ancient manuscripts of the books of the Hebrew Bible don't have even those four letters, but have replaced them with four dots . . . . instead. In deference to the sacred name of God, English translators have substituted the word LORD, for his name. When it signifies the name of God, "Yahweh," it appears in all capital letters (with its last three letters in a smaller font size), but when it is the translation for the Hebrew word of Lord, which is *Adonai*, only its first letter is capitalized. The proper pronunciation of YHWH was not discovered until the mid-twentieth century, when scholars learned that only particular vowels appear in Hebrew between certain consonant combinations. The proper pronunciation is as I have given it in this study, "Yahweh." Because I believe it is important that we know when and where God's name appears in the Hebrew Scriptures I have consistently replaced LORD, where it occurs in translation, with "Yahweh." Its meaning is as it is given in Exodus 3:14: "I AM WHAT I AM" or "I WILL BE WHAT I WILL BE" (both translations are correct). That is who God the creator is. He is whatever he wants to be. That is why he is God. Yet in American slang, in order to avoid sounding too religious, or pious, the creator God has been reduced to "Somebody up there," or "The Man upstairs," or simply "The Big Guy," or other silly euphemisms. Such abuses are so common we simply smile and go on. But they are part of our culture. We accept them for what they are. Yet, for the ancient Hebrews, the name YHWH was so sacred it was never pronounced, not even when the scriptures were being read. When those four letters appeared in a passage, the reader substituted the Hebrew word for Lord, which was *Adonai*. In the early years of English translations of the Bible, particularly the King James Version (KJV) of 1611, because it was not known how YHWH was pronounced, translators substituted the vowels in *Adonai*, Lord, for the spaces between the consonants of YHWH and arrived at YaHoWah, and rendered it into English as Jehovah (Exod 6:3; Ps 83:18; Isa 12:2; 26:4—KJV). Only the high priest, bearing the blood of sacrifice which he poured out on the mercy seat, ever uttered the name of God, "Yahweh." After all, he was in the presence of the divine glory of God (the *Shekinah*) which was believed to be his dwelling place. Shining right there between the tips of the wings of the Cherubim, winged bulls or oxen which were guardians of God's Presence. But we'll get into a fuller description of the temple, its functions, priests and assistants, a little later.

It was where the high priest prayed for the forgiveness of all the sins of Israel for the past year. And he prayed in the name of Yahweh.

THE PECULIAR GOD OF ISRAEL

There was nothing usual about Yahweh, the God of Israel. The peoples and nations surrounding Palestine were filled with pantheons of gods and goddesses. They all had both male and female deities. This was true among the Hittites far to the north in Asia Minor (today's Turkey), in Egypt to the south, and along the southwest coast of Palestine in Philistia, the name from which the name Palestine was derived. Canaan itself, before it became known simply as Palestine, was filled with its own gods and goddesses, leaders among which were *Baal* and *Asherah*, god and goddess. In the Assyrio/Babylonian empires which bordered Palestine on its north and east the people bowed to its chief deity *Marduk*, and his consort, *Ishtar*, the mother goddess. Other gods in its pantheon were *Nercal, Naku,* and *Ninturna.* These deities were important in Israel's history because in the eighth century BC the northern kingdom of Israel went into exile in Assyria, and in the sixth century the upper-class citizens of the southern kingdom were exiled in Babylon. The sixth century Babylonian exile was the period when the great writing prophets of Israel flourished, Second Isaiah (chs. 40–55 of Isa), Jeremiah, and Ezekiel. The prophets kept calling Israel back from being influenced by the plethora of foreign gods and goddesses and coming under their spell. Listen to the words of the prophets:

> To whom will you liken me and make me equal,
> and compare me, as though we were alike?
> Those who lavish gold from the purse,
> and weigh out silver in the scales—
> they hire a goldsmith, who makes it into a god;
> then they fall down and worship!
> They lift it to their shoulders, they carry it,
> they set it in its place, and it stands there;
> it cannot move from its place.
> If one cries out to it, it does not answer
> or save anyone from trouble.
> Remember this and consider,
> recall it to mind, you transgressors,
> for I am God, and there is no other;
> I am God, and there is no one like me . . .

Yahweh, God of Israel

> Listen to me, you stubborn of heart,
> you who are far from deliverance:
> I bring near my deliverance, it is not far off,
> and my salvation will not tarry;
> I will put salvation in Zion,
> for Israel my glory. (Isa 46:5–9; 12–13)

> As a thief is shamed when caught, so the house of Israel shall be shamed—
> they, their kings, their officials, their priests, and their prophets,
> who say to a tree, "You are my father," and to a stone, "You gave me birth."
> For they have turned their backs to me, and not their faces.
> But in the time of their trouble they say, "Come and save us!"
> But where are your gods that you made for yourself?
> Let them come, if they can save you, in your time of trouble;
> for you have as many gods as you have towns, O Judah. (Jer 2:26–28)

> The word of Yahweh [YHWH] came to me: "O son of man, set your face toward the mountains of Israel, and prophesy against them, and say, You mountains of Israel, hear the word of the Lord [*Adonai*] God! Thus says the Lord God to the mountains and the hills, to the ravines and the valleys: I, I myself will bring a sword upon you, and I will destroy your high places. Your altars shall become desolate, and your incense stands shall be broken; and I will throw down your slain in front of your idols. I will lay the corpses of the people of Israel in front of their idols; and I will scatter your bones around your altars . . .
> But I will spare some. Some of you shall escape the sword among the nations and be scattered through the countries. Those of you who escape shall remember me among the nations where they are carried captive, how I was crushed by their wanton heart that turned away from me, and their wanton eyes that turned after idols . . .
> And you shall know that I am Yahweh, when their slain lie among their idols around their altars, on every high hill, on all the mountain tops, under every green tree, and under every leafy oak . . . Then they shall know that I am Yahweh." (Ezek 6:3–5; 8–9; 13–14)

The contrast between idol and Yahweh is always striking. And it was confusing for all the powers of the Near East. They couldn't understand how the God of Israel could engender faith or worship. How do you worship a god who is never seen? Yahweh, Israel's God, allowed no pictorial representation of himself, either in idol form, or in drawing or in sculpture, nor could he be carried as an amulet (Isa 3:18–21; cf. Exod 32:3–4; Judg 8:21, 26; 2 Macc 12:40). The absence of any physical representation of a god was impossible for the average person in the Greco-Roman world to fathom. Yahweh has his temple, but no real evidence that he is there. The temple, as far as the Gentile observer could determine, was empty. It was a temple to nothing. Consequently, some in the ancient world believed that the people of Israel were atheists. It seemed ludicrous that a people could believe that their god existed in an empty temple.

On top of that there was only one temple for all the Jews, no matter where Jews might live. How, the foreign nations wondered, can a god of Israel have only one temple, and only in the capital city. Every city of any size in the ancient world had its temples for their gods and goddesses, and some cities had numerous temples, yet the God of Israel dwelt in just one place, the Jerusalem temple, the House of Yahweh? It was unthinkable. By the first century Jews had dispersed all across the Roman Empire, from Alexandria, in Egypt, north through Syria, East to West through Asia Minor, across Greece and into Rome itself, and perhaps even beyond. Yet there was only one temple! For the faithful Israelite that location might be hundreds or even thousands of miles away. Israel's God was certainly peculiar, like no other anyone had ever experienced.

But absolutely the most unique characteristic of Israel's faith was the daily prayer, the *Shema*, which the faithful prayed: "Hear, O Israel, Yahweh our God, Yahweh is one" (Deut 6:4). It is also quoted by Jesus in Mark 12:29 as the first and greatest commandment. All the other cultures had many gods and goddesses, each of which had functions of creation, procreation, ordering of nature, and ruling the affairs of mankind. How could one god, and one god alone, manage all of that? Yahweh was indeed a "puzzlement," as the King of Siam repeatedly says in the Oscar and Hammerstein musical, *The King and I*.

On one of the early days of our trip in the summer of 2011 through the Holy Land, not far from Tel-Aviv, we were privileged to sit down with an olive farmer under the shade of some of his olive trees. The farmer's name is Ehud Yonay, a former reporter who worked for several years in the United States. He is best known as the author of the article he wrote for *California* magazine in the 1980s, entitled "Top Guns." It inspired the 1986 blockbuster film starring Tom Cruise, *Top Gun*. For an hour and a

Yahweh, God of Israel

half we sat under the shade of Ehud's olive trees as he related the story of how his family immigrated to Palestine before Israel became a nation in 1948. He also summarized the amazing story of the ancient Israelites as told in the Hebrew Scriptures and its history since then. It was perhaps the best summary of Israel's long history I have ever heard. As he was telling his own story of the immigration of his grandfather and father and their families, he told us that today in Israel, approximately 85% of its population identify themselves as "secular Jews," which simply means they are non-practicing Jews. Most of them rarely, if ever, attend a synagogue, or eat according to the kosher laws, and may or may not observe the High Holy Days, or other feasts and festivals of Judaism. In fact Ehud identified himself and his family as "secular Jews." However, as he finished his beautiful narration of personal joys and sorrows, interwoven with a quick scan of the history of Israel as The People of God, he made one very moving comment. "For most of our history, Israel has been under the domination, or persecution of one or another nation, of one or another faith. We were dominated by the Assyrians, the Babylonians, the Greeks, the Romans, the Inquisitions of the Middle-Ages, the pogroms of the Soviet Union, the Holocaust of the Nazis. But through it all, we have never just vanished as a people. All the dominating forces through the centuries have come and gone. But we are still here. What has kept us as the Jewish people? It is our faith; our abiding faith!" He is absolutely right. Whether non-practicing Jew, or ultra-orthodox, its faith has remained strong, even through the worst of times.

The Jewish faith really began when a Mesopotamian sheik by the name of Abram, living in Haran, in Asia Minor (Turkey) listened to the voice of one God, who identified himself as "the Creator" to Abram/Abraham, and asked Abram to follow him to a land he would show him, the Promised Land. Abram and his family were living in a city of many gods. In fact it was the center of the cult of the northern Mesopotamian Moon god *Sin*, his wife *Ningal*, *Utu-Shamash* (Sun) and *Istar* (Venus). With all of these deities vying for recognition, it was the call of a deity he had never heard of that compelled him to follow him to an unknown land. That was nearly four thousand years ago! No faith, in all the world's religions, can rival that longevity. It is a faith that in many ways is unique. It is monotheistic. It is centered on the majesty and promises of God. It integrates the spiritual world of heavenly deity, with the physical material world in which we live. From it has spawned another great religion, Christianity, the religion of the faith of Jesus, the messianic visionary who taught his followers that the world is under the absolute rule of his Father, Yahweh God—the creator God of the universe. Through this Messiah Jesus, Yahweh is engaged in the renewal of creation to its original pristine state and will ultimately, in his own time, destroy wickedness.

Through the four thousand year history of the story of Israel, the faith of its people has been relatively united. I know of no other religion in history where its faith has been a unifying factor rather than a divider of one group from another. Yes, Jewish faith is also divided into denominations, most notable of which are Orthodox, Conservative, Reformed and Messianic, but the major premises of the faith of Israel have not fractured into many diverse peoples. All accept the canon of the Hebrew Bible. All accept it as God's Word, and are generally in agreement as to what that means. All believe it reflects the true history of the People of Israel. All accept Yahweh as the Creator God, and the God of Israel. All believe they are a people chosen by Yahweh who are under his care. Yes, there are nonbelievers within Jewish society, who are still ethnically Jews, but who do not share its faith, just as there are atheists and agnostics throughout the world, who share no faith. But the story of Israel is about the people of Israel who do have faith, and who identify themselves as the People of God, or God's chosen people. There is a unity between all of its denominations which is striking. As far as I can tell, it is a unique quality found nowhere else which embraces its life and culture, and which is based on the ancient stories contained in the Torah, the Prophets and the Writings (TaNaKh) of its scriptures.

Perhaps one of the most divisive of the world's great religions is the religion surrounding Israel's Messiah, Jesus. Christianity, the very community for which Jesus prayed so fervently on the night before his death, is perhaps the most fractured faith in the world today. In his prayer he prayed for that community that would grow out of the most intimate of his followers, his disciples: "I ask not only on behalf of these, but also on behalf of those who will believe in me through their word, that they may all be one. As you, Father, are in me and I in you, may they also be in us, so that the world may believe that you have sent me" (John 17:20–21). Today, they seem empty words, as a survey of world Christianity has so frightfully illustrated. In 2011 the "Center for the Study of Global Christianity," at Gordon-Conwell Theological Seminary, South Hamilton, Massachusetts, conducted a global survey of Christian denominations, and this is a summary of what they found:

The World Christian Database represents over 9,000 Christian denominations throughout the world. The data regarding denominations is reconciled against people groups and country of residence. Because of this, complex reports can be generated about people groups or countries based on hundreds of possible variables. Major traditions represented:

Anglicans
Catholics
Independents
Marginals
Orthodox
Protestants
Charismatics
Neocharismatics
Pentecostals

Each denomination is also coded by their membership of Christian World Communions and Christian councils at world, regional and national levels.[9]

These statistics are staggering. How did a people, supposedly emanating from the same faith, with their focus on the same Lord, end up so fractured? And shockingly, this fracturing began just a few short years after Jesus' crucifixion and resurrection. Early on, perhaps only 25 years following its beginning, the Apostle Paul cried out in his first letter to the Corinthians,

> It has been reported to me by Cloe's people that there are quarrels among you, my brothers and sisters. What I mean is that each of you says, "I belong to Paul," or "I belong to Apollos," or "I belong to Cephas [Peter]," or "I belong to Christ." Has Christ been divided? Was Paul crucified for you? Or were you baptized in the name of Paul? (1 Cor 1:11–13)

Yet that is nothing compared to Christianity being divided into 9,000 denominations! Christians were first divided when the question arose about whether Gentiles could become members of the People of God without first embracing Judaism. Paul preached and taught that they did not have to become Jews first. Yet some of the members of the church in Jerusalem, primarily Jewish converts to the Jesus movement, insisted that Gentiles had to first convert to Judaism. Since then the

---

9. World Christian Data Base. www.worldchristiandatabase.org/wcd/about/denominations.asp

divisions have increased exponentially over many and varied factors. What is the correct way to believe the scriptures are God's Word? Did God dictate their content word-for-word? Or did he inspire human writers in what he wanted them to say? Do the scriptures contain any factual errors, or contradictions? "Yes," some say. "No," is the reverberating response of others. Do the ancient creeds of the first four centuries of the church really define who God the Father, God the Son and God the Holy Spirit are? There are creedal denominations, and non-creedal denominations. Are certain rites of the Christian church sacred (i.e., sacramental) or more metaphoric and/or symbolic? There are sacramental denominations and non-sacramental denominations, and yet also disagreements among sacramental denominations about exactly which rites are sacraments, and which are not. There are further divisions about how to conduct these rites. Do you use wine, or grape juice in Communion/the Lord's Supper/the Eucharist? Should it be every week, once a month, or quarterly? Should you use a single chalice, or a tower of trays with many small glasses? And the list goes on and on. The bickering seems endless. Division and divisiveness are rampant, with each denomination believing it is the harbinger for the truth. "We are right," one denomination signals the other, and "You are wrong," the other signals back. Ironically, it is the Lord's Supper/Communion/the Eucharist where the church has had some of its most dramatic fights over the centuries. The word Eucharist means "Thanksgiving," yet one denomination cannot fellowship with an opposing denomination to celebrate "The Thanksgiving" together. It is mind boggling! To my way of thinking it is the *Great Sin* of the collective Christian Church.

In this little study it is my hope to show that these are petty arguments compared to the major issue which has kept the message of the universal Christian church focused almost exclusively on what I have called Christian Folk Religion. It is time to move beyond this focus. Recently biblical studies have turned toward that beyond, and it is not that far removed from where we are. In fact, it has been there all along. It is the understanding, as Anglican scholar N.T. Wright has correctly emphasized to us, that, in fact, the story of the Messiah, Jesus, is not the beginning of a new story, but the climax of the story of Israel, as it is revealed in the Hebrew Scriptures. Wright explains in more detail what he means by this:

> It is wrong to imagine that the gospels (or Jesus, for that matter) were concerned with founding the church, which is the way some people have said it. There already was a People of God . . .

> The gospels were telling the story of Jesus as the climax of that people's story. Jesus came, they indicate, to rescue and renew that people, not to destroy it and replace it with something else. Israel is to be fulfilled, not replaced[10].

To understand this great climactic event to the story of Israel, we must also understand how this occurred and where we go from here. But first, there is a little housekeeping we must do. For almost the first 400 years of Christianity, the church was so focused on who Jesus was and his relationship with God that it ignored the roots of the faith, namely Judaism. It wasn't until AD 381 that the Nicene Creed was finally completed, the main purpose of which was to declare the absolute dual character of Jesus as equally both divine (the second person of the Trinity), and fully human. Jesus is both God and man. None of the creeds of the ancient church go beyond that, including the Apostle's Creed, which is believed to have originally been formulated in the late second century (about 180), the Nicene Creed, completed in 381, and the Athanasian Creed, the date of which, and its point of origin, are both highly disputed. The Athanasian Creed although so lengthy it is rarely, if ever, read in Christian worship, spends most of its many words trying to define the meaning of Trinity: One God, yet three-in-one, an almost impossible task. The concept of the Trinity was so important to the early church that none of the three creeds even touch on the life and ministry of Jesus beyond affirming that he was born of the Virgin Mary and was crucified under Pontius Pilate, buried, and raised from the dead. There is no mention of Jesus' teaching, his miracles, his parables, the establishment of the kingdom of God, or Jesus' insistence that he is indeed The Son of Man, whatever that means, which I will explore at length in chapter 5. The foundational root of Christianity, so identified in Romans 11:8, as namely the Jewish heritage of the whole story of Israel, is ignored to the point that it has largely been forgotten within the church universal. Jesus' ministry leads us through that important message by his two greatest teachings which were about the kingdom of God (or the kingdom of heaven), mentioned 117 times, and The Son of Man, mentioned 73 times. And he probably spoke of them many more times than these, but these are only the sayings remembered at the time the gospels were written, somewhere between 50 and 70. It is time, therefore, to flip back the pages of scripture, to find out where we went astray.

---

10. Wright, *How God Became King*, 112.

Part One: Christian Folk Religion

THE HOUSE OF YAHWEH

Whenever the term House of God, is used in scripture, it means only one thing, the temple. When Moses came down from Mount Sinai with the tablets of stone engraved with the Ten Commandments, Yahweh commanded him to build a portable shrine so he could travel with them, and dwell in their midst. The shrine was to be a temporary tent, a portable temple (if you will), called the "tabernacle." The design of its building is given by Yahweh in Exodus 25:9–27:19. This shrine, built around 1,200 BC, served as a temporary House of God until a permanent temple could be built, which was done during the time of King Solomon. That first temple was completed by Solomon in 953 BC, but was destroyed by Nebuchadnezzar, king of Babylon, in 587 BC. The period of Solomon's temple's existence is known as the "First Temple Period." Following the Babylonian exile, a second temple was built by King Zerubbabel in 516, and then greatly enlarged by King Herod the Great, beginning in 20 BC, but was not completed until AD 63, only seven years before its total destruction by the Romans, along with Jerusalem on July 29, 70 by the Roman Tenth Legion under General Titus. The period in which Zerubbabel's and Herod's Temple existed is known as "The Second Temple Period." Its destruction occurred during what is known as the First Jewish Revolt. The Revolt began in 66 and ended with the taking of the Herod's Fortress (called Masada) near the Dead Sea by the Romans in 73. This monumental event plays a key role in understanding Jesus and his role within ancient Judaism. Unfortunately most Christians have only a cursory understanding of the significance of the temple, or how important it was in his ministry, and especially how its destruction in 70 became a decisive force in the way Christians interpret and understand the Hebrew Scriptures. I hope the following pages will shed new light on this subject, because without a clear understanding of its importance, several of Jesus' most important teachings will not, and cannot, be understood. I am speaking of his primary teachings concerning the "kingdom of God" or "kingdom of heaven," and calling himself "the Son of Man." Without a clear understanding of the role of the temple for Jewish faith, and its application to the teaching and actions of Jesus, any interpretation of the New Testament books of Hebrews and Revelation will be found wanting.

The tabernacle and subsequent temple were absolutely vital to the faith of Judaism. They were the residences of Yahweh, the God of Israel. Within their walls dwelt the Presence of God himself. It was in an inner

Yahweh, God of Israel

sanctuary known as The Most Holy Place, or the Holy of Holies. It was the most sacred spot in Judaism and was separated from the rest of the temple's structure by curtains surrounding it (cf. 2 Chr 3:14; Heb 9:2–3). No one had access to The Most Holy Place except the high priest who entered it once a year, on the Day of Atonement (*Yom Kippur*—Lev 16), and sprinkled the blood of sacrifice on the covering of the ark of covenant, the Mercy Seat. The ark of the covenant was a chest made of acacia wood (a native Mediterranean tree) which contained the two tablets of the Ten Commandments and Aaron's budding rod (Num 17:1–11) and a golden urn filled with manna (Exod 16:33–34). The ark is also called the ark of the testimony (Exod 25:22; 26:34; 30:6, etc.), the ark of the covenant of Yahweh (Num 10:33; Deut 10:8, etc.), the ark of Yahweh (Josh 6:6), or the ark of God (1 Sam 3:3). Its size was about 45 in. x 27 in. x 27 in. and it was suspended on poles that passed through rings on its side so it could be carried (Exod 25:10–22).

Above the mercy seat covering the ark of the covenant were two gold-covered images of mythological winged beasts known as cherubim (Exod 25:18–20; 37:6–9; Num 7:89). Cherubim have been found at archaeological sites throughout the Near East and have depicted numerous beasts including winged bulls, but the type of beast depicted in the cherubim above the mercy seat are not known. Yahweh instructed Moses that

> The cherubim shall spread out their wings above, overshadowing the mercy seat with their wings. They shall face one to another; the faces of the cherubim shall be turned toward the mercy seat . . . There I will meet with you, and from above the mercy seat, and from between the two cherubim that are on the ark of the covenant, I will deliver to you all my commands for the Israelites. (Exod 25:20, 22)

The cherubim were the guardians of the Presence of Yahweh. It was the most sacred spot in Judaism. Yahweh was far more than a spiritual presence. He was physically there and his glory was visible. The Hebrew word for his glory used in the Hebrew Scriptures is *kabod*, but later it is more generally known as the *Shekinah*, or God's tabernacling presence (1 Pet 4:14). In the Hebrew Scriptures Yahweh's glory is a devouring fire which will consume anyone who gazes directly upon it, and thus, in the story of the Exodus, led by Moses, when Moses ascends Mount Sinai and enters Yahweh's presence, the top of the mountain and Yahweh are shrouded in clouds (Exod 13:21). This was to preserve Moses' life. The same was true when God's glory accompanied Israel through the Sinai desert (Exod 13:21), and the tabernacle was covered by clouds when his glory filled it (Exod 40:35). There was even the time when the cloud in the temple was so thick the priests could not see to minister (1 Kgs 8–11). Whenever the high priest entered the Holy of Holies on the Day of Atonement with the blood of sacrifice, he also carried the incense pot (Exod 31:11) which surrounded him with the smoke of burning incense. This served as a cloud to shield him from God's glory. Throughout the scriptures, whenever a cloud is mentioned, it is usually to shield a mortal from that devouring glory. This is true in Daniel 7:13 when "one like a son of man" ascends to Yahweh on his throne, and it is likewise throughout Jesus' description of "the Son of Man" coming in power on the clouds of heaven. Clouds and God's glory almost always travel together whenever they are described.

The temple was divided into three units, the outer unit or *ulam* (porch or vestibule), *hekal* (nave), by which the whole building became known, and the *debir*, the inner sanctuary or Most Holy Place. The nave housed the golden lampstand, and the table of showbread.

The value of understanding the temple in Judaism cannot, and must not, be minimized, if we are to understand the mystery and ministry of Jesus. It is always the place where God dwells. It is where earth and heaven meet. As Wright so correctly observes:

> Not only was the Temple the center of the whole national life. It was, Jews believed (as many ancient peoples believed about their temples) the place where heaven and earth themselves interconnected and overlapped. It was therefore the place to which one might go for healing, forgiveness, and the renewal of fellowship with Israel's God. It was also—and a glace through the Old Testament will show what this means—the place in which God established his power base. "Heaven," after all, was seen as the throne room, the place from which "earth" would be ruled. But if "heaven" came to be linked with a particular point on "earth," then that point was where power was concentrated. Divine power. Theocracy. The kingdom of God. Long before anyone thought of linking kingdom and cross, the far more obvious link was kingdom and Temple.[11]

If God is in our presence, it is in his holy temple. It has been this way since the Exodus from Egypt. God wanted a house for himself, and he

---

11. *How God Became King*, 235–36.

gave instructions to build him a temporary house (the tabernacle) until a permanent house could be built for him. That permanent house is now and has always been the temple. Yes, the Jerusalem temple was destroyed in 70, but it still is very much in existence as a heavenly temple. You cannot see it, or hear it, but it's as real as God is real, or as Christ is real. It surrounds you; it is in you; and you are in it.

Psalm 11 says it so well:

> In Yahweh I take refuge, how can you say to me,
> "Flee like a bird to the mountains;
> for look, the wicked bend the bow,
> they have fitted their arrow to the string,
> to shoot in the dark at the upright in heart.
> If the foundations are destroyed,
> what can the righteous do?"
> Yahweh is in his holy temple;
> Yahweh's throne is in heaven.
> His eyes behold, his gaze examines humankind.
> Yahweh tests the righteous and the wicked,
> and his soul hates the lover of violence.
> On the wicked he will rain coals of fire and sulfur;
> a scorching wind shall be the portion of their cup.
> For Yahweh is righteous;
> he loves righteous deeds;
> the upright shall behold his face.

Yahweh is always in his temple, even when the foundations [of the temple] are destroyed, the righteous are shielded and protected by his presence. His throne is in heaven, which obviously is also within his holy temple. It is there that he examines and judges all of humanity, both the righteous and the wicked. While on the wicked he will rain coals of fire and sulfur, because he is righteous; he loves righteous deeds and the upright shall behold his face. Here the clouds are gone, and the righteous stand in his presence. It is where earth and heaven meet. Has the temple been destroyed? Only the physical and visible temple, but when scriptures and Jesus speak of the presence of God, it is in the temple.

THE FORK IN THE ROAD

As we travel through life, we are confronted by many forks in the road of our experience. This is part of the excitement of simply living our lives.

Part One: Christian Folk Religion

The same is true of our spiritual lives, both individually and as the People of God. Shortly after the birth of Christianity, a fork appeared in its early life cycle. One of those forks has been mentioned several times above. I'm speaking of the conflicted opinions between Jewish and Gentile believers, whether to admit Gentiles into the Jesus community without first ascribing to the way of life common in Judaism, with its many laws, feasts and festivals, and bearing the mark of that way of life by all its males' being circumcised. In about 48 an agreement was reached by Paul and his fellow missionaries, and the Jewish church in Jerusalem, which was by then under the leadership of James, the brother of Jesus. That decision is described in Acts 15 and the first 2 chapters in Galatians. Paul would carry on his mission among the Gentiles, without the need to convert them to Judaism first, and the Jerusalem church, along with one of Jesus' first disciples, Simon Peter, would focus on their missionary work to the Jewish communities. It was a good decision and it held great promise for a long lasting relationship between two very distinct cultures, each meeting the spiritual needs of its respective membership.

It was not very long, however, when due to two major conflicts the world stage changed. The two conflicts were (1) the shift of power within the Roman Empire to one of particularly brutal oppression, and (2) a revolt against that power within Israel itself. It is imperative that we take a look at each of these in turn, and then see how it affected the path the Christian church would take.

Nero and the Roman Empire

Israel was notorious across the Near East and Mediterranean region for its religious loyalty to its God and its way of life. This religious loyalty had, in the past, resulted in major uprisings. In about 200 BC Judea and its capital city Jerusalem came under the administrative control of the Seleucid dynasty based in Antioch, Syria. In 175 BC a new king came to power within that dynasty with the title: Antiochus IV Epiphany. He was a particularly brutal monarch who decided to uproot the peculiar religion of Judaism, with its invisible God, and replace it with the Roman religion and its gods. Thus, in 167 BC his forces entered the temple in Jerusalem and desecrated it by setting up a statue of the Roman god Zeus, outlawed traditional Jewish worship and then did the unthinkable: he had pigs sacrificed on its altar, knowing full well the Jewish laws

Yahweh, God of Israel

against pork in any fashion. The prophet Daniel called this despicable act, "the abomination that desolates" (12:11; cf. Matt 24:15; Mark 13:14). This event led to a major revolt, headed by five brothers of a very powerful family, the Hasmonean family, which raised a sizable army of rebels, threw the Seleucids out, cleansed the temple, and rededicated it in 164 BC. The cleansing of the temple after the Maccabean Revolt, as it came to be known, is celebrated today in the Jewish festival of Hanukkah. The history of this period can be read in 1 and 2 Maccabees, in the Apocrypha of the Hebrew Scriptures, as well as that above mentioned in Daniel.

The military victory by Judas and his brothers caused the Roman government to tread lightly when it came to dealing with the Jewish religion. Passions could be inflamed at any moment, and therefore Rome gave a waver in allowing Israel to continue its own religion, with a quasi-"hands off" policy. They became unique in that it was the only religion tolerated outside Roman religion. Thus, when Christianity was born, as long as it was believed to be a cult of Judaism, Rome left it alone. By the time Nero became Emperor in 57, and Christianity had grown to the point that it was recognized as a new religion, it began to experience Rome's brutality.

Before then, however, Judaism, while under the watchful, though wary eye of Rome, there was relative calm. During major festivals, such as Passover, however, the Roman presence increased dramatically, as religious pilgrims flooded into the capital city. The Roman army in occupied territory, which was usually a legion (ca. 6000 men) or more, was under the command of the regional Roman governor or prefect. This huge military force in Israel was normally based in the Mediterranean port city of Caesarea Maritima. During the week of Passover celebrations, however, the governor would move to Jerusalem, taking most of his army with him. They took up residence in the Antonio Fortress, which was on the northwest corner of the temple complex, overlooking the temple, watching for any troublemakers. Pontius Pilate, the Roman governor during Jesus' ministry, was governor only of the southern part of Israel, Judea. Antipas, the son of King Herod the Great, was the tetrarch and so-called "king" of the northern areas of Israel, including the Galilee region and Perea. A tetrarch was an emperor appointed vassal who retained local sovereignty, thus his title, "King Herod"—or simply "Herod"—in the gospels during the ministry of Jesus, although he should more properly be known simply as Antipas. His father, King Herod the Great, had died in 4 BC. Antipas had his palace in the city of Tiberius, on the western shore of the Sea of Galilee. During Passover he also took up residence in Jerusalem exercising authority over any citizen of his territory who might be charged with criminal acts, which could be fairly often because Galilee, which was in his territory, was known for its insurgents and terrorists. That's one of the reasons why Jesus was watched so closely when he was in Jerusalem. He and his disciples, all apparently from Galilee, were kept under surveillance and considered possible troublemakers. During Jesus' lifetime several events had occurred which made even the Roman Empire wary of a seething rebellion under the surface of its people. In AD 6 a census was announced by the newly appointed Governor Quirinius in Syria, which at the time was the regional authority for the control of Israel. The people of Israel knew that this census would be needed for just one purpose—to establish a tax base for the people, which would be followed by excessive taxes to fill the coffers of the Roman Emperor and his oppressive regime. The citizens were up in arms, and under the leadership of a man by the name of Judas the Galilean, an armed revolt took place. He began a movement of rebels known as Zealots which was a guerrilla band of Jewish peasants determined to convince the Roman army it would be wise to move out of Israel. They used various acts of primitive terrorism, such as assassinations, to achieve that aim. The Zealots were active right through Jesus' life. One of Jesus' lesser known disciples was a man named Simon who is mentioned as being a member of the Zealots, although we know nothing about him or his connection with the rebels. Also common throughout this period were bands of bandits who assaulted and robbed citizens, as Jesus' parable of the Good Samaritan illustrates.

Palestine was not a safe place to travel. There were thieves, thugs, and dangerous people lurking around almost every corner. One of the most notorious groups known for treacherous activities, and especially assassinations of Romans and Roman sympathizers, were a group of thugs known as *sicarii*, so named because of the curved dagger they carried under their robe, the *sica*. They would approach an unsuspecting Roman or sympathizer, stab the person from behind and then quickly blend into the crowd. The first century historian, Flavius Josephus, describes them in great detail in his *The Jewish War*:

> These men committed numerous murders in broad daylight and in the middle of the City. Their favourite trick was to mingle with festival crowds, concealing under their garments small daggers with which they stabbed their opponents. When their

victims fell, the assassins melted into the indignant crowd, and through their plausibility entirely defied detection. The first to have his throat cut by them was Jonathan the high priest, and after him many were murdered every day. More terrible than the crimes themselves was the fear they aroused, every man hourly expecting death, as in war. They watched at a distance for their enemies, and not even when their friends came near did they trust them; yet in spite of their suspicions and precautions they were done to death.[12]

It has been suggested that perhaps the surname of Judas Iscariot, the betrayer of Jesus, may have been derived from the word *sicarii*. But this seems impossible because Josephus says that the group was formed in the 50s during the governorship of Felix. Others think that Judas' last name comes from the name of a town in Judea, Kerioth. If Judas was from that town, however, he is the only known of Jesus' twelve disciples who may have come from southern Palestine. All the other major disciples seem to have come from Jesus' home town region of Galilee.

But Rome knew that any one of a number of bands of terrorists could inflame the people in an instant and break the Roman Peace (*Pax Romana*) and that was their foremost goal. Thus they let the Jews have their peculiar and strange religion with a degree of tolerance. In return, the high priest and the chief priests of the temple worked with the Roman government to help maintain that peace. It was an alliance which bothered the general populous, but it kept the status-quo fairly in check.

Because of the many and varied armed groups roaming the highways and byways of the countryside, it was dangerous business to travel alone. Most citizens going any distance at all traveled in groups, the larger the better. When Jesus was twelve years old and his family traveled the 85 miles from Nazareth in the Galilee during Passover to go to Jerusalem, presumably for Jesus' *Bar Mitzvah*, they traveled in such a large company of people that they had traveled a full day's journey on the way home before they realized he was not with the group and they had to turn back. They searched for three days before they found him in the temple, learning from the great teachers of the law there, the Pharisees. His parents were not amused and he went down with them and came to Nazareth, and "was obedient to them" (Luke 2:41–51). I think that's a safe statement.

---

12. Josephus, *War*, 147.

Part One: Christian Folk Religion

Nero became Emperor in 54 at the age of seventeen. He is perhaps best known as the Emperor who "fiddled while Rome burned" ten years after taking office. He has long been suspected of having started The Great Fire of Rome himself so he could clear an area for his planned palatial complex. Whether that is true or not is often debated, but he was an egomaniac who would stop at nothing to show his power. Very little that is written paints a positive picture of him. Regardless whether Nero started the fire himself or not, he blamed the Christians for igniting the blaze, that destroyed most of Rome. That led to the first and prolonged persecution of Christianity. It was known that he had Christian captives crucified, lined the roads of Rome with them, and then set them on fire to light the paths at night. He had captive Christians dressed in the skin of wild animals, and then let loose wild dogs which tore the Christians apart, limb by limb and then eaten. This great persecution, the first and perhaps the only truly universal persecution, is believed to have been the setting behind the book of Revelation. Rome had recently determined that Christianity was not a sect of Judaism, and thus not protected by the agreement between Judaism and Rome. If Christianity was not a Jewish sect it was an illegal religion under Roman law and fair game for sadistic sport. That first great persecution lasted about four years from 64 until Nero committed suicide in 68. Suetonius, a Roman historian at the end of the first century, does not mention that Christians had become scapegoats after the fire, but in a previous paragraph, mentions punishments inflicted on Christians, defined as men following a new and malefic superstition. Tradition says that it was during the Neronian persecution that the apostles, Peter and Paul were executed. Peter died by crucifixion, and Paul by beheading. Paul could not be crucified because it was illegal to crucify a Roman citizen because of its barbarity, and Paul was a Roman citizen. The book of Revelation is a book of hope and inspiration, and gave the message of perseverance to those enduring such suffering, assuring them that despite it all, God was still king. He ultimately would be the victor, and the world would be renewed, and there was a heavenly Jerusalem, waiting for them.

James the apostle, son of Zebedee, was already dead (Acts 12:2). Tradition also says Andrew, the brother of Peter, and the first disciple called by Jesus, was crucified around 70 in the city of Patras in Achaia. Thus within 40 years of Jesus' crucifixion most of the original disciples had died or been killed. Also dying about this time was James, the leader of the Jerusalem church, and brother of Jesus. He was killed in the temple in Jerusalem by being clubbed to death in about 62 Most of the major figures involved in the meteoric rise of the faith were lost within a ten year time span. It is little wonder that major changes were on the way. In fact, in the same period, the temple, Jerusalem, and the church there, would be gone, and with that the voice of Judaism was all but silenced within Christianity. Lost in the catastrophe of the decade of the 60s and early 70s was the instruction Jesus gave to his twelve disciples: "Go nowhere among the Gentiles, and enter no town of the Samaritans, but go rather to the lost sheep of the house of Israel" (Matt 10:5). Now the tables would be turned. The church would be almost totally controlled by Gentiles, and much of Jesus' Jewish message would be forgotten until the last quarter of the twentieth century.

The Fall of Israel

What truly determined the direction the church would take at the fork in the road were the catastrophic events which occurred in Israel itself. It began in 66 in a war perpetrated by militant rebels, Judea against the Roman Empire. Josephus, in his book *The Jewish War*, says that the rebellion broke out in Caesarea in 66 because Greeks (a term often used of non-Jews, and he probably meant simply, Gentiles) had been sacrificing birds in front of a local synagogue. The Roman garrison was quickly overrun by the rebels (*sicarii*) and the might of Rome came down heavily on the rebels, who could possibly also have been Zealots. Nero appointed General Vespasian to quickly crush the rebellion. He arrived in Palestine in April 67. He was soon joined by his son Titus, and the Roman garrison was rapidly increased to ten legions, or about 60,000 troops. The strategy was to sweep through the country from north to south. The serious operation, therefore, began in Galilee. Town after town fell to the Romans; many without even putting up a fight, but those who did were crushed almost immediately. Following Galilee, Vespasian moved his headquarters to Caesarea on the coast and swept through the coastal areas destroying everything in Rome's path. With victory after victory to his credit, Vespasian became very popular back in Rome. In 68 Nero had become increasingly erratic in his behavior and the Senate decided to remove him. The pressure on Nero caused him to commit suicide. He was followed by the Emperor Galba, who was murdered by his rival Otho after just a few short months, and quickly Vespasian was hailed emperor by his legions. This convinced him to return to Rome and claim the throne from yet another incompetent emperor, leaving his son Titus to finish the war in Judea. The 60s ended up having four emperors, Nero, Galba, Vitellius, and finally, Vespasian.

Although Jerusalem had been under siege near the beginning of the war, it had reached a stalemate. Titus and his tenth legion dug trenches around the walls of Jerusalem. Those who tried to escape the city and were caught were crucified and hung in lines on top of the dirt wall facing Jerusalem. As many as 500 Jews were crucified in a single day.

By the summer of 70 the walls of Jerusalem had been breached. The city was systematically being destroyed and burned. At the end of July the great temple was destroyed, and nothing was left except rubble. Jerusalem had totally fallen. Christian pilgrims traveling to Israel as late as the sixth century reported not knowing where the city even was, such was the devastation of the conflagration. The Arch of Titus can be seen in Rome to this day which shows the treasures of the temple being carried by Roman soldiers into Rome during Titus' triumphal procession there. The war went on for another three years, and only ended with the fall of the last stronghold, Herod's fortress Masada, along the southwestern tip of the Dead Sea, in 73.

Before the siege of Jerusalem reached its dramatic conclusion the remnants of the Jerusalem church had fled to Pella, now in Jordan. It had lost its voice and its influence. By 70 the only voice of the church was that of Gentile culture. The Jewish influence was gone. The temple was gone, and for all practical purposes, seemed irrelevant to the message of the church, most of the original apostles were gone, all of them Jewish, and in the centuries to follow the names of the early church fathers all had Gentile names: Clement, Ignatius, Policarp, Irenaeus, Tertullian, Origen, Justin, Athanasius, John Chrysostom. The Jewish voice had been silenced. Christianity's root had been effectively pruned off its branches, the very thing Paul warned against in Romans 11:17–21. If, as Christians, we think that the significance of the temple is in the past, that it belongs only to our mother religion, or faith, we are sadly misguided. In understanding the temple and its central place in the person of Jesus the Messiah we will better understand what the kingdom of God is, and why Jesus called himself the Son of Man. We will also understand what precipitated Jesus' crucifixion, and what the future holds for our own afterlife. These things are all bound up together in illuminating our faith so we can expand it beyond Christian folk religion.

We will learn why Jesus has sometimes been called a non-pious Torah believer; why so many of his parables were spoken in riddles; what his role was and is as the Son of Man; the real reason he healed the sick, made the blind to see, made the disabled whole again, and raised the dead; what it means that he is seated on the right hand of the Father; how he will come again in power and glory. And above all, we will get a glimpse of the heavenly Jerusalem. Is all of that possible in this little book? I hope so, but if not, it will start you on the way to self-discovery, which will fill your life with joy and hope until you experience it all yourself.

PART TWO

Moving Beyond
Christian Folk Religion

4

The Baptizer

LUKE IS THE ONLY gospel which tells us anything about the family and pedigree of John the Baptizer. We don't know exactly what Luke's sources were for this information (1:1–4) but in the space of only his first chapter we learn quite a bit about John's background. We learn that his parents were named Zechariah and Elizabeth. Zechariah was a temple priest (v. 5) who assisted at the temple periodically according to the custom of the priesthood where he offered incense (v. 9). Elizabeth was a descendent of Aaron, who was the brother of Moses, and the priestly family from which all the high priests of Israel were supposed to be descended. Thus, both John's parents descended from priests and by the laws of descent John also would have been a priest. It is informative that it was in the temple that the angel Gabriel appeared to Zechariah and told him that his wife Elizabeth would become pregnant with John. It was a shock to him because both he and Elizabeth were advanced in age and had been unable to have children.

We also learn that the name John was given to him in accordance with instructions from Gabriel (v.13). Elizabeth was a relative of Jesus' mother (v. 36), Mary, but we don't know the nature of that relationship. The assumption has usually been that John and Jesus were cousins, but it seems more likely that they were second cousins. We don't know where John was born, although a traditional site of his birth is Ein Karem, a hill southwest of Jerusalem, where there are two churches honoring him: the

Church of St. John the Baptist and the Church of the Visitation. In any case, his family must have been located very near Jerusalem so Zechariah could serve at the temple when scheduled to do so.

Family and friends considered John's birth and life ordained by God from the outset, according to Luke's account (v. 66–80). The first chapter of Luke ends by telling us that the child grew and became strong in spirit, and "he was in the wilderness until the day he appeared publically to Israel" (v. 80). This cursory statement which summarizes the young life of the Baptizer is typical of ancient biographies. Unlike modern biographies, ancient biographies do not show intellectual, psychological or moral development which occurs with maturity from child to adult. These developmental stages are simply omitted and if the biography includes an incident during a child's formative years he/she appears more adult-like than the child's actual age. This is clear in the Gospel of Luke. Even though Luke is the only source for a story of Jesus between his birth and his adult ministry, that being his visit to the temple when he was twelve years old (2:41–52), Jesus does not respond like a typical twelve year old. He is seen disregarding the concern his parents had for him, and answers curtly, "Did you not know that I must be in my Father's house?" (v. 49). It sounds like a fully developed adult's response.[1]

JOHN IN THE WILDERNESS

All of the gospels mention that John came out of the wilderness when he began his public career. The wilderness could mean one of two places: either the Judean desert which begins about thirteen miles to the southeast of Jerusalem by the Dead Sea, or the Negev desert directly south of Jerusalem, but that is a considerably farther distance. The most likely wilderness where John lived before appearing publically is the Judean desert. There are several reasons for making such an assumption. First, John identifies himself in all four gospels as the "voice of one crying in the wilderness" (Matt 3:3; Mark 1:3; Luke 3:4; John 1:23), a quote from Isaiah 40:3. In the Judean desert there was an ascetic community of priests which believed the temple priesthood was corrupt and Herod's temple in Jerusalem also illegitimate and void of the real presence of Yahweh in The Most Holy Place, the Holy of Holies. Therefore, even the sacrifices in the temple were not pleasing to God and basically meaningless. This group believed that the temple and

1. Burridge, *What Are The Gospels?*

its priesthood had become corrupt during the Hasmonean dynasty when they appointed one of their sons, Jonathan, high priest in 152 BC. Prior to that time the high priesthood had been an inherited position among the descendants of Aaron. Because this norm had been breached by the Hasmoneans, a group of temple priests, led by a man, presumably a fellow priest, simply known as The Teacher of Righteousness, walked out of the temple and formed their own community in the Judean desert along the northwest shore of the Dead Sea. The community was known as Qumran, and it was in this community of priests that the Dead Sea Scrolls were written. The community of Qumran believed themselves to be "the voice of one crying in the wilderness," the same quotation from Isaiah used by John. The use of that verse by both Qumran and John seems more than coincidental, but similarities go beyond that.

The second similarity is the fact that John was a baptizer. We are told the people of Jerusalem and all Judea were going out to him, and all the regions along the Jordan, and they were baptized by him in the river Jordan, confessing their sins (Matt 3:5–6; Mark 1:4–5; cf. Luke 3:1–18; John 1:24–28). Baptism was not a new practice. It had been practiced among Jews long before Qumran or John came on the scene, but it was especially prevalent in the Qumran community, where it is spoken of regularly in their writings (the Dead Sea Scrolls) and where a number of baths, *miqva'ot*, have been discovered. The baths were used daily as purification pools, which washed away sin and made a person acceptable to enter the presence of Yahweh. John's baptism of repentance accomplished the same thing. It is unknown whether John's baptism was a daily regular recurring event, or considered a one-time baptism, but it was by immersion (as were the purification baths at Qumran), and it was a baptism of confession and forgiveness, the same as at Qumran.

Third, one of the requirements for becoming an initiate into the community at Qumran was to be a descendent of priests which, of course, made John qualified. Qumran, it is believed, allowed no females within its membership. That is what its writings specified. Although some female skeletons have been found in the graveyard outside Qumran's ruins, it is probable that the female bodies had been buried there sometime after the community had fled and dissolved in AD 68. Some scholars believe they may even be the remains of Bedouin or Arab nomads from much more recent times.

Fourth, the nature of John's clothing of camel's hair and leather belt, and his peculiar diet of bugs and wild honey, suggest that he might well

Part Two: Moving Beyond Christian Folk Religion

have been an expelled member of Qumran. The daily dress of all members of the community was a white garment, the symbol of purity. One of requirements for becoming a member of the community was that the initiate give all of his worldly possessions over to the community (cf. the story of the organization of the early church in Acts 4:32–5:11), and all things were shared in common. During the first two years the initiate was on probation. It was only after that probationary period that a man would be allowed into full membership. During those two years if a person breached any serious requirements of the group such as questioning its leadership, or the group's authority, the person could be expelled. If expelled he was sent out of their midst into the hostile desert with nothing. All of his possessions were the property of the group. A man with no survival skills in that environment would certainly not survive. The desert for miles around was filled with poisonous snakes, scorpions, hyenas, wild dogs, lions, and numerous predators, most of which are there today. John however had lived in the wilderness for some time, and knew that environment well and what it would take to survive. A man with survival skills, could fashion his own clothing from whatever he found available, and eat whatever the land might provide, exactly the type of clothing John wore, and the diet he ate.

Even a quick reading of the accounts of John's teaching, and criticisms of others, makes it clear that he was not one for keeping his tongue in his head. One criticism against the tetrarch, Antipas, eventually cost him his head (Matt 14:1–12; Mark 6:17–29; Luke 9:7–9)!

John came out to the edge of the wilderness at the southern end of the Jordan River, which flows into the Dead Sea, somewhere around the year 28/29. It was there that he began to baptize and proclaim his message. His proclamation of judgment and call to repentance had great crowd appeal and people yearned to see and hear him. It was a refreshing change. It had been 400 years since a bona fide prophet had appeared and they were eager for the message, but the people would have to come to him. He would not go to the temple to teach, he was calling the nation to a new beginning. And that beginning would start at the edge of the wilderness.

John was enormously popular. His basic message was "Repent, for the kingdom of heaven has come near" (Matt 3:2), and also the call of Isaiah to "Prepare the way of the Lord, make his paths straight" (Matt 3:3; Mark 1:3; Luke 3:4; John 1:23). This message was crucial in his prophecy that the kingdom of heaven was near. The call to repentance signaled a new age was dawning where the purification of mankind and eventually

The Baptizer

all of creation would take place to bring Yahweh's creation back to its original state of purity; back to the way it was in Eden before the fall of mankind. Repentance and purification (the baptismal waters) would do that. It was the only way to prepare for the "coming of the Lord." This is one of the reasons John was such an important predecessor to Jesus. John's message and mission paved the way for the eventual path Jesus would take which became clear to Jesus in the wilderness where he spent a little over a month after his baptism.

John had gathered disciples of his own (John 1:35), two of which were Simon Peter and his brother, Andrew, both of whom would eventually become leaders among Jesus' own disciples. Jesus even said that among those born of women no one has arisen greater than John the Baptist (Matt 11:11; Luke 7:28), but then added, in the Matthew account, one of his many teaching riddles, "yet the least in the kingdom of heaven is greater than he . . . For all the prophets and the law prophesied until John came; and if you are willing to accept it, he is Elijah who is to come. Let anyone with ears listen." John is the culmination of the prophecy of Israel because all the prophets and the law prophesied until John came. John's sudden appearance was the marker that ended the era of prophecy up to that time. Yet at the same time, even after the great endorsement by Jesus that "no one has arisen greater than John the Baptist," Jesus ends it with a riddle so typical of his teaching, "yet the least in the kingdom of heaven is greater than he . . . let anyone with ears listen." Almost all of Jesus' riddles appear to have what seems reverse logic to Western ears. What Jesus meant by such riddles will be dealt with at length a little later. Suffice it to say here that in his riddles "the best is least," or "the highest is lowest," or "the first is last." Everything appears to be upside down from the way we Westerners understand reality. It will be very informative when we look at this in much more detail, but there is a specific truth here, a key which unlocks an amazing understanding about status in God's kingdom: who gets in or may be excluded, why Jesus performed miracles, and the meaning of the cross and resurrection.

John's popularity was probably due to the fact that his message was about the renewal of Israel. Though sounding harsh, it was also a message of hope, and became very popular among the people. Baptism signaled the beginning of that renewal, as did the call for judgment, repentance, confession, and forgiveness. This judgment, and all the rest, would fall on Israel itself. It was to be the salvation of Israel. As Meyer correctly points out,

Part Two: Moving Beyond Christian Folk Religion

> If it is Israel that is judged, it is Israel that is saved. But as judgment means the burning of the chaff, saved Israel is, in respect of its past collective selfhood, a remnant.
>
> Prophetic tradition had converted 'the remnant of Israel' into a powerful symbol of restoration. In and through the remnant of Israel God reconstituted his holy people.[2]

Of course the most prominent of John's baptized followers was Jesus himself. It marked the start of his ministry and public career. Because Jesus was crucified in the spring of 30, he was most likely baptized in late 28 or early in 29. It is doubtful that Jesus' ministry lasted a full three years as has been popularly thought. The assumption that Jesus had a three year-long ministry is based on the fact that the Gospel of John mentions Jesus going to Jerusalem to celebrate the Passover three times, but John does not follow a single chronology. Unlike the chronologies of the synoptic gospels which can easily be followed, he has set his gospel into themes and then fills these themes with incidents from various times in Jesus' life. It is unlikely, with the explosive nature of Jesus' ministry and message, that he could have survived an extensive ministry. It presented too great a threat to the religious powers within Israel, and they set off rather quickly to try to destroy him, especially once he arrived in Jerusalem.

Why would Jesus go to John to be baptized? That is an age old question and one for which there are no easy answers. Indeed, John himself asked such a question (Matt 3:14). Jesus simply said that it was a way "to fulfill all righteousness." Righteousness, in Jewish terminology was often synonymous with being pure before God. Purity, in God's eyes had little to do with being good, which is the nature of God alone (i.e., "perfection," Matt 5:48). Purity meant to be forgiven, or relieved, from your sins. Once that was accomplished, you were then ready and able to enter the temple complex. John's baptism meant repentance first for any sin committed or the willful violation of any of the many laws of Torah, and then of purifying yourself by immersing your body in water, which would wash away those impurities. In the New Testament it became known as baptism (Greek: *baptizo*, to bathe or wash as a ceremonial act of absolution). In Jerusalem there were a number of public *miqva'ot*, such as the Pool of Siloam (John 9:7–11), where pilgrims and citizens would go to purify themselves before they went into the temple. The ritual itself was an act of the purification of both body and soul. If Jesus believed his main aim

---

2. Meyer, 118.

to be the call of all Israel to repentance and forgiveness, leading to Israel's purification, could he rightly claim this unless he himself had undergone purification? His baptism (or purification) would fulfill all righteousness. He, therefore, would become one of the first to undertake the renewal ritual signaling the beginning of the purification of all mankind, and the start of the establishment of the kingdom of God. Because of his own purification he could therefore call for the purification of the whole nation. This was precisely his primary goal, and it would be accomplished through his teaching, his healing, and ultimately through his death on the cross.

THE WAY

According to Luke 3:2–9:

> The word of God came to John son of Zechariah in the wilderness. He went into all the region around the Jordan, proclaiming a baptism of repentance for the forgiveness of sins, as it is written in the book of the words of the prophet Isaiah,
>
> "The voice of one crying out in the wilderness:
> 'Prepare the way of the Lord, make his paths straight.
> Every valley shall be filled, and every mountain and hill shall be made low,
> and the crooked shall be made straight;
> and all flesh shall see the salvation of God.'"
>
> John said to the crowds that came out to be baptized by him, "You brood of vipers! Who warned you to flee from the wrath to come? Bear fruits worthy of repentance. Do not begin to say to yourselves, 'We have Abraham as our ancestor'; for I tell you, God is able from these stones to raise up children to Abraham. Even now the ax is lying at the root of the trees; every tree therefore that does not bear good fruit is cut down and thrown into the fire."

These few verses pack so much information in them that it is absolutely necessary to begin to unpack them. All the gospels introduce John the Baptizer as the precursor to the arrival of Jesus and his message. A careful analysis of these few words shows that to be the absolute truth.

When John, quoting Isaiah, says, "Prepare the way," he is telling Israel to get ready for a different kind of reality. A little later we will see just

Part Two: Moving Beyond Christian Folk Religion

how different God's reality is from ours. Suffice it to say that his reality is not our reality and it is difficult to understand until we have some keys to unlock it. Even then, much of that reality is truly baffling.

The term "the way" became a term Jesus also used to describe his own aims and purposes throughout his ministry. In response to his disciple, Thomas, who asked this question, "Lord, we do not know where you are going. How can we know the way?" Jesus replied, "I am the way, and the truth, and the life. No one comes to the Father except through me" (John 14:5–6). This has often been used as the proof text that it is only through belief in Jesus that we can achieve salvation. That is what we would like it to mean because it is then self-centered: "I believe in Jesus, therefore I am saved." There is more to be understood about what salvation really is. In the Bible salvation was always understood as the destiny precisely for Israel. Salvation and Israel were utterly inseparable. There was never a Savior apart from a saved Israel, and there would not be a Messiah apart from messianic Israel. This is true even when you read the passages in John which talk of believing in Jesus. If you read the gospels carefully, however, they contain a far more demanding message. Time and again, the primary call of Jesus for all his disciples is "Follow me." It is the demand that calls us to go wherever he leads. It may not be where we want to go, but we are to follow. It might be to do what we don't want to do, but because it is what Jesus does, we do it. It means to love someone we might not have any desire to love, but because Jesus loves that person, we do it. It might mean experiencing hardship, or persecution, which we certainly don't want to experience, but if that's what Jesus did, we do it. And he did it, and called on his disciples to do the same if necessary. Again, as mentioned in the previous chapter, our understanding of "believe" is static, but in Hebrew thinking it demands action. Jesus said, "If anyone wants to become my followers, let them deny themselves and take up their cross and follow me" (Matt 16:24; Mark 8:34; Luke 9:23). Dietrich Bonhoeffer, in his book *The Cost of Discipleship* written in 1937 said, "When Christ calls a man he bids him come and die."[3] If that's what he demands of us, we do it. Bonhoeffer knew full well the meaning of that statement he had made eight years earlier, when on April 9, 1945 he was hung by the Nazis for being complicit in the plot to assassinate Adolf Hitler. The way of Jesus is much more than just believing in him, it is a way of life. It describes Jesus' willingness to travel the path to suffering

---

3. *Op cit*, 44.

(Mark 3:31–34), and asks us to travel that same path. It is taking the narrow way (Matt 7:14). The term "the way" had such importance in the lives of the disciples and those who followed Jesus that the early church used the term The Way to describe themselves, their message, and their way of life (Acts 9:2; 19:9, 23; 22:4; 24:14, 22).

Among the Dead Sea Scrolls, written by the Qumran community which, if I speculate correctly, John the Baptizer was once a member, there is a fragment of a scroll designated as 4Q420, fr.[4] which speaks of "righteousness in the ways of God." And one of the primary scrolls found in the very first cave discovered above Qumran, *The Community Rule* (1QS[5]), written, it is believed, about 100 BC, has this remarkable passage:

> [The Master] shall conceal the teaching of the Law from men of injustice, but shall impart true knowledge and righteous judgement to those who have chosen the Way. He shall guide them all in knowledge according to the spirit of each and according to the rule of the age, and shall thus instruct them in the mysteries of marvellous truth, so that in the midst of the men of the Community they may walk perfectly together in all that has been revealed to them. This is the time for the preparation of the way into the wilderness, and he shall teach them to do all that is required at that time and to separate from those all who have not turned aside from all injustice.[6]

A little later, in the same scroll, is a song of thanksgiving, which includes these words:

> I will bear no rancour
> against them that turn from transgression,
> but will have no pity on all
> who depart from the way.[7]

The passage in Luke, still quoting Isaiah, goes on and describes how the way of the Lord is to be made straight, "Every valley shall be filled, and every mountain and hill shall be made low, and the crooked shall be made straight, and the rough ways made smooth; and all flesh shall

---

4. "4" indicates "Cave 4," "Q," it's from Qumran, "420 fr.," the 420th fragment from that cave.

5. The "S" in this designation means it is a "Scroll."

6. Vermes, *Dead Sea Scrolls in English*, 111 (English spelling of some words).

7. Ibid., 114.

Part Two: Moving Beyond Christian Folk Religion

see the salvation of God" (Luke 3:5–6). This is the renewal of all things, which Jesus will stress throughout his public career. When the kingdom of God becomes a reality, all mankind, the earth, and everything in it, will undergo a renewal which will purify it, cleanse it, undergo a figurative baptism, if you will, and everything: the material world, humanity, flowers, animals, all things, will be able to stand, purified, before the Creator God, and shall see the salvation of God.

John continues with his warning of the coming judgment:

> You brood of vipers! Who warned you to flee from the wrath to come? Bear fruits worthy of repentance. Do not begin to say to yourselves, 'We have Abraham as our ancestor'; for I tell you, God is able from these stones to raise up children to Abraham. Even now the ax is lying at the root of the trees; every tree therefore that does not bear good fruit is cut down and thrown into the fire. (Luke 3:7–9)

The renewal of all things is the final act of the judgment. You are not exempt from the judgment because of your pedigree, your nationality, your religious affiliation. In one of the most remarkable passages in the New Testament John calls his hearers, a "brood of vipers" who apparently are trying to flee the wrath to come. This "brood of vipers" is not identified by John, but it seems to be addressed to the crowd who had come out to hear him. According to John's gospel in 3:24, Pharisees were in the crowd. They were known for their high Torah piety. Their clothes, their actions, their judgments about other's actions (especially Jesus' actions), and a basic self-righteous attitude, were all based on meticulously following the Levitical laws. The Baptizer was well known for his asceticism (Matt 11:18; Luke 7:33) and as an ascetic would have been opposed to an outward sign of piety. In all likely hood, when he called people a brood of vipers who was trying to flee the wrath to come, he was referring to a such a group as the Pharisees and the scribes, who were the most pious of the pious (see Matt 23 for Jesus' seven woes against the piety of the scribes and Pharisees: more on that later). Such people displaying overtly their religion are chastised in Isaiah 29:13:

> Yahweh said:
> Because these people draw near with their mouths
> and honor me with their lips,
> while their hearts are far from me,
> and their worship of me is a human commandment learned
> by rote;

> so I will do amazing things with this people, shocking and amazing.
> The wisdom of their wise shall perish,
> and the discernment of the discerning shall be hidden. (Isa 29:13–14)

Jesus quotes this passage in Matthew 15:8-9. John, in his condemnation of such piety, is saying that rather than outward displays of faith, it is the question of bearing good fruit which determines a person's renewal. Good fruit has nothing to do with what Paul calls good works. Good works are things we do to curie favor from God and receive merit points from him (i.e., perhaps "works" of piety which show others that we are the proper good Christian).

As a child I remember hearing adults talk about people getting another "jewel in their crown" when they go to heaven for doing something nice for someone else as. That's good works. "Good fruit" is what God wants from all of us; it is exemplifying the acts of Jesus, acts of love for every child of God (the good and bad alike), acts of mercy and grace for all those who often receive no mercy or grace, healing the wounds and hurts of the world, suffering persecution, if necessary, in the place of someone else, all without any thought of some reward. It is selfless love. The Greek word for such selfless love is *agape*. It is the word the evangelist John uses in 1 John 4:16 when he says, "God is love," and it is also the word he uses for love in 1 John 4:11, "Beloved, since God loved (*agapeo*) us so much, we also ought to love (*agape*) one another". It is also the love of Christ described by Paul in Romans 8:35, "Who will separate us from the love (*agape*) of Christ? Will hardship, or distress, or persecution, or famine, or nakedness, or peril or sword?" The answer, of course, is "no." It is unconditional love, expecting nothing in return. The same is required of us. You see, this is the starting point for our traveling along the way of Christ. John the Baptizer then goes on to describe more specifically some of these acts:

> And the crowds asked him, "What then should we do?" In reply, he said to them, "Whoever has two coats must share with anyone who has none; and whoever has food must do likewise." Even the tax collectors came to be baptized, and they asked him, "Teacher, what should we do?" He said to them, "Collect no more than the amount prescribed for you." Soldiers also asked him, "And we, what should we do?" He said to them, "Do not

Part Two: Moving Beyond Christian Folk Religion

extort money from anyone by threats or false accusation, and be satisfied with your wages." (Luke 3:10–14)

This is the prescription for the beginning of the renewal and purification of the world, *agape* love.

And Jesus was then baptized, and heaven opened, and the Holy Spirit, in the form of a dove, descended on him, and a voice from heaven declared to him, "You are my Son, the Beloved; with you I am well pleased" (Luke 3:22). Jesus now became one of the first of humanity to be renewed and purified. It was the way into the kingdom of God. Repentance, forgiveness, and purity: that is the way, there is no other!

THE TEMPTATIONS OF CHRIST

Leaving John the Baptizer and his disciples behind, Jesus went deeper into the wilderness and there faced his greatest temptations. Years ago the comedian Flip Wilson used to say, "The devil made me do it!" It was always good for a laugh, but there was a thread of truth there. The devil often gets blamed for whatever we do. The truth is not that the devil made Flip Wilson do whatever he was accusing the devil of, but the truth is that most of us want to blame the devil for whatever we're caught doing, or even the thoughts we have. Actually the temptations we have are most often the result of what we want to do. That's why they're temptations. In Genesis 8:21 God says to Noah, "the inclination of the human heart is evil from youth." No mention of "the devil" there! Temptations seem like a pretty good plan at the time, but they often arise out of our own belief that a certain action may be the best solution to whatever it is we want to do. When the Bible says that Jesus went into the wilderness and was tempted by the devil, there was no figure with cloven hoofs, horns on his head, and a spear headed tail leaning over and whispering in his ear. It was an honest thought that certain actions could make sense in the knowledge that God had said to him, "You are my Son, the Beloved." It was the revelation that what lay before him was a responsibility beyond all human understanding. Behind that statement from heaven implied a divine mission accompanied by divine power and compassion. "If you are the Son of God," two of the three temptations begin. Yes that was it: the big *if*: "*if* you are the Son of God," can I believe it? That thought was accompanied by doubt, What if it's not true? Perhaps I was having a hallucination! If it is true, what does it mean? Ideas, anxiety, questions, doubt. But then, What if it is true, what then? Yes, What then! When you have lived your whole life surrounded by peasants, the poorest of the poor, you have witnessed their suffering and pain. People, who work their whole life on a piece of land that they don't own, and will never own, and who, from day to day don't even know if they'll have food tomorrow. "Give us *this* day our daily bread," Jesus taught his disciples to pray. Yet we ask, "But what about tomorrow?" Every morsel is a pittance for today. Hopefully there will be a morsel tomorrow. But if you are the "Son of God, the Beloved," then all of that can change. The power of God, coupled with the mercy and compassion of God could change all that! Feed the hungry. Alleviate their suffering. It is the divine, loving thing to do! It is the right thing to do. How many times when they have suffered tragedies have Christians asked, "Why did God let this happen?" Well, that's the point. Jesus was faced with the compassionate idea that it didn't have to happen. "If you are the Son of God, command these stones to become loaves of bread" (Matt 4:3). It was a good plan, a great plan, but the wisdom of mankind may be foolishness in God's eyes! The Apostle Paul said it, "For God's foolishness is wiser than human wisdom, and God's weakness is stronger than human strength" (1 Cor 1:25). Here is that upside down logic we're going to see many times in Jesus' teaching, and here it is again in Paul. God may be foolish but his foolishness puts human wisdom to shame, and what appears to be God's weakness in human eyes is more powerful than any human power.

The answer to the question of bread for the world was that there are greater things than that, and only God knows what that is. "One does not live by bread alone, but by every word that comes from the mouth of God" (Matt 4:4). Again, the answer comes in the form of a riddle: Can words fill a hungry belly? Yet, the temptation had to be rejected, because God may have other plans. If you are the Son of God you have been given the power above every other power. You can do anything, and nothing can stop you. You can eradicate sickness, blindness, muteness, deafness, mental illness, paralysis, skin disease, and every kind of human malady. You can raise the dead, and stop death from happening. Never again would any human being need purification before entering the temple because they would all be purified, from the least of them to the greatest of them. And no one could stop you from doing so. It could be done in the blink of an eye. No one could block your way, or bring you to harm. In your mind's eye, you can envision yourself on the pinnacle of the temple, standing on top of the wall surrounding the temple complex, the highest point on the Temple Mount

Part Two: Moving Beyond Christian Folk Religion

in Jerusalem. In front of you is a cliff that looks down into the Kidron Valley hundreds of feet below. "If you are the Son of God, throw yourself down; for it is written, 'He will command his angels concerning you', and 'On their hands they will bear you up, so that you will not dash your foot against a stone'" (Matt 4:5–6). Never in human history has anyone had such absolute power, but what if that's all wrong? Jesus, in his thoughts, considered: "The Bible was quoted to me, Psalm 91:11, so I'll decline the offer and quote the Bible right back, "Again it is written, 'Do not put the Lord God to the test'" (Matt 4:7 from Deut 6:13).

Power and compassion, are known qualities of the Creator Yahweh. But what is his plan? How can anyone know? Is it possible to know the will of God? Those are the decisions Jesus faced in the wilderness. But there is one temptation yet to go, and it holds the key. The temptation, in essence is this, "No matter how noble it is, no matter how compassionate it is, no matter what it is, if it is not God's plan, it is wrong! In the end it is worshiping the wrong god; it is serving your own belief in what you think is the right thing to do. You become your own god." So Jesus rejected it too: "Worship Yahweh your God, and serve only him." Then suddenly angels came and waited on him (v. 11). He had made the right choice.

When he emerged from the wilderness after more than a month Jesus' mission was set before him. It would, for the first time in his life, change everything. His Father's will transcends his own. Jesus' purpose, his mission, his destiny was in the hands of the Creator God.

THE BAPTIZER AND JESUS IN PERSPECTIVE

With the appearance of John the Baptizer and his call for repentance and purification, preparations were made for the Messiah so expected by Israel, and the mission he would bring. The gospels make the assumption that it was at his baptism that Jesus first learned of his messianic calling. The implications of that calling were terrifying, just as the calling of the prophets before Jesus were terrifying for the prophets: Moses pleaded with God, "The Israelites have not listened to me; how then shall Pharaoh listen to me, poor speaker that I am?" (Exod 6:12). Isaiah cried out, "Woe is me! I am lost, for I am a man of unclean lips, and I live among a people of unclean lips, yet my eyes have seen the King, Yahweh of hosts!" (Isa 6:5). Jeremiah was called while only a lad and protested, "Ah Yahweh God! Truly I do not know how to speak, for I am only a boy." (Jer 1:6). Then, at the age of about 35, Jesus went to John for baptism. It was an unlikely match.

Jesus, the builder from the small village of Nazareth, met the ascetic priest lately reemerged from the wasteland Judean desert, and both converged at the waters of the Jordan River. Yes, it was an unlikely match indeed. But instead of Jesus being the protester, it was the Baptizer who protested to Jesus, "I need to be baptized by you, and do you come to me?" (Matt 3:14). John had told his own disciples, "I baptize you with water; but one who is more powerful than I is coming; I am not worthy to untie the thong of his sandals" (Luke 3:16). Yet here was Jesus, explaining to John, "It is proper for us in this way to fulfill all righteousness" (Matt 3:15). Thus began the journey along the way. In the chapters that follow we'll look at the steps he took along the way:

In the next chapter we'll explore "the Son of Man": who "the Son of Man" is and what the peculiar title means, and find out that this mysterious figure would be Jesus' constant companion showing him the way and directing all of his actions according to God's divine will.

In chapter 6 we'll be introduced to the kingdom of God. We'll see that Jesus called Israel back to repentance, just as John was doing, preparing them for entrance into the kingdom. Only after that process had begun could Jesus inaugurate what God had promised from the beginning, the kingdom.

In chapter 7 we'll learn that in God's kingdom there is a new reality, and new rules, with which we are going to have to contend. Jesus trained and taught his followers about how God sees the world which is often totally different from what we know, or think we know. In Isaiah 55:8 Yahweh told Isaiah that "my thoughts are not your thoughts, nor are your ways my ways." Instead in God's ways there is power in weakness, not in strength, and wisdom in apparent folly; it is indeed the humble who are the holy, and piety alone is not the mark of righteousness. It is a riddle few will understand, but it is the key to unlock the new reality with its new rules in the kingdom of God.

Chapter 8 will help us understand who the opponents of Jesus really were and consider what the renewal of God's creation really entails and how Jesus begins to bring it about. He does this through his teaching in parables, which are often in the form of riddles. We will also learn how his miracles, which are rarely performed solely out of compassion, bring this about.

Part Two: Moving Beyond Christian Folk Religion

Chapter 9 is all about "quiet piety," the mysterious truth that Jesus rejected an attitude that was intended to make one look and feel "religious." He didn't act the way religious people expected him to act. He didn't pray in public, he didn't seek the accolades of those he came to help. He told those who were healed not to tell anyone who had healed them, but only to go to the priest and get certified that they were indeed healed. When crowds seeking healing were too large he went off by himself to pray. Such actions were, and are, perhaps the most mysterious, and peculiar acts of God's Messiah.

We'll then conclude the bulk of this study with the tenth chapter which deals with the greatest sin the world has ever known: Jesus' crucifixion. The cross became the throne where God's power and glory would shine beyond all expectation. The world may believe the cross was where God showed his vulnerability, and that the resurrection was the declaration that God could not be defeated, but God's greatest power was displayed in the cross and in Jesus dying on it. How this happened is one more riddle in the mix, and would signal the establishment of the kingdom of God when Jesus uttered, "It is finished" (John 19:30 cf. John 17:4) and breathed his last breath.

This was the path that lay ahead in Jesus' ministry. It was the only path he could take, this way of the Lord where "the rough ways [are] made smooth. " It is the only way where "all flesh shall see the salvation of God" (Luke 3:5–6; cf. Isa 40:3–5).

To end the study we'll conclude with a few brief final observations to, hopefully, bring many of these subjects into focus.

5

The Son of Man[1]

THE SECOND MOST SPOKEN of topic in Jesus' teaching, is the term the Son of Man. The only subject he spoke more about than the Son of Man was the kingdom of God. The assumption has usually been that the Son of Man is a designation for the humanity of Jesus, while Son of God is the designation for his divinity. In other words, it fully describes his dual nature: Jesus, the God/Man. While the early church fathers expressed that belief, today that idea is rejected by most biblical scholars for various reasons, the prime reason being that the use by Jesus of the term is clearly based on the figure seen in the prophecy of Daniel in 7:13, and that figure is not a human figure, but a heavenly one. To sort out the issue and come to a conclusion of the identity of the Son of Man in Daniel, various proposals over the years have been made, from just ignoring the issue all together, or assuming that the Son of Man is a circumlocution Jesus uses for the personal pronoun "I," or simply responding to the issue by saying, I don't know what it means. What follows is a solution that I believe to be plausible.

---

1. Adapted from my article "The Mystery of Jesus' Teaching about "The Son of Man," *BTB*, 70-80.

Part Two: Moving Beyond Christian Folk Religion

THE STATE OF THE PROBLEM

About midway through Jesus' ministry, he asked his disciples this question: "Who do people say that the Son of Man (*ho huios tou anthropou*) is?" This question has never been adequately answered. The early church fathers believed the title The Son of Man had to do with the human/divine nature of Christ himself. Toward the end of the first century the titles The Son of Man and The Son of God became linked together as Ignatius of Antioch did in the late first century in his letter to the Ephesians (chapter 7): "There is one only Physician, of flesh and of spirit, generate and ingenerate, God in man, true life in death; Son of Mary and Son of God; first passible and then impassible, Jesus Christ our Lord." By the second century the ante-Nicene fathers became even more convinced that both The Son of Man and The Son of God revealed that he is both human and divine. Late in the century Tertullian reaffirmed this interpretation in his *Adversus Praxean*. In chapter 2 he wrote: "Him we believe to have been sent by the Father into the Virgin, and to have been born of her both Man and God, the Son of Man and the Son of God, and to have been called by the name of Jesus Christ." The debate concerning the dual nature of Christ continued unabated until the fourth century when the matter was resolved at the Council of Nicaea.

Today, the speculation of the early church fathers is considered no longer tenable for the reason stated above. In almost all usages of the term Son of Man outside the gospels, the reference is to a heavenly being, and not an earthly mortal. This is so in Daniel 7, in the apocryphal books of 1 Enoch and 4 Ezra, and in the New Testament where the term appears only three times outside the gospels: Acts uses the term once, and Revelation twice. In the Hebrew Scriptures the one exception to this usage is in Ezekiel, which will be discussed at length below.

Exactly what Jesus meant when he spoke of The Son of Man has become somewhat of a baffling mystery among scholars. In fact, it has variously been described as "The Son of Man Debate,"[2] "The Son of Man Tradition,"[3] or "The Son of Man Concept,"[4] but especially "The Son of Man Problem."[5] According to Wright, an Oxford colleague muttered in

---

2. Vermes, *Jesus in His Jewish Context*, 81.
3. Hare, *The Son of Man Tradition*.
4. Casey, *Solution to the 'Son of Man' Problem*, 82-115.
5. Wright, *Jesus and the Victory of God*, 512.

a seminar they were attending, "Son of Man? Son of Man? That way lies madness."⁶ E.P. Sanders correctly analyzes the evidence in this way:

> There were no hard definitions of Messiah, Son of God or Son of Man in the Judaism of Jesus' day. Even if he had constantly called himself by all three titles, we could learn what he thought of himself only by studying him not by studying the titles in other sources. The evidence is that he rejected the title Messiah. As far as we know, he did not call himself Son of God. He did refer to himself as Son of Man, but we do not know in what sense.⁷

The result of this is the conclusion that "The Son of Man" presents a major dilemma for the bible student. This is especially so since it is presumed that Jesus spoke of "The Son of Man" in Aramaic rather than the Greek of the New Testament.

One scholar, Casey, has done a recent comprehensive study comparing the three usages of "The Son of Man," in Greek, *ho huios tou anthropou*, in Aramaic, *bar enash(e)*, and in Hebrew, *ben adam* (without the definite article). Although Casey's book is entitled *Solution to the Son of Man Problem*, his solution never answers the basic question Jesus asked, "Who is 'The Son of Man'?" Instead, he engages in a linguistic analysis of the use of the words within the text of the gospels to reach a conclusion as to how the Aramaic *bar enash* of Daniel 7.13 became the Greek *ho huios tou anthropou* of Jesus' sayings in our Greek versions. His argument is almost impossible to follow. I cannot comprehend how four first century gospel writers, each writing separately in different parts of the ancient world, could have followed the same series of linguistic processes a twenty-first century scholar has concluded, to try to figure out the exact phrase Jesus used in Aramaic. I believe the addition of the definite article in the Greek, "The Son of Man," expressing the idiom in the third person, is part of the key to the solution of its meaning, and not part of the problem. The phrase where Jesus borrowed the term occurs in Daniel 7:13. The phrase in Daniel reads, "one like a son of man," while Jesus' phraseology is "the Son of Man." There is a marked difference. Aramaic does not have a definite article, and there is only one way Aramaic can indicate a specific thing, which the definite article does, is by adding a suffix at the end of the noun. The suffix is an *e*. Thus the Aramaic *enash*, which as is, means "a son of man" becomes *bar enash(e)*, indicated by

6. Ibid.
7. *The Historical Figure of Jesus*, 248.

the suffix, which in the transliteration is put in parenthesis, (*e*), and then becomes "*the* Son of Man," and must have been in the original Aramaic spoken by Jesus, which was then translated by all the gospel writers into the familiar Greek of the New Testament.

"The Son of Man" occurs seventy-one times on the lips of Jesus in the four gospels. It appears five other times, but either summarizes a teaching of Jesus (Mark 8:31; 9:9; Luke 24:7), or Jesus is questioned by a crowd, "How can you say that the Son of Man must be lifted up? Who is this Son of Man?" (John 12:34). The mere fact that the gospels alone put it on the lips of Jesus indicates that it must have been original with him and not the product of the early church. The term appears only three times in the rest of the New Testament (a lone exception is Hebrews 2:6, where the author quotes Psalm 8:4). The other occurrences are all in visions: by Stephen in Acts 7:56, where he proclaims, "Look . . . I see the heavens opened and the Son of Man standing at the right hand of God"; and by John the Seer in Revelation 1:13 where in the midst of the (seven golden) lampstands "I saw one like the Son of Man, clothed with a long robe and with a golden sash across his chest"; and then again in Revelation 14:14, where John says, "Then I looked, and there was a white cloud, and seated on the cloud was one like the Son of Man, with a golden crown on his head and a sharp sickle in his hand!"

Putting aside linguistic analysis, I believe the solution to The Son of Man Problem lies within the context itself. To do this we must note the context in which "The Son of Man," or simply "Son of Man," is used in both the Hebrew Scriptures and the New Testament.

THE HEBREW SCRIPTURES

Ezekiel

Besides the Aramaic of the saying in Daniel 7:13, which I will consider presently, the other prominent use of the term in the Hebrew Scriptures is in Ezekiel, where it occurs more than ninety times in Ezekiel's forty-eight chapters. The almost unanimous consensus of scholars is that the Hebrew (*ben adam*) in Ezekiel simply means "human being," and is translated by the NRSV as "mortal" or "O mortal": "O mortal, stand up on your feet and I will speak with you" (2:1). The fact that the term is repeated with such frequency in Ezekiel, and not in the writings of the other prophets, leads me to believe that its purpose is more than just one prophet's particular style. It appears to be a title. Ezekiel is addressed as *ben adam*, "son of man." Its usage as a title will become clear as we work through to a solution. In the latter chapters of Ezekiel the title is more significant, especially in chapters 40—46 where Ezekiel is given a description of the temple to be built upon the return of citizens of Judea from exile:

> In the twenty-fifth year of our exile, at the beginning of the year, on the tenth day of the month, in the fourteenth year after the city was struck down, on that very day, the hand of Yahweh was upon me, and he brought me there. He brought me, in visions of God, to the land of Israel, and set me down upon a very high mountain, on which was a structure like a city to the south. When he brought me there, a man was there, whose appearance shone like bronze, with a linen cord and a measuring reed in his hand; and he was standing in the gateway. The man said to me, "Son of man, look closely and listen attentively, and set your mind upon all that I shall show you, for you were brought here in order that I might show it to you; declare all that you see to the house of Israel." (Ezek 40:1–4)

What follows this are the measurements and descriptions of the temple. As Ezekiel is given these specifications he is consistently addressed as ben *adam*.

"One like a son of man" in Daniel

Daniel 7:13, on the other hand, is an apocalyptic vision of Yahweh's throne room. Chapters 2.4b–7.28 are written in Aramaic, while the rest of the book is written in Hebrew. Aramaic became the language of the people of the Near East during the Babylonian exile, while Hebrew became primarily the language of worship. The apocalyptic vision of Daniel begins in 7:9:

> As I watched,
> thrones were set in place,
> and an Ancient of Days took his throne,
> his clothing was white as snow,
> and the hair of his head like pure wool;
> his throne was fiery flames,
> and its wheels were burning fire.

Part Two: Moving Beyond Christian Folk Religion

In vv. 13 and 14 Daniel sees the ascension of "one like a son of man" from earth to the throne room where the "Ancient of Days" (the NRSV translates this as "Ancient One") is enthroned:

> I saw one like a son of man
> coming with the clouds of heaven.
> And he came to the Ancient of Days
> and was presented before him.
> To him was given dominion
> and glory and kingship,
> that all peoples, nations, and languages should serve him.
> His dominion is an everlasting dominion
> that shall not pass away,
> and his kingship is one
> that shall never be destroyed.

Apocryphal Books

Among the apocryphal books, 4 Ezra is a book little known outside academia. 4 Ezra is imbedded within the apocryphal book of 2 Ezra (sometimes titled 2 Esdras). 4 Ezra is actually chapters 3–14 of 2 Ezra. It is in chapter 13 Ezra where the figure son of man is seen. It is similar to one like a son of man in Daniel 7. This time Ezra sees "something like the figure of a man come up out of the heart of the sea (13.3–4) who flew with the clouds of heaven; and wherever he turned his face to look, everything under his gaze trembled, and wherever his voice issued from his mouth, all who heard his voice melted as wax melts when it feels the fire." This is clearly a messianic figure because in v. 32 he is identified as God's Son "whom you saw as a man coming up from the sea." Although most extant early translations are in Greek (completed before 190 BC), the original language of the passage was most likely Aramaic or Hebrew and composed near the end of the first century AD.[8] This messianic figure is judicial in that he destroys nations with the Torah, symbolized by fire in the vision (13:10–11, 38). Although written after the New Testament, it is doubtful that it carries much early Christian influence, although it became popular in regional Christian churches in the Middle-Ages. Today it is known to have been translated into Latin, Syriac, Ethiopic, Georgian, Armenian and Coptic (of which only fragments survive).

---

8. Hogan, "Ezra, Fourth Book of," *EDEJ*, 623-626.

The Son of Man

One of the most important sources for any study of "The Son of Man Problem" is the extra canonical book of 1 Enoch, especially chapters 37—71 which comprise the *Book of Parables* or *Similitudes of Enoch*, the date of which has been widely disputed over the years, although the consensus seems to be favoring the first century AD. *The Similitudes* is especially important because it is an early source outside the gospels where "Son of Man" appears to be a title. He is called "the Elect One" numerous times, "the Son of Man" (46:2, etc.), "Mine elect" (48:9), and "the Anointed" (the "Messiah": 48:10 and 51:4). This figure is

> mighty in all the secrets of righteousness, And righteousness shall disappear as a shadow . . . because the Elect One standeth before the Lord of Spirits, And his glory is for ever and ever, And his might unto all generations. And in him dwells the spirit of wisdom, And the spirit which gives insight, And the spirit of understanding and of might, And the spirit of those who have fallen asleep in righteousness. And he shall judge the secret things, And none shall be able to utter a lying word before him; For he is the Elect One before the Lord of Spirits according to His good pleasure. (49:2–4)

In 51:2–3,

> the Elect One shall arise, And he shall choose the righteous and holy from among them: For the day has drawn nigh that they should be saved. And the Elect One shall sit on My throne, And his mouth shall pour forth all the secrets of wisdom and counsel; For the Lord of Spirits hath given them to him and hath glorified him.

These are clearly messianic and apocalyptic images because eventually the unrighteous are destroyed and the world is renewed: "And the righteous and elect shall be saved on that day, And they shall never thenceforward see the face of the sinners and the unrighteous. And the Lord of Spirits will abide over them, And with that Son of Man shall they eat And lie down and rise up for ever and ever." Chapter 71 contains the vision which has reminiscences of Daniel 7 and the heavenly visions of Revelation 20–22:

> And he translated my spirit into the heaven of heavens, And I saw there as it were a structure built of crystals, And between those crystals, tongues of living fire. And my spirit saw the girdle which girt that house of fire, And on its four sides were

> streams full of living fire, And they girt that house. And round about were Seraphin, Cherubic, and Ophannin: And these are they who sleep not And guard the throne of His glory . . . And they came forth from that house . . . And with them the Head of Days, His head white and pure as wool, And His raiment indescribable. And I fell on my face, And my whole body became relaxed, And my spirit was transfigured. (Enoch 70: 5–11)

The Similitudes concludes with a doxology to the Son of Man:

> (The angel) came to me and greeted me with His voice, and said unto me This is the Son of Man who is born unto righteousness, And righteousness abides over him, And the righteousness of the Head of Days forsakes him not. And he said unto me: He proclaims unto thee peace in the name of the world to come; For from hence has proceeded peace since the creation of the world, And so shall it be unto thee for ever and for ever and ever. And all shall walk in the ways since righteousness never forsaketh him: With him will be their dwelling places and with him their heritage, And they shall not be separated from him for ever and ever. And so there shall be length with that Son of Man, And the righteous shall have Peace and an upright way in the name of the Lord of Spirits for ever and ever. (71:14–16)

The Similitudes are especially significant because here "the Son of Man" is clearly a title and is not counted among the angels. For the first time it has a ring to it not unlike Jesus' use of the idiom in his teaching.

The Dead Sea Scrolls

Before we attempt to find a solution to The Son of Man Problem we must consider one more source which may have played a vital role in Jesus' understanding of himself as "The Son of Man." That source is contained in several writings found among the Dead Sea Scrolls. Before the scrolls were discovered in the mid-twentieth century it was not known that from the second century BC to the turn of the era there was the belief that at least some Jews at the time were expecting two Messiahs, rather than one. The two Messiahs are a "Priest Messiah," and a "King Messiah." The first Messiah is variously called the "Messiah of Aaron," the "Priest Messiah," "Priest" or "Interpreter of the Law," and the second Messiah is called the "Messiah of Israel," the "King Messiah," the "Branch of David" (cf. Jer 23:51; Zech 3:8; 6:12), the "Prince of [all] the Congregation" or

The Son of Man

the "Sceptre." They are mentioned in at least five of the Qumran documents: *The Damascus Document* (4Q265–73), *The Community Rule* (1QS), *The Messianic Rule* (1Q28a), *The Blessings* (1Q28b), and *The Book of War* (4Q285). For a complete understanding of this discovery, I will quote most of the passages pertaining to the two Messiahs. It must be pointed out, however, that this belief in two Messiahs is introduced in the scrolls as though it is not a new concept, but rather common knowledge. Though there is no indication in the New Testament that *Messiah*, or its Greek equivalent *Christ*, was ever plural, it can be assumed that it was not totally foreign to the thinking within the Judaism of the early first century AD that the expectation might be for more than one Messiah. All translations of the Dead Sea Scrolls are by Vermes[9].

The Damascus Document (CD):

> Those who follow these statutes in the age of wickedness until the coming of the Messiah of Aaron and Israel shall form groups of at least ten men, by Thousands, Hundreds, Fifties, and Tens. And where the men are, there shall never be lacking a Priest learned in the Book of Meditation; they shall all be ruled by him. [Parchment Sheet XII, Line 20—XIII Line 4]
>
> *This is the exact statement of the statutes in which they shall walk until the coming of the Messiah of Aaron and Israel who will pardon their iniquity.*[Sheet XIV, line 19].

It should be noted that in each of the references to the two Messiahs in the scrolls, the "Messiah of Aaron" (the "Priest Messiah") is listed first, which is the order of priority, as will become apparent below.

The Community Rule (1QS)

> As for the property of the men of holiness who walk in perfection, it shall not be merged with that of the men of injustice who have not purified their life by separating themselves from iniquity and walking in the way of perfection. They shall depart from none of the counsels of the Law to walk in all the stubbornness of their hearts, but shall be ruled by the primitive precepts in which the men of the Community were first instructed

---

9. *The Complete Dead Sea Scrolls in English*,

> until there shall come the Prophet and the Messiahs of Aaron and Israel [Sheet IX, line 10–12].

Exactly who "the Prophet" is that was expected, is not known. Some scholars believe it may be a third Messiah, but there is no clear evidence for that and the topic is debated.

The most curious description of the function of the two Messiahs is in *The Messianic Rule* [1QS28a Sheet II, lines 10–25]:

> [*This shall be the ass*]*embly*[10] *of the men of renown called to the meeting of the Council of the Community*
> When God engenders [the Priest-] Messiah, he shall come with them at the head of the whole congregation of Israel with all [his brethren, the sons] of Aaron the Priests, [those called] to the assembly, the men of renown; and they shall sit [before him, each man] in the order of his dignity. And then [the Mess]iah of Israel shall [come], and the chiefs of the [clans of Israel] shall sit before him, [each] in the order of his dignity, according to [his place] in their camps and marches. And before them shall sit all the head of [family of the congreg]ation, and the wise men of [the holy congregation,] each in the order of his dignity. And [when] they shall gather for the common [tab]le, to eat and [to drink] new wine, when the common table shall be set for eating and the new wine [poured] for drinking, let no man extend his hand over the firstfruits of bread and wine before the Priest; for [it is he] who shall bless the firstfruits of bread and wine, and shall be the first [to extend] his hand over the bread. Thereafter, the Messiah of Israel shall extend his hand over the bread, [and] all the congregation of the Community [shall utter a] blessing, [each man in the order] of his dignity.

What is so interesting about this passage is how closely it parallels Jesus' Last Supper in the gospels. If Jesus was aware of this document, which is neither impossible, nor improbable, how did he envision his role as Messiah, assuming that is what he believed his destiny to be?

---

10. The bracket(s) indicate holes in the mss. which have been completed by scholars according to the content and size of the breaks.

The Book of War (4Q285)–The Messiah, Branch of David (fragment 7)

> [As it is written in the book of] Isaiah the Prophet, [The thickets of the forest] will be cut [down with an axe and Lebanon by a majestic one will f]all. And there shall come forth a shoot from the stump of Jesse [. . .] the Branch of David and they will enter into judgement [. . .] and the Prince of the Congregation, the Br[anch of David] will kill him [. . . by strok]es and by wounds. And a Priest [of renown (?)] will command [. . . the s]lai[n] of the Kitti[m . . .]

The Kittim are presumed to be the Romans, especially in *The War Scroll* (1QM).

In the *Blessings* (1Q28b) there are prayers of blessing for both the "Messiah of Aaron" (the "Priest Messiah"), Sheet III, lines 1–20, and for the "Messiah of Israel" (the "King Messiah," or the "Prince of the Congregation"), Sheet V, lines 19–30.

RECENT ATTEMPTS AT A SOLUTION

As has already been discussed, in recent years attention has centered more on a linguistic analysis of the term "Son of Man" and its syntax rather than its context. Vermes concluded that Jesus term "The Son of Man" was primarily a circumlocution for Jesus himself, simply a humble way of saying "I".[11] I agree that the title often refers to Jesus himself, but I believe it is much more than this.

A SOLUTION BEGINS TO EMERGE

With this survey now before us of the sources so important in any study of the meaning of The Son of Man, it is time to consider a possible solution to "the Problem." We will do this by looking, in order, at each of five assumptions:

1. Laying aside Ezekiel's use of the term "son of man" for the moment, there can be no question that "son of man" has some origin in, or with, the Divine (Dan 7:13, 4 Ezra 13:25, 37; 1 Enoch 47:3; Matt 24:30–31 and its parallels, Mark 13:26 and Luke 21:27).

---

11. *Jesus in His Jewish Context*, 160–66.

Part Two: Moving Beyond Christian Folk Religion

2. In Daniel 7.13 "one like a son of man" ascends to the "Ancient of Days," or "Ancient One" (NRSV), obviously a euphemism for Yahweh, where the "son of man" figure is "given dominion and glory and kingship." This implies a messianic role of regality and kingly power. The fact that "His dominion is an everlasting dominion that will not pass away," also has messianic overtones. In 4 Ezra 13:3–4 "a figure of a man" arises out of the sea and flies "with the clouds of heaven." In V. 32 he is identified as "God's Son." In the Similitudes of Enoch the Son of Man (46:2), or the Anointed (48:10) "standeth before the Lord of Spirits, And his glory is forever and ever, And his might unto all generations . . . For he is the Elect One before the Lord of Spirits according to. His good pleasure (49:2–4).

3. In nearly every passage where the "Son of Man" appears it is in association with the temple, whether the temple in Jerusalem, or the heavenly temple that it is believed will ultimately replace and/or renew the earthly temple (Dan 7:9–14; Ezek 40–46; Matt 24:1–27; Mark 13:1–27; Luke 21:5–28; Rev 1:12–16; 14:14–16). Daniel 7–12 was composed in the early second century BC during the reign of Antiochus IV, who posed a direct threat to the Jerusalem temple cult. Thus, it plays a central role in chapters 8–12 of Daniel. Its author envisions that the end of days has come and renewal is immanent as prophesied by Jeremiah and Ezekiel. We see this especially in Daniel 9:24, "Seventy weeks are decreed for your people and your holy city: to finish the transgression, to put an end to sin, and to atone for iniquity, to bring in everlasting righteousness, to seal both vision and prophet, and to anoint a most holy place".

4. It is fitting, therefore, that the "son of man" figure, when he ascends to the Ancient of Days, enters Yahweh's throne room (7:9) which can be nowhere else but the Holy of Holies of the heavenly temple, accessible only by the high priest. Crispin Fletcher[12] identifies "one like a son of man" in Daniel as the heavenly high priest. It is the atoning spot where iniquity is forgiven, sin is ended, and "everlasting righteousness" begins.

5. In Isaiah 6:2 and 4, Seraphim stand guard around the temple, as do cherubim in numerous other biblical passages (1 Kgs 6:23–29; 7:29, Ezek 8:1–10:14, etc.). In Ezekiel cherubim are major angelic-like figures which accompany the throne of Yahweh and protect him as it moves from place to place (described in chapters 9, 10, 25, 26, 28, 36 and 37). Working with the cherubim are wheels (Hebrew *ophan*) which transport Yahweh's throne in chapter 10 of Ezekiel. The description of the *ophan* in

---

12. "The High Priest as Divine Mediator in the Hebrew Bible: Dan 7:13 as a Test Case." *SBL Seminar Paper*, 170.

Ezekiel makes it abundantly clear that they are also angelic-like guardians of the throne. They have eyes all around (10:12) and each had four faces. In later literature the *ophanim* or *ophannin* are linked with the *seraphim* and the *cherubim* as they are in the *Similitudes of Enoch* which describes "the throne of His glory" as being guarded by *Seraphin, Cherubic,* and *Ophannin.* "And they came forth from that house (the temple) . . . And with them the Head of Days" (71:4–5). The throne of God was, as emphasized earlier, always in the Holy of Holies of the temple, and was God's residence. It was there, we are told, his *Shekinah,* or "glory," dwells. Again, *Shekinah* does not appear in biblical texts, but it does in later rabbinic literature. His glory has traditionally been associated with the Ark of the Covenant in the tabernacle and the mercy seat in the Holy of Holies in the temple (Exod 40:34; 1 Sam 4:21; 1 Kgs 8:11; 2 Chr 7:1f). In Ezekiel "the glory of Yahweh" departs the temple and hovers over "the mountain east of the city" (the Mount of Olives) before the scene shifts "to Chaldea," (Babylon) and the exiles there (10:18–11:24).

In the synoptics, immediately after visiting the temple with his disciples, a debate is sparked when Jesus speaks of the temple's eventual destruction. His disciples want to know when that will happen and "what will be the sign of your coming and of the end of the age," and he begins teaching about the "coming of the Son of Man" (Matt 24:3, 27; Mark 13:3, 26; Luke 21:7, 27) when people "will see the Son of Man coming in a cloud with power and great glory" (Luke 21:28; Mark 13:26).

In Revelation 1:12–13 the apocalyptic seer has a vision of a scene with seven golden lampstands "and in the midst of the lampstands I saw one like the Son of Man, clothed with a long robe and with a golden sash across his chest." In Exodus when the plan for construction of the tabernacle is described, it was to contain a lampstand "of pure gold with seven lamps for it" (25:31–38), which was then put in the tabernacle "opposite the table on the south side of the tabernacle" (40:24). In 1 Kings, Solomon made golden lampstands for the temple (7:49) which burn "every evening for Yahweh our God" (2 Chr 13:13). The scene which John envisions, therefore, is the Son of Man within the heavenly temple. The same is true in John's second vision of "the Son of Man" (14:14), who is dressed wearing a crown (*stephanos*) of gold and carrying a sickle, because an angel exits the temple and calls out to the Son of Man seated on "the cloud."

The imagery of the cloud, present in most apocalyptic visions (Dan 7:13; Ezek 10:4; 4 Ezra 13:3, Matt 24:30, 26:64, Mark 13:26, 14:62, Luke 21:27, 1 Thess 4:17, Rev 1:7) is almost always associated with the throne

Part Two: Moving Beyond Christian Folk Religion

of God, or his presence. It shielded the Israelite army, and the Israelites, from the glory of Yahweh's presence in Exodus 14:19, and 16:10. The cloud accompanies almost all visions of God in the Hebrew Bible and New Testament (Exod 19:16, 24:15, 40:34; Lev 16:2; Num 9:15; 1 Kgs 8:10; Isa 19:1; Ezek 10:4; Matt 17:5 and parallels; Rev 11:12). The cloud appears to be shielding the visionary from the burning glory of his presence. As the Son of Man ascends to, or descends from, the presence of God, he does so "on the clouds of heaven." The throne, or thrones (Dan 7:9), of God must therefore reside either in the heavenly or earthly temple. The thrones also include a second throne, presumably for the "son of man" (v. 13) who ascends to the Ancient One on his throne (v. 9). The only location for the throne must be within the "Most Holy Place" or Holy of Holies, accessible only by the high priest. In 1Samuel the location of God's throne is made clear,

> Let us bring the ark of the covenant of Yahweh here from Shiloh, so that he may come among us and save us from the power of our enemies. So the people sent to Shiloh, and brought from there the ark of the covenant of Yahweh of hosts, who is enthroned on ("between"—KJV) the cherubim (1 Sam 4:3–4).

Later, after Solomon's temple was completed one of the temple songs, calling God "the Shepherd of Israel," makes it clear exactly where his throne is:

> Give ear, O Shepherd of Israel,
> you who lead Joseph like a flock!
> You who are enthroned upon ("between"—KJV) the cherubim,
> shine forth
> before Ephraim and Benjamin and Manasseh.
> Stir up your might,
> and come to save us! (Ps 80:1–2 [cf. Ps 90:1])

The cherubim guard the mercy seat in the Holy of Holies, and is the dwelling place of the glory of the Lord. It is the Most Holy Place where the high priest of Israel enters on the Day of Atonement, prays to Yahweh using the unspeakable sacred name, and sprinkles the sacrificial blood on the sacred lid (the "mercy seat") of the Ark of the Covenant. To survive the brilliant glory of God, which shines immediately above the mercy seat, the high priest also carries a container of hot coals and incense causing a thick haze (a "cloud") to obscure the glory of God, lest eyes who behold it should die. The sprinkling of blood was to purify the

The Son of Man

contamination of the Holy Place by the sins of the people of Israel. The Son of Man, who both ascends and descends from the throne of God, whether spoken of by Daniel, mentioned in 1 Enoch and 4 Ezra, or in the teachings of Jesus, is, therefore, none other than the heavenly high priest (cf. Heb 4:14; 5:5, 10; 6:20, etc.), either seated on, or accompanied by, a cloud. "The Son of Man", then, when spoken of by Jesus is synonymous with "heavenly high priest."

To confirm the identity of "The Son of Man" as the heavenly high priest, the vestments worn by "one like the Son of Man" in Revelation 1:13 and 14:14 correspond closely with the vestments of the high priest of Israel, the construction of which are described in detail in Exodus 39:1–31. They include a robe (vv. 22–24), a golden diadem (v. 30), and a golden sash (v. 29). One variation of the description is the color of the sash. In the Exodus account of the vestments of the high priest the sash is made of "fine twisted linen, and of blue, purple, and crimson yarns, embroidered with needlework," all colors which symbolize the royal authority of the high priest, while the heavenly high priest ("the Son of Man") visions in Revelation the "crown" and "sash" are both gold, the prominent color of the heavenly realm in apocalyptic literature (Dan 10:5; Rev 4:4, 9:7, 17:4, 18:16, 21:18–21).

In Ezekiel, the "son of man" title carries far more meaning than just the designation "mortal" as it is translated in the NRSV. In nearly every case, it's more than ninety usages of the term is in connection with the sins of Israel (2:3; 3:4; 3:17; 4:4; 6:1 7:1, etc.) or with the functions or sins of the temple (8:5; 8:14; 21:2; and especially 22:23). In chapters 40–46 Ezekiel has visions of a new temple, with its description and measurements, all particulars which concern priests and especially the high priest. The description of the temple begins with this order, "Son of man, look closely and listen attentively, and set your mind upon all that I shall show you, for you were brought here in order that I might show it to you; declare all that you see to the house of Israel" (40:4). In 43:7 he is told, "Son of man, this is the place of my throne and the place for the soles of my feet, where I will reside among the people of Israel forever." The fact that Ezekiel, addressed as "son of man" in this verse, is shown the place of "my throne," implies that he is shown the Holy of Holies, the Holy Place accessible only to the high priest. These pieces of information are especially suited for a high priest. In addition, in 43:18, where Ezekiel is called "the son of man," he is given the ordinances for the altar, again of particular concern only to a priest. The same is true in 44:5: "Son of man, mark well, look closely, and listen attentively to all that I shall tell you concerning all the ordinances of the temple of Yahweh and all its laws; and mark well those who may be admitted to the temple and all those who are excluded from the sanctuary."

In 46:20–21 and 48:10–14 there are specific instructions for priests which only a high priest would have the authority to enforce. The result of this is that, in my opinion, where "son of man" is used in Ezekiel, it should simply be translated "priest" and in a few places even the title "high priest" would be appropriate. Substituting the titles "son of man" or "mortal" (NRSV) with "priest," or "high priest," gives the prophecy of Ezekiel rich meaning which may not have been apparent before.

In numerous places where Jesus speaks of "The Son of Man" it is in connection with his impending suffering (Matt 17:12, 20:17, Mark 8:31, 9:12, 10:33, 45, Luke 9:22, 17:24–25, John 3:24, 8:28). In Hebrews 2:17–18 the author has connected all the dots to make this statement:

> Therefore (Jesus) had to become like his brothers and sisters in every respect, so that he might be a merciful and faithful high priest in the service of God, to make a sacrifice of atonement for the sins of the people. Because he himself was tested by what he suffered, he is able to help those who are being tested.

And in 9:11–12 the faithful high priest makes the sacrifice of atonement with his own blood:

> When Christ came as a high priest of the good things that have come, then through the greater and perfect tent (not made with hands, that is, not of this creation), he entered once for all into the Holy Place, not with the blood of goats and calves, but with his own blood, thus obtaining eternal redemption."

In anticipation of the Messiah's atonement for the sins of the world with his own blood as "the Great High Priest," Hebrews begins his description with this observation:

> In these last days he (Yahweh) has spoken to us by a Son, whom he appointed heir of all things, through whom he also created the world. He is the reflection of God's glory and the exact imprint of God's very being, and he sustains all things by his powerful word. When he had made purification for sins, he sat down at the right of the Majesty on high. (Heb 1:1–3)

Continuously throughout the literature "the son of man" is the judge of the wickedness of humanity (4 Ezra 13:3–4; 13:37–39; 1 Enoch 38:3; 49:2–4; 51:1–2; 69:27; Matt 19:27–30; 25:31–46; Rev 1:12–3.21). In 4 Ezra whoever heard the voice of the son of man "melted as wax melts when it feels the fire" (13:4), and in verses 37 and 38 he will reprove the assembled nations for their ungodliness . . . and will reproach them to their face with their evil thoughts. In the *Similitudes* "the secrets of the righteous shall be revealed and the sinners judged' by the Son of Man ("the Righteous One") (37:3). In chapter 49 "unrighteousness shall disappear as a shadow and he shall judge the secret things, And none shall be able to utter a lying word before him" (v. 2 and 4). Finally, in the *Similitudes* "the sum of judgement was given unto the Son of Man, And he caused the sinners to pass away and to be destroyed from off the face of the earth, And those who have led the world astray" (69:27).

In the New Testament, Matthew describes "the Son of Man . . . seated on the throne of his glory" who then gives those who have followed him "twelve thrones" where they are "given authority to judge the twelve tribes of Israel" (19:28). A few chapters later a detailed description is given of the Son of Man who gathers "all the nations before him, and he will separate people one from another as a shepherd separates the sheep from the goats" (25:31–46). In Revelation 1:12–3:21 "one like the Son of Man is given the keys of Death and Hades" (1:18). This is followed by his judgement of the seven churches of Revelation.

6. The literature portrays the royalty of the "son of man" (Dan 7:13–14; 1 Enoch 45:3; 51:3; 55:4; 61:8; 62:4–9; 69:26; Matt 16:28; 19:27–30; 25:31; Mark 9:1; Luke 9:26–27; Rev 3:21). In the seminal image of "one like a son of man" in Daniel 7:13–14, the figure is "given dominion and glory and kingship and it is everlasting and shall never be destroyed." The same basic theme is repeated in the *Similitudes* where "Mine Elect One" sits "on the throne of glory" (45:3; 51:3; 55:4; 61:8, cf. Dan 7:9 and Matt 19:28), where "the mighty and all who possess the earth shall bless and glorify and extol him who rules over all" (62:6).

The many teachings and parables about the kingdom of God/heaven which so dominate the ministry of Jesus need not be enumerated here, but he often speaks of "the Son of Man coming in his kingdom" (Matt 16:28; 19:27–30; 25:31; Mark 9:1; 9:26:7–27; Rev 3:21, etc.).

As an addendum to the above, it must be mentioned that when Jesus instituted the Eucharist at the Last Supper, he blessed the bread and wine (Matt 26:26 and parallels; cf. 1 Cor 11:23–26). This action emulates the

Part Two: Moving Beyond Christian Folk Religion

action of the Priest Messiah mentioned in *The Messianic Rule* among the DSS where the covenanters, when gathering for "the common [tab]le", are instructed to "let no man extend his hand over the firstfruits of bread and wine before the Priest (Messiah); for [it is he] who shall bless the firstfruits of bread and wine, and shall be the first [to extend] his hand over the bread."

All of this raises the question as to the role Jesus envisioned for the Messiah: whether the Messiah was "King of the Jews", or heavenly high priest, and which role he assumed as Messiah. I believe he considered himself primarily as Priest Messiah. When Pilate asked him this question outright, "Are you the King of the Jews?" (Matt 9:11, Mark 15:2; Luke 23:3) his only response was, "*You* say so." In John's gospel (18:34) Jesus' response is different. He responds with, "Do you ask this on your own or did others tell you about me?" Jesus then adds in vv. 36: "My kingdom is not from this world. If my kingdom were from this world, my followers would be fighting to keep me from being handed over to the Jews. But as it is, my kingdom is not from here." Either response is evasive, never answering the question. The "kingdom" he refers to is the kingdom of God which he came to inaugurate, and which we will discuss at length in the next chapter. It is informative to mention at this point, however, that the kingdom of God, which "is not from here," will, however, be inaugurated *here*. It will be God's realm and under his reign, not "the Son of Man's". Thus Jesus is not, strictly speaking, a king. John's gospel continues, however, with this exchange (vv. 37–38): "Pilate asked him, 'So you are a king?' Jesus answered, "You say that I am a king. For this I was born, and for this I came into the world, to testify to the truth. Everyone who belongs to the truth listens to my voice.' Pilate asked him, 'What is truth?'" Jesus has turned the question about being a king into a declaration about "the truth." It is for that one purpose he "came into the world." He never ascribed to being a king, but he most certainly ascribed to being "the Son of Man", which by extensive evidence must be the Priest Messiah.

His ministry displayed the actions of a priest, more often than a king, such as, his teachings, miracles, forgiving sins, and making the lame, weak, sick, dead or dying, blind, mute, or leper whole again (the Greek term *lepros*, always translated "leper," is believed to be a generic term for "skin disease"). He was a priest of compassion, but also a priest of judgment, and a suffering priest. He also possessed direct access to the presence of the Creator God, and only one other figure in all of Israel had that direct access, the high priest. Yes, the prophets were often in God's presence, but it was by God's initiative. You do not find the prophets on their own approaching the throne of God. Only Moses does so, and that is because the tabernacle was not yet built, and an abode for his abiding presence did not yet exist. The tabernacle/temple, on the other hand, was the abode of the visible presence of the Lord, who dwelt in the midst of his called People of God.

Today, the earthly temple no longer exists, but for Jews everywhere, Yahweh's house is still the House of the Lord, the temple, but it is a temple beyond this realm, invisible to us, yet so very real. N.T. Wright refers to this real, but invisible, temple as "the eschatological Temple."[13] The four prophetic books of Zephaniah, Haggai, Zechariah and Malachi, all point to the restoration of the temple under the leadership of a royal (Davidic), or possibly a priestly figure. Elsewhere, in Wright's books *Simply Jesus* and *How God Became King*[14], he says that the temple is always where "heaven and earth meet." And in Wright's *New Testament and the People of God*: "The Temple thus formed the principle heart of Judaism . . . it was the organ from which there went out to the body of Judaism . . . the living, and healing presence of the covenant God."[15] The book of Hebrews has it so right when it refers to Christ as "the great high priest" (4:14).

Jesus was ultimately crucified under Roman law as "The King of the Jews," just like the titular above his head read, but in actuality his accusers, the high priest and the chief priests of the religious council, the Sanhedrin, condemned him as falsely claiming to be high priest, and heavenly high priest at that (Matt 26:65). It was a role Caiaphas, the high priest, claimed only for himself. To usurp that role was blasphemy and justified the sentence of death. So in the eyes of the religious elite, Jesus hung on the cross as the defeated high priest, and good riddance! But that is not the end of the story, as you well know.

"THE SON OF MAN" SPOKEN OF IN THE THIRD PERSON

In conclusion, the peculiar third person construct in the New Testament of "The Son of Man" must be addressed. There has been a lot of ink and paper expended attempting to explain its purpose. It is not necessary to

---

13. *Jesus and the Victory of God*, 499, and *How God Became King*, 171.
14. *How God Became King*, 173, 235–36.
15. 226.

review all the many theories as to why Jesus referred to the Son of Man as "the Son of Man." The fact of the matter is that Jesus seems to be referring to a figure outside of himself, while at the same time it is often clear that he is referring to himself, and himself alone. How can that be?

Because all four gospels quote Jesus as speaking of " the Son of Man" it must have been the usage of Jesus in his own language, Aramaic. Thus he must have used the Aramaic term *bar enash(e)* with the emphatic suffix, indicating the third person usage. It is my belief that this was intentional. "The Son of Man" was separate from Jesus, yet was most certainly to be identified *with* Jesus. So who was "the Son of Man," besides being the high priest? The high priest is the identity of the Son of Man sayings in both Jesus' sayings, and in the figure of Daniel 7:13, but that title was more than that. "The Son of Man" accompanied Jesus throughout his ministry, and it will be the "the Son of Man" who, at the end of days, will return in power and glory on the clouds of heaven. "The Son of Man," is quite simply, the Will of God. It is that destiny which, as God's will, leads Jesus everywhere, including the cross. It is "the Son of Man" who Jesus prayed God would remove from him ("this cup") so fervently on the night before his crucifixion, and the heavenly answer was simply, "No." Thus it is "the Son of Man" who accompanied Jesus to the cross, and when Jesus cried out, "My God, my God, why have you forsaken me?" (quoting Ps 22:1), he thought at that moment "the Son of Man left him." But he was wrong. "The Son of Man" was with him to the end (or was it really the beginning) when Jesus uttered his last, "It is finished." Yes, Jesus, accompanied by "the Son of Man" (God's Will), had accomplished everything he came to do. The kingdom of God had indeed been inaugurated at that moment, and while to the world it was the most catastrophic event which ever occurred, it was actually God's greatest display of power. At that moment death had been defeated, Satan had lost all of his power, and the Priest Messiah had ushered in the forgiveness of sins, the cleansing of the human heart, and had begun the renewal of the earth. And it is that figure, "the Son of Man" and Jesus in total union, who will return again on the clouds of glory where heaven and earth will be totally renewed, and everyone, everywhere, will behold its glory.

During his lifetime, Jesus had denied his own will to follow the Will of his Father. It is the same requirement Jesus demands of his followers (Matt 16:24 and parallels). We also do not know where following him will go, but go we must. For the vast majority of us the requirement is not as harsh as it was for Dietrich Bonhoeffer. He was a German pastor during Germany's most awful past. It was during the dictatorship of Adolf Hitler that Pastor Bonhoeffer was faced with a terrible decision: does following Jesus mean that I must just "obey the governing authorities" as Paul said, and thus do nothing? That's what many of the clergy of Nazi Germany believed. "All authority is given by God," Paul had said. Bonhoeffer, however, believed he had been given a different message. You must actively work to stop the madman. With a great feeling of guilt, and confusion of conscience within him, he believed the message he was receiving was right. He therefore joined in with fellow pastors who opposed Hitler. They called themselves the "Confessing church" and began a program to stop Hitler, and eventually Bonhoeffer actively worked toward Hitler's assassination. But before the plot was fully hatched, some of its leaders were identified, and Bonhoeffer was one of them. He was imprisoned at Flossenbürg Prison, and eventually sentence to death. On April 8, 1945, the Sunday after Easter that year, one of his fellow prisoners recalled events in this way:

> He had hardly finished his last prayer when the door opened and two evil-looking men in civilian clothes came in and said: "Prisoner Bonhoeffer. Get ready to come with us." Those words Come with us—for all prisoners they had come to mean one thing only—the scaffold.
> We bade him good-bye he drew me aside "This is the end, he said. For me, the beginning of life."[16]

The journey to the scaffold was about a hundred miles north-northwest and it would take a day to get there. He was hung in the early hours of April 9th but little did he know at the time, that was the actual date and approximate time of Jesus' resurrection, "Early in the morning," April 9, 30. Yes, Bonhoeffer was absolutely right, while it was truly the end, it for him "the beginning of life." It was his resurrection! He had fulfilled everything he had preached about. In his 1937 book, *The Cost of Discipleship*, he had said, "When Christ calls a man he bids him come and die."[17] And in a sermon he preached while he was a pastor in London, he said,

> Life only really begins when it ends here on earth . . . all that is here is only the prologue before the curtain goes up . . . Death is grace, the greatest gift of grace that God gives to people who believe in him . . . it beckons to us with heavenly power, if only

16. Metaxas, *Bonhoeffer: Pastor, Martyr, Prophet, Spy*, 528.
17. *Op cit.*, 44.

we realize that it is the gateway to our homeland, the tabernacle of joy, the everlasting kingdom of peace.[18]

It is not only Jesus, following "The Son of Man" to his destiny, who knows suffering. Hundreds and thousands, and perhaps hundreds of thousands have endured such suffering, but whatever that destiny is, we are called to follow. That destiny, the Will of God, was "The Son of Man" for Jesus, and the role of "The Son of Man" was the heavenly high priest. It was his constant companion, this denial of self, and it ultimately resulted in the cross. Paul, I believe, speaks of this in Romans 3:28 when he speaks of the faithfulness of Jesus (Matt 16:24). It was Jesus' faithfulness in denying himself, and accepting the destiny laid out for him by "The Son of Man," that took him to the cross. Thus, "The Son of Man" leads and Jesus follows.

And so it is that "The Son of Man," Jesus' constant companion throughout his ministry, whom he followed to his final destiny, fulfilled the dual role of the Messiah: both the "Priest Messiah" and the "King Messiah." Both were expected in the end of days by the ascetic community at Qumran who authored what today are known as the Dead Sea Scrolls. Their expectations were fulfilled in Jesus of Nazareth.

---

18. Ibid., 531.

6

The Kingdom

"THE KINGDOM": THESE WORDS alone bring to mind many images, and evoke various emotional responses, depending upon our cultural upbringing, our sense of values, our biases, our prejudices, our fears. They're apt to bring to mind fears of absolute power, or perhaps the pomp and ceremony of golden carriages, beaver hats, and palaces. Today, throughout the world, there are few absolute monarchies controlling the political power of nations. Most are constitutional monarchies with parliamentary forms of government run by coalitions of various political parties, and headed by a prime minister. The monarchy of such a nation is primarily a figurehead, a unifying factor in the government. The prime example, of course, is the United Kingdom, but there are approximately twenty-three countries throughout the world, which have constitutional monarchies, including Norway, Sweden, Denmark, the Netherlands, Morocco, and Jordan.

One of the first decisions the Continental Congress in America made when it was debating the issue of independence from Britain was whether they would want a monarchy or not. A few advocated it, but the vast majority did not. A religious kingdom is something else again. Suddenly thrown into the mix of the image of kingdom is a kingdom ruled by religious values which may evoke feelings of terror in some, and just laws in others. There have been fringe politicians in many countries, including the United States, who have occasionally advocated enforcing the Biblical laws, but just the thought of that can bring to mind inquisitions, pogroms,

Part Two: Moving Beyond Christian Folk Religion

perhaps even ethnic cleansing. Many on the extreme right of religious faith have perhaps thought enforcing Biblical laws a good idea. The great fear of most religious people under such a system is the establishment of a theocracy, where God's law becomes the law of the land and leads to oppression, violence against anyone who is thought to have violated God's law, and worse. This is a major issue in a number of contemporary countries, including most recently the change of government in Egypt. While many in the western world advocated Egypt becoming a democratic state, few people realized that a truly democratic election could go in just about any direction. My wife and I have traveled to Egypt twice and know that in 2005 and 2008 a topic discussed among Egyptians was whether they were in favor of a secular state (which they were under during the dictatorship of Hosni Mubarak), or preferred an Islamic state. The election of 2012 somewhat settled the issue when they elected a president who was a member of the Muslim Brotherhood. At the time of this writing it is not yet clear whether Egypt under the rule of the Muslim Brotherhood will remain at least a semi-secular state, or placed under Islamic law which will restrict the role of women in the government and in private life, and impose harsh penalties on violators of the law. According to the current news the emotions are high on both sides of the issue within Egypt. In 1969 I was stationed for a year in southeastern Turkey, and my wife and I have traveled through Turkey in 2010. Turkey, although it has a Muslim population of more than 90%, is generally proud of the fact that they are one of the most secular of the Muslim countries.

THE KINGDOM—ITS MEANING

With this brief introduction there can be numerous interpretations of the meaning of the kingdom of God, yet it is the one subject at the focal point of most of Jesus' teaching. In the recorded sayings and teachings of Jesus the term occurs 125 times, more than any other subject. Many of his parables begin with "the kingdom of God is like . . . " or something similar. It should be made clear from the outset, however, that the terms "kingdom of God" and "kingdom of heaven" are synonymous. The latter occurs most frequently in the Gospel of Matthew. It is believed he preferred this term over "kingdom of God" in respect for the sensitivity of his primarily Hebrew audience who might be offended at the use of the divine name, especially if his gospel was originally composed in Hebrew

The Kingdom

or Aramaic, for which there is some evidence that it was. If it was written in Hebrew or Aramaic, its original form might have been "kingdom of Yahweh," a term that occurs in 1 Chronicles 28:5 and in 2 Chronicles 13:8. The popular concepts that Jesus' teachings about the kingdom of heaven have to do with the afterlife are mistaken. This is made clear in the prayer Jesus taught his disciples, which has this petition, "Your kingdom come. Your will be done, on earth as it is in heaven" (Matt 6:10). The prayer is that the kingdom of God/heaven would come on earth just as it exists in heaven. The heaven here spoken of has a separate existence. Where it exists is another subject we will explore a little later.

Although the Hebrew Scriptures speak of kingdom frequently it is usually used to refer to political divisions which are under monarchical rule (Gen 10:10; Num 32:33; 1 Kgs 2:12; 1 Chr 10:14). The land of Palestine was a united monarchy under kings Saul, David, and Solomon, but after the death of Solomon, who died in 933 BC, Palestine was divided in 930 BC into the kingdoms of Judah (2 Chr 11:17) in the south, and Israel (1 Sam 15:28; 24:20) in the north. Following the Assyrian conquest of the northern kingdom of Israel during the Assyrian king Tiglath-pileser III (745–727 BC), there was a massive deportation of its citizens in the northern kingdom of Israel. Its citizens were deported from towns and villages all over its territories, and the result was that tribal unity among the ten northern tribes was lost, and they became known as the "Lost Tribes of Israel." Only the Judahites of the south and the tribe of Levi, which was a priestly tribe and held no tribal area, survived as tribes. The tribe of Judah gave its name to the southern kingdom, known as Judea in Jesus' day, and also gave its name to the religion of Yahweh, "Judaism," and its adherents, "Jews."

THE CONFLICT OVER GOD'S SOVEREIGN RULE

Within the Hebrew Scriptures there was a major conflict over whether Israel should even have a king if Yahweh is indeed king of the whole world. This issue is debated on several occasions in the books of the Former Prophets, or early prophets, such as Joshua (book of Joshua), Samuel (in Judges, 1—2 Sam), and the lesser known Jeremiah (1—2 Kgs). This last named person is not the well-known prophet who lived in the sixth century BC and wrote the book of Jeremiah, but a man in the eighth century BC, from the town of Libnah, and grandfather of two of the kings of

Part Two: Moving Beyond Christian Folk Religion

Judah, Jehoahaz and Zedekiah (2 Kgs 23:31; 24:18; Jer 52:1). The Hebrew Bible lists these books under The Prophets, while in Christian Bibles they are regarded as historical books. The books of the Former Prophets tell of the progression of the ruler ship of Israel as a nation from being ruled by judges to a full-blown monarchy beginning with King Saul, then King David, and King Solomon, who built the first temple. The most pronounced of the debates over establishing a monarchy is in 1 Samuel. It speaks of God being uneasy with the national outcry for a human king, because Yahweh sees it as a rejection of him as king. Starting in chapter 8 there is a prime example of this conflict:

> All the elders of Israel gathered together and came to Samuel at Ramah, and said to him, "You are old and your sons do not follow in your ways; appoint for us, then, a king to govern us, like other nations." But the thing displeased Samuel when they said, "Give us a king to govern us." Samuel prayed to Yahweh, and Yahweh said to Samuel, "Listen to the voice of the people in all that they say to you; for they have not rejected you, but they have rejected me from being king over them. Just as they have done to me, from the day I brought them up out of Egypt to this day, forsaking me and serving other gods, so also they are doing to you. Now then, listen to their voice; only you shall solemnly warn them, and show them the ways of the king who shall reign over them." (1 Sam 8:4–9)

First Samuel 8:10–18 describes the ways of the king who will reign over them. The ways of the king, of course are the human kings who will rule, and Samuel warns them that he will draft their sons to become the nation's warriors (10:11), and will make their sons commanders over the armies (v. 12), and will conscript their daughters to be housemaids, cooks and bakers (v. 13). Samuel then goes on to say that the king will confiscate their best fields, vineyards, and orchards for his own use (v. 15). He will even confiscate their best slaves, cattle, and donkeys for himself (v. 16). On top of all this he will take a tithe, a tax, of one-tenth of everything they own and for all practical purposes they will become slaves to the king (v. 17). Following this dire prediction Samuel also makes this prophecy: "And in that day you will cry out because of your king, whom you have chosen for yourselves; but Yahweh will not answer you" (v. 18). In other words, Samuel was saying, "Your own king will become your oppressor, but when that day comes and you realize you have become like a slave to your king, don't turn to Yahweh in your anguish and expect him to answer. You have rejected him as your king." Yet even with that warning, the people were adamant, they wanted a king so they would be like other nations: "But the people refused to listen to the voice of Samuel; they said, 'No! but we are determined to have a king over us, so that we also may be like other nations, and that our king may govern us and go out before us and fight our battles'" (vv. 19–20). And there was the final rub that "we also might be like other nations." They didn't want to be different, or stand out from the crowd. They wanted to be just like everyone else. It is a common human emotion. Yahweh had always declared that they were not like other nations. They were the people of God. Yahweh had time and again identified himself as: "the God of Abraham, Isaac, and Jacob." He repeatedly had told them, "I brought you out of the land of Egypt." In other words, he has all along been the God who identified them as his nation. He had been their protector, guide, and their warrior. They could never be like everyone else. They were his. But it was the voice of the people in the long run that won out over the will of Yahweh: Yahweh said to Samuel, "Listen to their voice and set a king over them." Samuel then told everyone to go home (v. 22). A little later on in 10:17–19, 25 Samuel delivered Yahweh's message to the people:

> Thus says Yahweh, the God of Israel, "I brought up Israel out of Egypt, and I rescued you from the hand of the Egyptians and from the hand of all the kingdoms that were oppressing you. But today you have rejected your God, who saves you from all your calamities and your distresses; and you have said, 'No! but set a king over us! Now therefore present yourselves before Yahweh by your tribes and by your clans . . . " Samuel told the people the rights and duties of the kingship; and he wrote them in a book and laid it up before Yahweh. Then Samuel sent all the people back to their homes. Saul also went to his home at Gibeah, and with him went warriors whose hearts God had touched. But some worthless fellows said, "How can this man save us?" They despised him and brought him no present. But he held his piece.

The kings of other nations have been the oppressors over Israel, yet the people of Israel want a king other than Yahweh? Do they not realize that in doing so the oppressed might very well become the oppressor? That is the argument Yahweh makes with Samuel. It was Yahweh who has rescued Israel from the king (pharaoh) of Egypt, yet the people in asking for their own king were rejecting Yahweh as king.

Part Two: Moving Beyond Christian Folk Religion

That is where the story ends in 1 Samuel 10. It has been known for decades that the story is incomplete and that apparently its ending has been lost. But when the Dead Sea Scrolls were found, among them was the fragment of a scroll of Samuel containing this story and includes the ending which had been lost. It completes the story in that it is an illustration of the brutality of the king of Ammonites, who was a tyrant, and how he mistreated Israelites who lived in the regions of Gad and Reuben to the east of the Jordan. Regions the king of the Ammonites considered his territory. He abused these foreign Israelites by gouging out their right eyes. "No one," the passage from the Dead Sea Scrolls says, "was left of the Israelites across the Jordan whose right eye Nahash, king of the Ammonites, had not gouged out." The New Revised Standard Version of the Bible (NRSV) has inserted the paragraph, which had been lost, following 1 Samuel 10:27 to complete the story, but omitted any verse numbers in the paragraph to avoid confusion. The manuscript of Samuel found among the Dead Sea Scrolls was a thousand years older than any of the previous manuscripts in the world's possession, but it is important to the story. It lends further evidence of why Israel's insistence in having a monarchy may, in the long run, become a disaster for them, and how a demand for an earthly king is actually a rejection of Yahweh's benevolent rule.

Ultimately Israel did institute a monarchy, but it produced only two significant kings, David and Solomon. The first king, Saul, was weak and ineffective. He was of the tribe of Benjamin and although anointed by Samuel as king over the northern tribes, he was essentially a warrior primarily for the tribe of Benjamin. When he proceeds with a sacrifice that Samuel was supposed to conduct before battle (1 Sam 13:7–14), Samuel condemns Saul and declares a judgment that Saul's descendants cannot ascend to royalty. Tensions flare up when Samuel declares that David will become the future king. Saul is filled with jealousy against David, and the situation deteriorates to the point that Saul falls on his own sword (1 Sam 31:1–13; 2 Sam 1:1–10). But it was under David that the country became truly united. At the beginning of David's reign he was king of just the southern tribe, which formed the nation called Judah (2 Sam 2:1–7). Later he also became king of the ten northern tribes of Israel (5:1–5). It was David, therefore, who unified the tribes of the north, with the tribe of Judah to the south, and it became one nation, Israel. This unified Israel only existed from the tenth into the ninth centuries BC. The southern area containing Judah, eventually became known as Judea, as it is called to this day. But the days of David and Solomon were exceedingly short lived glory days. After Solomon's reign schisms began to dissolve the unity and the northern and southern kingdom separated. Each had a succession of kings until Israel in the north fell to Shalmaneser V, king of the Assyrians in 722/1 BC (2 Kgs 17) and the south fell to Nebuchadnezzar, the king of the Babylonians in 597 BC (2 Kgs 24–25). Each of these defeats resulted in exile for many of the leading citizens of these divided kingdoms. Thousands of the citizens of Israel, the northern kingdom, were led into Assyrian exile and the elite from the south to the Babylonian exile. The most important of these exiles was the Babylonian because it had lost its leaders who gave it its culture and social stability. During that critical time it also caused the rise of the great writing prophets of Second Isaiah, Jeremiah, and Ezekiel. It was Ezekiel, the priest/prophet, who described seeing the glory of Yahweh leave the temple in Jerusalem and then hover over the Mount of Olives (Ezek 10:18–19, 11:16–25) and depart toward the east to dwell with the true Israel in exile (11:16–17). The prophets of the exile paved the way for the expectation of someone who would redeem them from their plight and once again make them into a great nation. Only a renewal of the covenant would lay the foundation for the true emergence of God's kingdom.

There has long been a debate over whether that kingdom was to be understood in a merely spiritual sense, or whether God truly has sovereignty over the rule of nations as Daniel 4:31–32 seems to suggest:

> A voice came from heaven: "O King Nebuchadnezzar, to you it is declared: The kingdom has departed from you! You shall be driven away from human society, and your dwelling shall be with the animals of the field. You shall be made to eat grass like oxen, and seven times shall pass over you, until you have learned that the Most High has sovereignty over the kingdom of mortals and gives it to whom he will."

The Wisdom of Solomon 6:1–3, in the Apocrypha, expands on this:

> Listen therefore, O kings, and understand;
> learn, O judges of the ends of the earth.
> Give ear, you that rule over multitudes, and boast of many nations.
> For your dominion was given you from the Lord,
> and your sovereignty from the Most High;
> he will search out your works and inquire into your plans.

It is clear from these passages that when God rules, he becomes the monarch under which all human monarchs rule. Although toward the

Part Two: Moving Beyond Christian Folk Religion

end of the Hebrew Scriptures the kingdom of God was becoming more fully defined, it was not until the New Testament that God's reign really began to be understood. Jesus placed it at the forefront of his teaching. Saying after saying, and parable after parable, begins with words similar to "the kingdom of God is like . . ." He wanted his disciples and those who came after them to truly understand what the kingdom of God means.

Almost immediately after his baptism by John in the Jordan River, Jesus relocates the center from which his ministry will take place to the town of Capernaum, along the northwestern shore of the Sea of Galilee. It was a fishing village and the home of Simon (later renamed "Peter") and his brother Andrew, both of whom were disciples of John the Baptizer (John 1:43–51). Though Simon and Andrew had been born in Bethsaida, a village along the north shore of the Galilean lake, they now were from Capernaum. Also from the same village were the sons of Zebedee, James and John, all of them fishermen. It is now believed that Jesus actually lived with Simon and his wife and family in Capernaum. These four became the core of twelve disciples (so named in Matt 10:1–4; Mark 3:16–19; and Luke 6:14–16). The other named among the twelve included Philip and Bartholomew, Thomas and Matthew/Levi (a tax collector), James (also called "The Less" or "son of Alpheus") and Thaddeus, Simon (also called "the Zealot" in Luke 6:15 and Acts 1:13), and Judas Iscariot, the betrayer. The list of the twelve varies somewhat in Luke 6:16 where he replaces the name of Thaddeus with "Judas son of James." This Judas is probably the same as the person called "Judas, not Iscariot" in John 14:22. Though sometimes identified as another name for Thaddeus, there is no evidence for this identification. If he is a different person from Thaddeus, then the number of named disciples expands to thirteen, in addition to these, John's gospel mentions the call of Nathanael (John 1:43–51). Nathanael was from the town of Cana (John 21:2) about 20 miles from Capernaum, where, according to the second chapter of John, Jesus performed his first miracle at a wedding, turning water into wine. It is not beyond speculation that the wedding in Cana might well have been Nathanael's or a relative of his, as the story immediately follows the call of Nathanael. At any event, Jesus' whole family was in attendance (John 2:3) and Jesus' mother appears to be helping the family of the wedding with the multi day celebration.

It is obvious, throughout the gospels, that Jesus was constantly surrounded by a cadre of "disciples" who traveled with him throughout his ministry and his trip to Jerusalem and became witnesses to his death and resurrection. These included numerous women including Mary Magdalene,

Joanna who was the wife of a servant of Herod Antipas, Susanna and other women of means who actually financed his ministry (Luke 8:1–3). In addition to these three named women disciples, Luke also adds the addendum "and many others." This would indicate that Jesus had a large group of followers around him from which the Twelve Disciples were chosen, and within this group was an inner circle of three, Peter, James, and John, who accompanied him during important, intimate, moments of his life, such as the transfiguration (Mark 9:2–13), and his prayer in Gethsemane the night before his crucifixion (Matt 26:36–46).

Though the exact list of names of the Twelve Disciples may have changed some over the period of his ministry, the number of "twelve" is constant because they became symbolic figureheads, each over one of the twelve tribes of Israel, which constitutes a new kingdom Jesus was inaugurating, "the kingdom of God." This is made clear in Matthew 19:27–30:

> Then Peter said in reply, "Look, we have left everything and followed you. What then will we have?" Jesus said to them, "Truly I tell you, at the renewal of all things, when the Son of Man is seated on the throne of glory, you who have followed me will also sit on twelve thrones, judging the twelve tribes of Israel. And everyone who has left houses or brothers or sisters or father or mother or children or fields, for my name's sake, will receive a hundredfold, and will inherit eternal life. But many who are first will be last, and the last will be first.

The last part of this statement has several key points. The first is that "everyone who has left houses or brothers or sisters or father or mother or children or fields, for my name's sake . . . will inherit eternal life." This is exactly what the twelve had done, as did Jesus himself, thus they have followed his own example. The second is the riddle at the end that "many who are first will be last, and the last will be first." This strange saying will be dealt with at length in the next chapter.

The selection of an inner council of twelve was one of Jesus' first steps in signaling that a new kind of kingdom was dawning upon Israel, unlike anything the people of Israel had ever experienced. Unfortunately very little of the church's effort has been directed towards this prominent aspect of Jesus' ministry. As has already been pointed out, the first three hundred years of the history of the church was primarily invested in defining who Jesus was and is, and not what he wanted us to learn from him.

Part Two: Moving Beyond Christian Folk Religion

THE FORGOTTEN KINGDOM

The ancient creeds totally ignore anything about Jesus' teachings. They focus primarily on the makeup of the Trinity: Father, Son, and Holy Spirit. The early church fathers were obsessed with defining how Jesus could be both divine and human. The creeds they formulated tell us that Jesus is "God's only Son, our Lord, who was conceived by the Holy Spirit, born of the virgin Mary" (Apostles Creed), that he is "the only Son of God, eternally begotten of the Father, God from God, Light from Light, true God from true God, begotten, not made, of one Being with the Father; through him all things were made. For us and for our salvation came down from heaven, was incarnate of the Holy Spirit and the virgin Mary and became truly human" (Nicene Creed). The creeds then go right to Jesus' suffering and crucifixion under Pontius Pilate, his death, burial and resurrection on the third day "in accordance with the scriptures" (Nicene Creed). The creeds which supposedly define Christian belief and faith fail to tell us one word about the kingdom of God, his most important mission in his sayings and parables, or the Son of Man, who he was, and why Jesus spoke so constantly about him, or even anything about his miracles and why he performed them. These precious subjects by Jesus are lost in the Hellenized church. Over the centuries most of his teachings and sayings have been used (and abused) instead, as separate commands and demands to prove our "Christian" culture's approval or disapproval of the actions of others, i.e., they have become proof texts of judgment or justification. They tell us that we must have faith so we will go to heaven when we die. Thus the kingdom of God/heaven has been largely relegated to the afterlife, or the eschaton, which refers to the end of the present age or final judgment. This despite Jesus' prayer to his Father that "your kingdom come, your will be done, *on earth* as it is in heaven."

The common belief that the kingdom is yet in the future, is contrary to what Jesus actually taught. Throughout his teachings, the kingdom of God is being inaugurated in the here and now. Jesus clearly spoke of the kingdom of God as being "at hand" (Matt 4:17; 10:7; Mark 1:15), "prepared for you" (Matt 25:34), "come near to you" (Luke 10:9), "come to you" (Luke 10:11), "within you" (Luke 17:21), etc. This is the expansion of the Hebrew Scriptures' understanding that God became the king of the whole world, and actually all of creation (Ps 22:8; 47; 103:9; Dan 4:32). The kingdom of heaven is *not* "pie in the sky, by and by." It has been observed that this conception, however, generates problems, for it

The Kingdom

is obvious that God's will is not consistently done by any government or individual, and so in what sense is God the ruler of all? It is the question that deserves a careful study of Jesus' teachings as we have them recorded in the gospels. It evidently played such an important role in his ministry that the bulk of his recorded teachings address this very issue. The gospel writers are the ones who have been responsible for these sayings being remembered and recorded. Obviously that is because they were his sayings most often repeated by those who walked with him, or talked with him, or listened carefully to everything he said.

Matthew remembered that one of the earliest things Jesus said was to seek first the kingdom of God (Matt 6:33), and Luke remembered him saying, "I must proclaim the good news of the kingdom of God to the other cities also; for I was sent for this purpose" (4:43). Luke also remembered Jesus saying, "What is the kingdom of God like? And to what should I compare it? It is like a mustard seed that someone took and sowed in the garden; it grew and became a tree, and the birds of the air made nests in its branches" (13:18–19). Obviously from these sayings, the "kingdom of God" doesn't just burst upon the scene. It is a process occurring over great spans of human time, perhaps many millennia. Yet we are human. We want satisfaction *now*! It must happen within *our* short span. So we wait eagerly for Jesus to return, *now*! "Destroy this old creation of yours, *now*! It's been corrupted and is no longer good!" That's the blaring message broadcast from one pulpit after another and from televangelists all across the airwaves. "Get on with it, God Almighty; send Jesus back to establish your Kingdom!" Think, though, for a moment, what this message is also saying—it is proclaiming that Jesus' first coming did not complete what he came to do. Oh, yes, many Christians think, he died for me so that I can go to heaven! But from the cross, his last utterance was, "It is finished!" He had completed *all* he came to do. His mission was a success, through and through. Yes, he'll return all right, and he'll return in triumph, but it will not be to destroy the world and inaugurate the kingdom of God. He's already inaugurated the kingdom. That task was complete when he uttered, "It is finished." When he returns, he will return leading the multitude of the unified "People of God" who have passed before and will gather those who remain—they'll meet to greet him "in the air" as Paul so beautifully affirms in 1 Thessalonians 4:17. Jesus will not be coming to take the People of God *out* of the world, but to unify *all* the People of God and bring them all to earth where the kingdom of heaven is:

Part Two: Moving Beyond Christian Folk Religion

> Then I saw a new heaven and a new earth; for the first heaven and the first earth had passed away, and the sea was no more. And I saw the holy city, the new Jerusalem, coming down out of heaven from God, prepared as a bride adorned for her husband. And I heard a loud voice from the throne saying,
>
> > "See the home of God is among mortals.
> > He will dwell with them; and they will be his peoples,
> > and God himself will be with them;
> > he will wipe every tear from their eyes.
> > Death will be no more;
> > mourning and crying and pain will be no more;
> > for the first things have passed away."
>
> And the one who was seated on the throne said, "See I am making all things new." Also he said, "Write this for these words are trustworthy and true." Then he said to me, "It is done! I am the Alpha and the Omega, the beginning and the end." Rev 21:1–6a

Note the words, "I am making all things new." It is the renewal of the earth, not its destruction. Also note that he repeated Jesus' final words from the cross, "It is done," the same as Jesus said, "It is finished!" The world hasn't "passed away," it is corruption, sin, wickedness, pain, distress, that have passed away. In vv. 6b to 8 he goes on to say,

> To the thirsty I will give water as a gift from the spring of the water of life. Those who conquer will inherit these things, and I will be their God and they will be my children. But as for the cowardly, the faithless, the polluted, the fornicators, the sorcerers, the idolaters, and all liars, their place will be in the lake that burns with fire and sulfur, which is the second death.

In all the parables Jesus told where he said, "the kingdom of God is like..." he was building an expectation toward this final scene. Revelation was written to bring hope and expectation to those who were experiencing horrific persecution, crucifixion, being torn apart by wild dogs, being set afire to be human torches lighting the streets of Nero's Rome. "You will be part of my children," God was telling them, "persevere and death will be no more." God will "wipe every tear from their eyes. Death will be no more; mourning and crying and pain will be no more, for the first things [these sufferings] have passed away." Few of us (hopefully none of us) will undergo what those people suffered in the mid-sixties AD, but it is the supreme picture of the kingdom of God, when it is complete.

The Kingdom

The evangelists wanted us to remember that Jesus had told the crowds who surrounded him that the kingdom of God was to be received just like a little child's faith, or we cannot enter it (Matt 18:4; Mark 10:15; Luke 18:17); it is not for the rich (Matt 19:23–26; Mark 10:23; Luke 18:24–25), nor for the pious who "lock people out of the kingdom of heaven" (Matt 23:13). It is God alone who has determined the order of things to which persons could be admitted and from which they might be excluded. It is not the prerogative of any other king, government, or person to make such a judgment (Matt 7:1; Luke 6:37). We will address the issue of the priority of the underclasses for admittance to the kingdom over the wealthy in the next chapter. We will see there that under God's rule, there is a new reality, one which those of us from the western hemisphere find difficult to understand. And in chapter 8 we will examine Jesus' conflict with the pious of Israel, especially the Pharisees, and his own attitude toward religious piety in chapter 9.

In 1979 Ben F. Meyer, in his book *The Aims of Jesus* emphasizes the supreme focus of Jesus on the reign of God. Meyer asks this question, "What do the sayings of Jesus say about the kingdom of God?"

> They say "free gift." The reign of God is not achieved or developed or controlled or disposed of by men. It "is near," "comes," "appears"; it "overtakes" or "comes upon" one; one may be "in" it or "not far from" it; one "expects" or "looks for" it and lives to "see" it; one is "called" or "invited" to it, "attains" or "enters into" or is "cast out" of it; one "seeks after" it and is or is not "fitted" for it. God "gives" it, man "accepts" or "takes" or "inherits" (i.e., enters into specifically gratuitous possession of) it.[1]

When God rules he becomes Lord over mankind, nations, and events. There is no king, president or national assembly who can trump that rule. It can also be said that when God is king there is also no human interpretation of any recorded Word of God that takes priority over how God acts. His lordship is over the Bible, history, and world nations. Thus, his lordship is not a theocracy where priests, pastors, or church hierarchies become his intermediaries to administer his justice. The kingdom of God is independent from all ecclesiastical intervention. The kingdom of God is independent of human structure. Entering into it is by invitation only, and remaining in the kingdom is dependent on a person's activity within it. Any form of wickedness is cause for being expelled from it.

---

1. *Op cit*, 131.

Part Two: Moving Beyond Christian Folk Religion

While the kingdom of God is already present in the world, it will also be the order of things in the world to come at the end of the age where those who were already in the kingdom during their lifetimes will be sealed there eternally because evil will no longer exist. In other words, while the kingdom of God is now, it is also eschatological, the reality of the end of time.

The Baptizer clearly expected that he was announcing the start of the eschaton, the coming of the kingdom of God at the end of the age, when he said,

> I baptize you with water for repentance, but one who is more powerful that I is coming after me; I am not worthy to carry his sandals. He will baptize you with the Holy Spirit and fire. His winnowing fork is in his hand, and he will clear his threshing floor and will gather his wheat into the granary; but the chaff he will burn with unquenchable fire. Matt 3:11–13.

But then John was arrested: "When John heard in prison what the Messiah was doing, he sent word by his disciples and said to him, 'Are you the one who is to come, or are we to wait for another?'" (Matt 11:2–3). He began to have his doubts about whether the end of the age was about to happen, or would the world have to wait for yet another Messiah to usher it in. But then Jesus sent word back to him telling of the signs already happening: "Go and tell John what you hear and see: the blind receive their sight, the lame walk, the lepers are cleansed, the deaf hear, the dead are raised, and the poor have good news brought to them. And [happy] is anyone who takes no offense at me." (Matt 11:4–6)

The signs of the coming of the kingdom of God were already happening. The disenfranchised and the underclasses of society were now being purified, and receiving the good news that they have indeed been invited into the kingdom. The answer to John's question was an emphatic "yes, the kingdom is already on its way." John had prepared the way and it was now a reality.

Jesus came to minister "only to the lost sheep of the house of Israel" (Matt 15:24). Thus God's kingdom was intended, first and foremost for Israel. This is what Jesus meant when he said, "many will come from east and west and will eat with Abraham and Isaac and Jacob in the kingdom of heaven" (Matt 8:11). Abraham and Isaac and Jacob *and* their heirs are already inheritors of the kingdom. Others are invited in to also join them, but only because some of the heirs of the kingdom will be thrown into outer darkness (v. 12).

Paul, in his letters, when speaking of Jews and Greeks, invariably uses terminology similar to that in Romans 1:16 where he speaks of the gospel as "the power of God for salvation to everyone who has faith, to the Jew first and also to the Greek." The term "Jew" in Paul is always in a position of priority (i.e., the Jew first) when it is coupled with Greek (i.e., Gentile), as it is here, and in Romans 2:9, 10, 17, 10:12 and Galatians 3:28.

Of primary importance here is understanding that the kingdom of God, in all of its meanings and nuances signals the restoration of Israel:

> Then the moon will be abashed, and the sun ashamed;
> for Yahweh of hosts will reign on Mount Zion and in Jerusalem,
> and before his elders he will manifest his glory. (Isa 24:23)
> For Yahweh is our judge, Yahweh is our ruler,
> Yahweh is our king; he will save us. (Isa 33:22)
> How beautiful upon the mountains
> are the feet of the messenger who announces peace,
> who brings good news, who announces salvation,
> who says to Zion, Your God reigns.
> Listen! Your sentinels lift up their voices,
> together they sing for joy;
> for in plain sight they see the return of Yahweh to Zion.
> Break forth together into singing, you ruins of Jerusalem;
> for Yahweh has comforted his people,
> he has redeemed Jerusalem.
> Yahweh has bared his holy arm before the eyes of all the nations;
> and all the ends of the earth shall see the salvation of our God.
> (Isa 52:7–10)

> Sing aloud, O daughter of Zion; shout, O Israel!
> Rejoice and exult with all your heart, O daughter Jerusalem!
> Yahweh has taken away the judgments against you,
> he has turned away your enemies.
> The king of Israel, Yahweh, is in your midst;
> you shall fear disaster no more.
> On that day it shall be said to Jerusalem;
> Do not fear, O Zion; do not let your hands grow weak.
> Yahweh, your God, is in your midst, a warrior who gives victory;
> he will rejoice over you with gladness, he will renew you in his love;
> he will exult over you with loud singing as on a day of festival.

Part Two: Moving Beyond Christian Folk Religion

> I will remove disaster from you, so that you will not bear reproach for it.
> I will deal with all your oppressors at that time.
> And I will save the lame and gather the outcast,
> and I will change their shame into praise and renown in all the earth.
> At that time I will bring you home, at the time when I gather you;
> for I will make you renowned and praised among all the peoples of the earth,
> when I restore your fortunes before your eyes, says Yahweh.
> (Zeph 3:14–20)

This is the root Paul is talking about in Romans 11:18, when he says: "The root supports you" (i.e., "you" is the Gentile Christian). And "To the Jew first and also to the Greek" (Rom 1:16). When Jesus taught his disciples to pray:

> Hallowed be your name,
> your kingdom come,
> your will be done,
> on earth as it is in heaven

in Matthew 6:9 it was the public proclamation that the arrival of the kingdom of God would be the final saving act of God, that his reign did indeed signify the consummation of human history; but at the center of this consummation stood, as in Torah and prophets, the prime beneficiary of God's saving act: his people Israel. Contrary to western philosophy and Hellenized Christianity, salvation is not an individual act, but a corporate one. We who are not members of the people of Israel, join them in salvation, and follow their lead into salvation (Rom 9–11). If we are to understand Jesus and his public ministry, we must have a firm grasp on the meaning of the kingdom of God. It is the renewal of God's People, the Jew first and then the Gentile also. It is the renewal of the kingdom God which is being established, but to do so we must understand that it begins like a grain of mustard seed (Matt 13:31). How many millennia it will take to blossom into a great bush is known only to Yahweh God. But blossom it will. At some point in the eons, God will rush in and complete the renewal begun by Christ, but God is timeless and, as such, our time means nothing to him. Eternity is a timeless concept, sometimes expressed as an "eternal now," where there is no past and no future; where everything is present. When Jesus proclaimed the coming of the kingdom of God to Israel, it was to the nation as a whole. When Jesus performed his miracles of healing it

The Kingdom

was not simply an act of compassion for the afflicted, it was a renewal *out* of affliction, a sign of what the kingdom of God would be like. They were actually the first recipients of that kingdom (e.g., Jesus' famous, if puzzling, statement, "The first shall be last, and the last shall be first"). It is the underclasses, the forgotten, the often abused, ridiculed, the excluded, who are to receive the blessings of the kingdom, just as Jesus said in the Beatitudes: "Blessed are you when people hate you, and when they exclude you, revile you, and defame you . . . Rejoice and leap for joy, for surely your reward is great in heaven" (Luke 6:22–23). It was a sign for all of saved Israel and those who would join them in salvation. It was an invitation to every hearer to accept salvation in simplicity, like a child.

For Jesus, in one of his parables, the kingdom of God is like a great banquet (Matt 22:1–14; Luke 14:15–24; cf. Matt 26:29) where many are invited with the words, "Come; for everything is ready now." But then everyone invited began to make excuses. And Jesus says that the owner of the house became angry and said, "Go out at once into the streets and lanes of the town and bring in the poor, the crippled, the blind and the lame." And when that was done, the owner was told that there was still room for more, and the master then ordered the servant to go out into the roads and lanes, "and compel people to come in so that my house may be filled" (Luke 14:17, 21, 23). In this parable, it seems, the kingdom of God is not just for the invited guests, which most of us would assume to be the religious, the pious, or the "good" Christians, like *us*. In fact, these same "invited" guests are the ones who want to accept the invitation only on their own terms: "I have just bought a piece of land, and I must go out and see it" (v.18), and "I have bought five yoke of oxen, and I am going to try them out" (v. 19), and "I have just been married, and therefore I cannot come" (v. 20). This is a harsh message for all of us. Let's assume that most of us who read these words *are* the religious, the pious, and the "good" Christians (i.e., perhaps the bulk of church members), and let's assume we read this parable with a blind eye, only seeing the characters in the parable but not realizing that we, ourselves, are those characters, who want the kingdom, but on our own terms. If we don't see ourselves in the story, we have missed its primary point. The parable *is* about us if we believe we are members of the kingdom of God: Church denominations block other church denominations from participating in sacraments, in sharing pulpits, in common fellowship, in the joy of faith and certainly in the love of the Messiah. Most often it is because a particular denomination does not agree with the way

Part Two: Moving Beyond Christian Folk Religion

we believe down to the last dotted "I" or crossed "t" Jesus chastised us good for that (Matt 23:13): "Woe to you _____ (fill in the blank with your own name or denomination). For you lock people out of the kingdom of heaven." Yes, I know that Jesus addressed this woe to the scribes and Pharisees, hypocrites! But who were the scribes and Pharisees? They were the religious (the most religious), the pious (the most pious), the truly good of society. The scribes were the men who preserved the Word of God for us by meticulously copying letter by letter every word we read *in* the Word of God. They knew every syllable of the scriptures. They were the experts on its wording and on its meaning. No one knew it better than the scribes. The Pharisees were laymen, not priests, but they were the great teachers of Israel.

It was the Pharisees who Jesus, as a twelve year old boy, listened to so intensely so that he lost all sense of time, and wanted to stay in their presence and learn from them, all the while his frantic parents were trying to locate him. Yes, both the scribes and the Pharisees were extremely pious. They prayed constantly just as Paul, a proud Pharisee himself his whole life long (Acts 23:6; Phil 3:5–6), told us to do (1Thess 5:17; 2:13). There was no group in all of Israel more religious than the scribes and Pharisees and they showed it! Yet Jesus included them in the category called "hypocrites" (*hupokrites*, actors who take a part other than their own) because their religion was more style than substance. Their piety is not necessarily because they love God more, but rather because it makes them *feel* like they love God more. Notice that in this list of woes in Matthew 23 there is no mention of priests. Temple priests ran the daily affairs of the temple and conducted sacrifices, and lesser priests, such as the Levites cleaned up the temple from the carnage left by the sacrifices. Most of the chief priests, who really controlled all of the functions of the temple, were political appointees to the job, and their faith and loyalty to Yahweh, and Israel, were highly questioned and disputed among the most religious, pious, and the "good" in the first century. And notice, the word hypocrites does not necessarily assume that Jesus meant that the scribes and Pharisees were the hypocrites of the day. It could just as correctly mean, "scribes, Pharisees" *and* hypocrites, which could include us. Every word Jesus said, every statement he uttered, every woe he pronounced in Matthew 23, and every judgment he made was personally aimed at those who heard him or read his words. We are the scribes, Pharisees, and hypocrites! We are the religious, the pious, and the good people of faith.

The Kingdom

For most of my life I have considered the German pastor, Dietrich Bonhoeffer, the epitome of what Jesus would consider a child of God to be. He became one of the most important theologians of the last century, a scholar of first rank, a pastor to pastors, and above all, a man who exemplified what it means to follow Christ, even if that leads to one's own death, which is exactly what happened to him on April 9, 1945. There is an irony to his life, however, as he was growing up his entire family were essentially non-practicing Lutherans in that they rarely, if ever, went to church. The family was deeply spiritual, however, singing hymns at home, accompanied by Dietrich's mother on the piano. Despite the non-piety of the family, at the young age of fifteen Dietrich announced to his family that he had decided he wanted to study theology. His decision created quite a controversy in his family, especially with his older brother, Klaus, who had chosen a career in law.

Klaus was astounded that Dietrich wanted to study theology instead of law and stressed his opinion that the church is a "poor, feeble, boring, petty bourgeois institution." To which fifteen-year-old Dietrich responded, "In that case, I shall have to reform it."[2] Dietrich eventually became one of the church's most important writers and theologians who wrote extensively on what it meant to follow Christ. In 1937, eight years before he would be martyred by the Nazis, in his groundbreaking book, *The Cost of Discipleship*, he famously said, "When Christ calls a man he bids him come and die." And in a book of letters he sent from his prison cell to his friend and former seminary student, Eberhard Bethge, *Letters and Papers From Prison*, he one time mused, "By the way it is remarkable how little I miss going to church, I wonder why." I believe he was looking for a Christianity which transcends piety, and all the trappings of Christian demonstration, and, in fact, is replaced with deep and true spirituality. On December 11, 1928, Bonhoeffer gave a lecture at a German school in Barcelona where he

> began provocatively; putting forth the notion that Christ has been exiled from the lives of most Christians. "Of course," he said, "we build him a temple, but we live in our own houses." Religion had been exiled to Sunday morning, to a place "into which one gladly withdraws for a couple of hours, but only to get back to one's place of work immediately afterward." He said that one cannot give him only a "small compartment in our spiritual life," but must give him everything or nothing. "The religion of

2. Metaxas, *Bonhoeffer*, 38.

Christ," he said, "is not a tidbit after one's bread; on the contrary, it is the bread or it is nothing. People should at least understand and concede this if they call themselves Christian."[3]

Thus, as Jesus told us in his parable of the master who gave a great dinner where the invited guests all made excuses, it is often the most religious who walk away from the invitation to the banquet, and yet the banquet will be filled with the underclasses of society, and those who have been excluded from the great feast.

The kingdom of God, while the hope of the world, and signaling the dawn of a new age, carries with it great demands of the faithful who must "deny themselves, take up their cross and follow me" (Matt 16:24). It is also a kingdom where the norms are not human norms of "good" or "bad", or "proper" or "improper", or "class" distinction, or "success" or "failure." The norms of the kingdom are norms of the divine: "infinite", rather than "finite", of "grace", rather than "worth", of "forgiveness", rather than "retribution", of "love unmerited", rather than "love returned" Is that "just"? For those who believe their faith *deserves* entrance into the kingdom, the answer may seem unjust, for why should the "rabble" of the world have access to the blessings of the kingdom, when the "good" of society may be excluded? It's not because *they're* good, but because God is good. That's what grace and mercy are all about. When Bonhoeffer wrote *The Cost of Discipleship* he began talking about cheap grace which he defined as a type of grace passed out by churches like trinkets passed out on the street corner. Grace is never cheap, as Bonhoeffer's life amply proves. It demands our unfailing loyalty toward God, love of the loveless, devotion to a deep spirituality which transcends piety and outward show of "how religious I am." In the pages that follow we will see how upside down the logic of God can be, and how Jesus, the Messiah of God and our optimal model of spirituality, shunned piety and turned his greatest criticism toward the model of the most religious of his land. Finally, we will begin to understand why the world wanted his death most of all, and when he appeared his weakest, he was actually displaying the most powerful message God could give, as he ushered in the reality of the kingdom of God.

3. Ibid., 82.

7

A New Reality, New Rules

THINGS ARE DIFFERENT WITHIN the kingdom of God–things often not realized by the modern reader. The difference is this: when God is king, the rules have changed. God's ways are simply not understood by the human mind. Remember what we said in the first chapter of this book? Albert Einstein defined God as "the illimitable superior spirit who reveals himself in the slight details we are able to perceive with our frail and feeble minds." This "illimitable superior spirit" constantly has to deal with our "frail and feeble minds." It is just as Isaiah reported when he quoted Yahweh as saying, "my thoughts are not your thoughts, nor are your ways my ways" (Isa 55:8). What we think of as common sense, or logical, is often just the other way around in the wisdom of God. It might even be possible to conceive of God's ways as upside-down logic in the human mind. When John the Baptizer cried out, "Prepare the way of Yahweh!" he was signaling a new age that was about to dawn. That new age was beginning with the appearance of Jesus in Israel. Nothing would ever be the same again. When Jesus returned from the wilderness and began his teaching, it was a different kind of message from any heard before, and when he began his healing miracles, something new was being experienced. There were exorcisms and demons being forced out of people. These were indications that indeed a new age was dawning. It was not an age to come in the future, it was right there happening in front of them. It was the triumph of Yahweh over evil. "No one can enter a strong man's house," Jesus said, "and plunder his property without first tying up the strong man; then indeed the house can be plundered" (Mark 3:27). When Jesus exorcized a demon out of a person he was plundering Satan's house. It was the sign that already the evil one had been bound up. He was already losing the battle. A new age was indeed dawning and the rules were changing. Someone had taken control of the world in a way never seen before. It seemed that Israel had suddenly been introduced to what appeared as a topsy-turvy world.

THE TOPSY-TURVY WORLD

One time Jesus was approached by a man who asked a favor of him. He asked Jesus to intercede and request that his brother be instructed to divide the family inheritance with him. But Jesus answered the man by saying, "Friend, who set me to be a judge or arbitrator over you?" And Jesus turned to those around him and said, "Take care! Be on your guard against all kinds of greed; for one's life does not consist in the abundance of possessions" (Luke 12:13–15). This is another indication that a new value system was in play in the new kind of kingdom Jesus was introducing. The rules which seem logical in our world were changing in God's reign. The man who approached him obviously believed that he was being treated unjustly because he was being locked out of sharing the family inheritance. It was a reasonable request; an intercession even a parishioner might ask a pastor to do. You would think Jesus could have inquired about it. But he didn't. Instead, Jesus assumed that the request was inspired out of the man's greed. So he told a well-known parable:

> The land of a rich man produced abundantly. And he thought to himself, "What should I do, for I have no place to store my crops?" Then he said, "I will do this: I will pull down my barns and build larger ones, and there I will store all my grain and my goods. And I will say to my soul, 'Soul, you have ample goods laid up for many years; relax, eat, drink, be, merry.'" But God said to him, "You fool! This very night your life is being demanded of you. And the things you have prepared, whose will they be?" So it is with those who store up treasures for themselves, but are not rich toward God. (Luke: 12: 16–21)

This seems to be reverse logic. What is wrong with preparing for the future? Why must we always do without? This man was the epitome of an early capitalist: become a success, expand your business, and increase your wealth. Remember the phrase in Jesus' prayer, "Give us this day our daily bread?" Why must life always be like that? Most of you reading this, I presume, are constantly planning for the future. You are saving for your retirement; or you have a rainy day account with a little money for unexpected expenses. You probably know you will have enough to buy food for tomorrow, or you probably already had enough food in your pantry for tomorrow's meals.

It is good not to have to worry about a possible crisis tomorrow. Why be constantly consumed by thoughts and fears "Where am I going to get the money to buy my food for tomorrow?" Yet Jesus becomes even more explicit with instructions we don't quite understand or want to hear:

> Therefore I tell you, do not worry about your life, what you will eat, or about your body, what you will wear. For life is more than food, and the body more than clothing. Consider the ravens: they neither sow nor reap, they have neither storehouse nor barn, and yet God feeds them. Of how much more value are you than the birds! And can any of you by worrying add a single hour to your span of life? If then you are not able to do so small a thing as that, why do you worry about the rest? Consider the lilies, how they grow: they neither toil nor spin; yet I tell you, even Solomon in all his glory was not clothed like one of these. But if God so clothes the grass of the field, which is alive today and tomorrow is thrown into the oven, how much more will he clothe you—you of little faith! (Luke 12:22–28)

And there you have it! The word faith drives everything in the kingdom. It's not so much about what you have, or don't have. It's about new values in the kingdom. In the world's kingdom, to which we belong, values play a major role. Success is often measured by what we own: the house we live in, the car we drive, the clothes we wear. At a gathering of ministers the small talk between casual acquaintances often turns to questions on how many members their churches have (i.e., how successful a pastor or priest or rabbi has been in building up a particular congregation). It is never, at least that I've heard, about what the congregation is doing for the underprivileged, the poor, the sick. Most people want to at least appear successful to those around them. In the 1990s there was a hilarious British comedy series called *Keeping up Appearances*. It's about a lady named Hyacinth, who was brought up on the wrong side of the "tracks," the side where the rest of her family still reside, but she married

Part Two: Moving Beyond Christian Folk Religion

a well-established middle-class gentleman who had middle-class values (whatever that might be). In the meantime, the other side of the family, was, and is, slovenly, living in a broken down house, and the middle-class lady's brother slouches around, in front of the "telly" bellowing constantly at his wife to bring him another beer, while another sister, of questionable reputation, lives upstairs. Hyacinth, the middle-class lady, is busy trying to make herself seem refined, even though it's not in her genes. Every time the telephone rings she drops whatever she's doing and rushes to the phone because, "It might be somebody impawtant!" It isn't. It's usually one of her relatives from the "other side of the tracks" relating this crisis or that crisis happening now. This, from the side of the family she hopes the world will never know is from her family, and her past. The antics of Hyacinth trying to hide her past make for great comedy. Like every good comedy, though, it plays on at least a modicum of truth. The modicum here is our desire to be "proper." It's not so much about wealth versus poverty, although there's a suggestion of that, but rather about being "proper" versus "improper," a theme that appears often in British literature where values in the past were always centered on a person's station in life. "Masterpiece Classics," the BBC's highly successful television series, usually broadcast on the PBS stations in America, has had numerous stories about this class distinction. Examples are: "Upstairs, Downstairs," and the immensely popular "Downton Abbey," which has drawn an audience of more than 70 million viewers in the United States alone. Both of these series address the class differentiation between the upper class family managing an inherited family estate, always residing in the "Upstairs," and the servant class running the daily operation of the estate from "Downstairs." Co-mingling between the two classes is unheard of, and if or when it happens, especially if it involves romance, it causes a major scandal. Even the British government's parliament is divided into The House of Lords, and the House of Commons.

In America such class distinctions might not be quite as "in your face" as the British, but "the haves" are distinctly separated from "the have nots." Since our inception as a nation we have been known for our tolerance of human possession (slaves), and our racism. Today we are divided into "blue collar" workers, and "white collar" workers. In our society, there is the 1% truly rich, then a declining middle-class, and finally, the underclasses, the "have nots," who, besides being poor, also have no power and are often looked upon with scorn by "the haves." Yet we pride ourselves on being a "Christian nation," with "Christian values." Are we? Read on.

JESUS AND HIS "SCANDALOUS" BEHAVIOR

When Jesus began teaching, preaching, and performing miracles, it became clear that all of that was changing. He seemed to welcome the scandal which was often leveled against him, why does he eat with tax collectors and sinners? (Mark 3:16; Luke 15:1; cf. Luke 19:7). Jesus never shied away from controversy, and he was not immune from breaking the decorum of proper people. His dining habits certainly fell into this category. He actually ate with the irreligious, or at least those who were the "common people" ("people of the land"–'*amme ha-arets*, Heb.).[1] who did not observe the high piety laws of the Pharisees. The Pharisees observed the laws required of the priests, which were more stringent than those required of common people. The people of the land or "the common people" were considered of lesser social standing than the religious elite. Most of them were peasant farmers who tilled the land for wealthy land owners. In all likelihood they were unschooled, illiterate, uncouth, and perhaps wretchedly dirty, and could not, or would not, differentiate between the 613 Mosaic laws governing the religious elite, many of which only applied to the priests. Thus "sinners" became a pejorative term for people who are not of the caliber acceptable to the highly religious. The commoners ('*amme ha-arets*) were only considered "sinners" in the eyes of the Pharisees. They were "sinners" because of their lower level of observation of the laws. Of course, Jesus' disciples were commoners and one, Matthew/Levi, was also a tax collector. Therefore Jesus regularly "ate with tax collectors and sinners." Dining fellowship held a special place within the first century culture. It was a time of fellowship between friends and associates who were close to each other (see Ps 41:9). If invited guests refused an invitation it was considered a major snub of hospitality, and highly offensive to the host (Matt 22:1–14 and Luke 14:16–24). Your social ties signaled to those around you the kind of company you kept. Table fellowship sometimes also had religious significance. The burnt offering of sacrifice was eaten with others to celebrate festal occasions (Exod 18:12; 24:11; 1 Kgs 3:15). Who you ate with could also determine whether or not you were maintaining ritual purity, if the person(s) at table were, or were not, ritually pure. Gentiles, for instance, were not (Deut 14:21). The same was true of the religious or the irreligious in Judaism. The irreligious could be false prophets (Matt 7:15; Mark 6:26), persons possessed by demons (Matt 8:16; Mark 1:32; Luke 8:33), and the unclean.

---

1. Sanders, *Jesus and Judaism*, 176, 385 n. 14.

Part Two: Moving Beyond Christian Folk Religion

For the religious elite, this could exclude nearly everyone who was not of their class. Scribes and Pharisees ate with scribes and Pharisees; the elite with the elite. It was the right and proper thing to do, or risk scandal.

Proper table fellowship was also determined by moral character. Tax collectors were not ritually unclean but were excluded because they were considered immoral people. They collected taxes for an occupying and oppressive government and were also suspected of corruption, bribery, and/or extorting money from the citizens, rich and poor, to line their own pockets. Also in the immoral class were prostitutes, but the woman in Luke 7:36–50, though it is assumed she was a prostitute, is never called that, only that she is "a woman in the city." Her actions indicate her deep remorse for some great sin, and that has usually led to the assumption that she was a prostitute, but that is only speculation. Therefore, when Jesus was accused of "eating with tax collectors and sinners" their charge was that he didn't care who it was he dined with, or with whom he kept company. In addition to scurrilous charges about Matthew, the tax collector, another of Jesus' disciples was a man named "Simon," who, as he is listed in Matthew (10:4) and Mark (3:18), is called a Zealot (Canaanite—KJV), a revolutionary ("terrorist"). Thus there were members of the twelve disciples who were of dubious character and easily fell into the category of "tax collectors and sinners." And in addition to the twelve, Jesus had numerous other followers in his cadre, including quite a few women, especially Mary Magdalene, from whom Jesus had cast out seven demons, (Mark 16:9), and altogether many of them would also be considered persons of dubious character. The passage in Luke 5:29–31 is the story about dinner at Matthew/Levi's home, with many other tax collectors and others reclining[2] and eating together. It was a classic case of Jesus shunning the rules of proper decorum.

In Matthew 22:1–14, Jesus told a parable about a king who gave a banquet for a wedding feast and killed his oxen and his fat calves for the great celebration, yet the invited guests refused the invitation and made light of it, ridiculed the whole affair, and some even turned violent against the king's slaves and servants. The remaining servants were then instructed to go out in the streets and gather all whom they found good and bad; so the wedding hall was filled with guests. This is the same theme Jesus told elsewhere (Luke 14:17, 21, 23). However, in the parable in Matthew, when the banquet was filled with people from the streets

---

2. In the first century it was common to recline when eating, with the food either on a low table or on the floor.

A New Reality, New Rules

both good and bad it was noticed that one man did not have on a wedding robe, and the man was chastised by the king and thrown out of the banquet. It is a curious end to the story. It seems to make no sense. The doors had been flung open to everyone on the street, yet one man was not properly dressed? But the issue was not one of being properly attired, it was not being ready for the wedding and the great banquet. There was no excuse for that in Jesus' parable. The invitation was, "You're invited," but the expectation was "be ready for the feast!" The rules during the reign of God are different, and often seem out of place.

GOD'S VALUES, NOT OUR VALUES

Yes, when God reigns, the rules change. God's values are not our values. Sometimes he intrudes into our lives in ways we neither expect, nor want, yet he expects and demands our absolute faith in him, we must be ready for him. Throughout the story of Israel we see that demand for faith constantly in play. The basic message of the story of Israel is the faithfulness of Yahweh, and the persistent unfaithfulness of Israel. When Yahweh first called the Mesopotamian desert sheik Abram, later named Abraham, he and his family were living in southeastern Asia Minor (present day Turkey), in the village of Haran. Haran was a Sumerian city and the center for a pantheon of pagan gods, the chief god of which was the moon god *Sin*. There was even a temple to the moon god there. Abram was surrounded by all these gods in Haran vying for allegiance. While *Sin* was the god of the moon, there were 90 other gods and goddesses throughout Mesopotamia, each having their own cult, and the people tried to please as many of these deities as they could so their homes would be protected against any and all evils, and they wanted to be assured of a good harvest of crops that year, etc. Sumer was the first area of Mesopotamia to be civilized. It had its own extensive list of 33 gods and goddesses among the whole Mesopotamian pantheon. Besides *Sin*, the moon god, there was *An*, the god of heaven, *Antu* and *Ishtar*, the gods of creation, *Anu*, the god of the sky, *Apsu*, god of sweet waters, etc. Each deity assured prosperity in a different part of life. Without naming each one, in addition to those above, there were also deities of grain, of dawn, god of sun and crop fertility, a goddess of the kings of Sumer, a goddess of the womb, god of vegetation, mountain god, goddess of the dead, god of war, god of light and fire, goddess of healing, goddess of love and fertility and war, god of

Part Two: Moving Beyond Christian Folk Religion

storms and rain, etc. These were the deities surrounding Abram, and yet it was one God, unknown and unnamed before, who spoke to him. This unknown God eventually identified himself simply as "Yahweh." Later on he became known as the God of all creation and in the centuries following consistently identified himself as the "God of Abraham, Isaac and Jacob" (Exod 3:6,15 –16; 4:5; 6:3; Deut 9:27; 1 Kgs 18:36; 1 Chr 29:18, etc.). It was this previously unknown God who spoke to Abram:

> Now Yahweh said to Abram, "Go from your country and your kindred and your father's house to the land that I will show you. I will make of you a great nation, and I will bless you, and make your name great, so that you will be a blessing. I will bless those who bless you and the one who curses you I will curse; and in you all the families of the earth shall be blessed." So Abram went as Yahweh had told him. (Gen 12:1–4)

Notice what Yahweh was asking of Abram/Abraham. He was asking him to abandon his culture, his faith, his whole family environment, the region and town he lived in, and where his ancestors lay buried, and was told to travel to some far off land he had never even heard of before. In return Yahweh said he would make of him a great nation, whatever that might mean (no specifics are given), and that he would be a blessing. All this was promised, with no more assurances than that. There were no assurances of fertility for either his family or his livestock, of good crops, personal wealth, good weather, safety from floods, or famine, or any of the hazards of life. This vague promise was made by an unknown God he had never heard of before, who told him to travel to a strange land. Yet he obeyed the call. Then there is the amazing story in Genesis 22 where Yahweh commands Abraham to sacrifice his son Isaac as a burnt offering unto him. Isaac was Abraham and Sarah's first-born son when Abraham was already 100 years old (Gen 21:1–7). Yet it was this son, born in their old age, that Yahweh commanded to be sacrificed: "Take your son, your only son Isaac, whom you love, and go to the land of Moriah, and offer him there as a burnt offering on one of the mountains that I shall show you" (22:2). And Abraham did exactly as Yahweh commanded. Cutting wood for the sacrifice, and saddling a donkey, Abraham took Isaac, along with two other young men, and set off for Moriah. After worshiping with Isaac, Abraham laid wood on Isaac's back, carried a knife for the slaughter of his son, and they walked together toward the place of sacrifice. Along the way Isaac asked his father, "The fire and the wood are here, but where

A New Reality, New Rules

is the lamb for the burnt offering?" To which Abraham responded, "God himself will provide the lamb for a burnt offering, my son" (vv. 7–8). Isaac made no response to this explanation. Abraham then built an altar, laid his son on it, bound him, and raised his knife to kill him, but an "angel of Yahweh" stopped him and "Abraham looked up and saw a ram, caught in a thicket by its horns. Abraham went and took the ram and offered it up as a burnt offering instead of his son" (vv. 11–13). This is one of the most symbolic stories in the Hebrew Bible. Jews call it *Aqedah Isaac*, the "binding" of Isaac. In Christian theology it has always been considered a parallel story to the crucifixion of Christ, with the significant difference that the Messiah Jesus *was* the sacrifice himself and no substitutionary sacrificial animal was provided. One Jewish scholar, Richard Friedman,[3] when relating this story, said in a lecture that he theorizes that when Abraham tells Isaac "God himself will provide the lamb for a burnt offering" and Isaac does not respond, Isaac *knew* he would be "the lamb" and consents to his own sacrifice! I believe he may be right.

Is it any wonder Abraham's faithfulness was compared to the faithfulness of Jesus in the writings of the Apostle Paul, the book of Hebrews, and in the letter of James? In Romans Paul says of this patriarch of the nation of Israel, "Abraham believed God, and it was reckoned to him as righteousness" (4:3), and Abraham's faith is again mentioned in 4:12, 16, in Galatians 3:6, 9, Hebrews 11:8 and in James 2:23, where Abraham is also called "the friend of God."

God's New Rules

The first absolute rule in God's reign is faith in him (i.e., the wedding robe in the parable in Matt 22:11). This is the confidence that he will protect you and shield you. On our trip to Israel in 2011 I met a Jewish woman who was a survivor of the holocaust. She told me about a series of amazing events where one person after the other was there to help her and shield her from the ever-present Nazis, and it kept her from being exterminated with the rest of her family. After relaying this series of miraculous rescues, I remarked to her, "You were surrounded by angels!" She responded immediately by saying, "Yes. You're absolutely right!" I believe, without reservation that there are times, for various reasons,

---

3. "The Death of the Gods—or Why a Monotheistic God Speaks in the Plural," in a lecture given at *Bible and Archaeology Fest XIII*, sponsored by *BAR*, 2010.

Part Two: Moving Beyond Christian Folk Religion

when God shields us. I believe that this lady was preserved because she had to tell her story to the rest of the world. God did this, not because she was necessarily good (though I have no doubt that she is), but because God is good. There were many people who survived the holocaust for that reason. It is impossible to know why certain people are singled out for direct action like that on God's part. We can only attribute it to God's unfailing knowledge and goodness.

Even the underclasses of society experience that goodness for reasons we cannot imagine. In the world we know and understand, the world in which we live, the underclasses are exactly that, they are underclasses. They are the poor, the mentally and physically disabled, the diseased, and anyone usually referred to as the underprivileged. Unfortunately, they are also often the butt of our scorn, and even of our unfeeling humor. Of the poor: "get a job," or if we are unusually caring and empathetic we might say, "give them a hand-up, not a hand-out." Of the handicapped, if we have any empathy at all, we probably think, "Oh, that poor creature." Or, if we're brutal in our nature, we probably think to ourselves, "You, poor devil, you can't do anything!" Of course, such reactions are no longer considered politically correct. Note: that expression is qualified by the term "politically," which implies that we will be judged by how we express ourselves to or about the underclasses, not out of any particular love for those who are the underprivileged. That's a far cry from Jesus' admonition that we should love (*agapeo*) our neighbor as we love ourselves. Remember, *agapeo* means unconditional love: love without any reason whatsoever, simply that the person is one of God's created children, whom he declared good (Gen 1:28, 31). It is the same standard God applies even to our enemies. "Love (*agapeo*) your enemies, and pray for those ("bless them"—KJV) who persecute you." Enemies are not just people we don't like, but people we despise for any number of reasons: enemies who threaten our national way of life, or who have personally and maliciously hurt or wounded us physically or emotionally, or persons we believe are enemies of our faith. The list is endless, and the reasons we despise them may seem endless and justified, but in the logic that is not our own, but rather the logic of the creator God, Yahweh, and his beloved Son, there is no out, nothing that is justified except love (*agapeo*). Again, in God's kingdom, the rules have changed from our logic to his. In Psalm 14 (cf. Ps 53 which is almost identical):

A New Reality, New Rules

> The fools say in their hearts, "There is no God."
> They are corrupt, they do abominable deeds;
> there is no one who does good.
> Yahweh looks down from heaven on humankind
> to see if there are any who are wise, who seek after God.
> They have all gone astray, they are all alike perverse;
> there is no one who does good, no, not one.
> Have they no knowledge, all the evildoers
> who eat up my people as they bread,
> and do not call upon Yahweh?
> There they shall be in great terror,
> for God is with the company of the righteous.
> You would confound the plans of the poor,
> but Yahweh is their refuge.
> O that deliverance for Israel would come from Zion!
> When Yahweh restores the fortunes of his people,
> Jacob will rejoice; Israel will be glad.

It is a strange language we hear from the psalmist. It is the fool (v. 1) who denies the existence of God, yet it is Yahweh who gives refuge to the poor and is in the company of the righteous. It is the fool who has no knowledge (4) and who does no good (3). The fool is obviously not among the wise, who seek after God. Apparently the fool's so called "wisdom" is folly, for the wise are with God who is in the company of the righteous, as are the poor who are mentioned in their own category. The poor do not necessarily have any great knowledge, or great wisdom. They are not necessarily the righteous, nor are they even the good, for "no one . . . does good, no, not one" (3). Yet Yahweh is their refuge (6). It is a strange mix, devoid of what most of us would consider common sense. God is in the company of the wise who seek after God, and those who call upon Yahweh, and the righteous, and the poor. The poor always and forever have the strange protection of God wherever he reigns. What is their qualification, other than that they are poor?

There seems to be no qualification at all. The underclasses of society, whether poor, or diseased, or lame, or mentally retarded, or even possessed of demons, are all under the divine protection of a loving God. The only reason given for this unique status throughout scripture is that they are the underclasses of society. In the world in which we live the best they can hope for and expect is that they will survive. Though the rich are told over and over again it is their responsibility to care for the poor, the care is minimal, while the rich get richer. Thus it is Yahweh, no mortal and

Part Two: Moving Beyond Christian Folk Religion

no special requirements, who invites them in. The doors to the kingdom have been flung open to the underclasses on the roads and lanes whether good or bad (cf. Matt 22:10; Luke 14:23). But then there is the closing (7):

> O that deliverance for Israel would come from Zion!
> When Yahweh restores the fortunes of his people,
> Jacob will rejoice; Israel will be glad.

Now we get a glimpse of why the rules are so different, the psalmist is looking ahead to when God will truly reign, when deliverance for Israel will come from Zion. Zion is where the temple is located, and God's glory always resides in the temple, and deliverance for Israel must come from Zion! It is when Yahweh restores the fortunes of his people that Jacob will rejoice and Israel will be glad. It is the kingdom of God.

The rules have been changed, and human logic has been turned on its head. The doors to the great banquet, a common metaphor for the kingdom, are thrown open and filled with invited guests we would never expect. Psalm 68:10: "In your goodness O God, you provided for the needy." Psalm 69:30, 33: "I will praise the name of God with a song; I will magnify him with thanksgiving . . . For Yahweh hears the needy, and does not despise his own that are in bonds." Psalm 107:1, 39–43:

> O give thanks to Yahweh, for he is good; for his steadfast love
> endures forever.
> Let the redeemed of Yahweh say so, those he redeemed from
> trouble
> and gathered in from the lands,
> from the east and from the west,
> from the north and from the south . . .
> When they are diminished and brought low
> through oppression, trouble or sorrow,
> he pours contempt on princes
> and makes them wander in trackless wastes;
> but he raises up the needy out of distress,
> and makes their families like flocks.
> The upright see it and are glad;
> and all wickedness stops its mouth.
> Let those who are wise give heed to these things,
> and consider the steadfast love of Yahweh.

Notice here that when Yahweh raises up the needy out of distress the upright see it and are glad while "all wickedness stops its mouth." It is the wicked who are shocked. Here is the same logic Jesus used in the parable of the rich man and the beggar Lazarus (Luke 16:19–31) who reclines in Abraham's arms, while the rich man is in torment. The rich man begs father Abraham for mercy and pleads for him to send Lazarus to him with a moistened finger, just to release him somewhat from his torment. But Abraham's response is, "Child, remember that during your lifetime you received your good things, and Lazarus in like manner evil things; but now he is comforted" (24). The story seems unjust as Lazarus, who received evil things during his lifetime, only experienced the evil temporarily, while the rich man would be in torment eternally (27–31). Even the miraculous would not necessarily save the rich man's brothers, for "if they haven't listened to Moses and the prophets, neither will they be convinced even if someone rises from the dead." The onus is on our own backs. Everything that is said is all that needs to be said. There is no more proof that you need than that! Abraham had responded to God's call to follow him, *with no proof*, but follow he did. That is "faithfulness." It is a tough lesson, and it defies our logic, but there we have it: logic that seems topsy-turvy to us. It is important that we pay attention to the last statement in the parable where Jesus says that if they don't listen to the scriptures, people won't believe even if someone rises from the dead. This statement is particularly telling because it sheds light on the reason Jesus performed exorcisms, healings, and raising the dead. It was not to prove he was the Messiah, or that he had great compassion (although he certainly did), but rather because the renewal of all flesh was begun as the kingdom of God was being established. When the Baptizer sent word to Jesus from prison asking if he was the one who is to come, or are we to wait for another, Jesus' response to John is this: "The blind receive their sight, the lame walk, the lepers are cleansed, the deaf hear, the dead are raised, and the poor have good news brought to them (Matt 11:5).

These are the signs of the renewal of all flesh. The new Eden is dawning, everything will one day be new again, and Jesus is saying, in effect, I am starting with those least able to take care of themselves. This is just one of the major riddles Jesus taught: "Many who are first will be last, and the last will be first" (Matt 19:30; 20:8; 20:16; Luke 13:30). It is the upside down logic of the kingdom.

And this is just the beginning of the story of how God views and deals with the underclasses of society, often at the expense of the proper, the religious, the power brokers of society. This disparity occurs in so many passages besides the Psalms it would be redundant to list them

Part Two: Moving Beyond Christian Folk Religion

all. But there is one more that simply has to be seen which sums up all the rest, it is Psalm 82:

> God has taken his place in the divine council;
> in the midst of the gods he holds judgment:
> How long will you judge unjustly
> and show partiality to the wicked?
> Give justice to the weak and the orphan;
> maintain the right of the lowly and the destitute.
> Rescue the weak and the needy;
> deliver them from the hand of the wicked.
> They have neither knowledge nor understanding,
> they walk around in darkness;
> all the foundations of the earth are shaken.
> I say, "You are gods, children of the Most High; all of you;
> nevertheless, you shall die like mortals,
> and fall like any prince."
> Rise up, O God, judge the earth;
> for all the nations belong to you!

Here is Yahweh God who rules the earth because, "all the nations belong to you." He is the king who from his throne in the divine council holds judgment. He calls us gods because we, who are children of the Most High, hold the power of our world in our hands. And he warns us that we are nothing but people who shall die like mortals, and fall like any prince. We are they who have "neither knowledge nor understanding" and who "walk around in darkness." We are the wicked from which the weak and the needy must be delivered. It is a scathing indictment of the human condition. It has nothing to do with how religious we are, whether we are among the most pious of the world, or whether our speech is constantly peppered with God talk: "The Lord bless you," "if it is the father's will," or "God willing," or "the Lord be praised!" It has to do with one thing, and one thing only, *agapeo*, "love" which is simply that: love, with no conditions or modifiers. There is a story which tells of the time Jesus, was visiting a man by the name of Simon, who is a leper in Matthew's (26:6–13) and Mark's version (14:3–9), but a Pharisee in Luke's (7:36–50). Though it seems like a contradiction that is not necessarily so. He may be a Pharisee who has a skin disease (all skin diseases in Jesus' day were called "leprosy"). It makes no difference anyway because the point is basically the same. I am going to take a little license and co-mingle the three accounts, although the bulk of my

A New Reality, New Rules

example will come from Luke because the attitude of the home owner makes more sense if indeed he *was* a Pharisee or Pharisee/leper. In any event Jesus is in the owner's house upon the man's invitation to dine with him, when a woman of the street brought an expensive jar of ointment with her. She began to weep because of a profound sense of guilt and bathe his feet with her tears and to dry them with her hair. Then she began to anoint his feet with the expensive ointment. Then Simon, began thinking to himself of how crude it was that Jesus would allow a woman of such disrepute to touch him and make such a fuss over him. A Pharisee knew the law better than most, and knew that the woman was considered ritually unclean in God's eyes, and a prostitute besides, and must never come in contact with a righteous man. And in Mark's version others at table began to whisper among themselves, "Why was the ointment wasted in this way? For this ointment could have been sold for more than three hundred denarii, and the money given to the poor." And the other guests began to scold the woman.

> But Jesus said, "Let her alone; why do you trouble her? She has performed a good service for me. For you always have the poor with you, and you can show kindness to them whenever you wish; but you will not always have me. She has done what she could; she has anointed my body beforehand for its burial. Truly I tell you, wherever the good news is proclaimed in the whole world, what she has done will be told in remembrance of her." (Mark 14:6–9)

How many times have you heard Christians (very good Christians) quote this saying of Jesus, "You always have the poor with you"? Unfortunately, what she has done has not been remembered by the bulk of the world. What Jesus said in response to what she did is what has been most remembered. I have heard the quote of Jesus that "you always have the poor with you" as the justification by good Christian people for not taking responsibility to care for the needy or others in the underclass. This is one verse extracted from a whole Bible of verses which lay the responsibility for the care of the underprivileged directly on the shoulders of the People of God. And that is exactly the point of the story. Read Jesus' whole sentence: "For you always have the poor with you, *and you can show kindness to them whenever you wish.*" We are held accountable for the status of the poor. Their plight is *our* fault. There are no excuses, as the sampling above shows. The situation with the woman of the street is a unique situation which involved great remorse for sins committed,

Part Two: Moving Beyond Christian Folk Religion

a plea for mercy (her anointing his feet), and Jesus' interpretation that it was also a prophetic act anticipating his own crucifixion and death.

It was a once in a lifetime experience. No one else did this for him, or would be able to do this for him while he was alive. This woman of the street, now forgiven and redeemed had indeed performed a great, and unique, service for him. It was the "woman of the street" who showed her great love (*agapeo*) while the "righteous" Simon and other guests poured scorn on Jesus for allowing her to do so with her "expensive perfume." It has nothing whatever to do with being a modifier of our responsibility for the underprivileged, which is one of the main themes of the entire Bible, and especially in the preaching and teaching of Jesus, the Messiah of Yahweh, God of Abraham, Isaac, and Jacob. In addition it is once again a fact that Jesus welcomed into his presence "sinners." He eats with "tax collectors and sinners." The rumor was true. Sin does not necessarily mean wickedness.

When Jesus was judged for eating "with tax collectors and sinners" it was a judgment made by the religiously pious, who believed they had proven they were above all that. But Jesus' warning to them is "the first will be last, and the last will be first" (Matt 19:30; 20:8; 20:16; Luke 13:30). "Blessed are the poor" (Luke 6:20), and translate that to "Happy are the poor." "The first will be last, and the last will be first"; upside down logic, but as a Christian friend pointed out recently, if it's God's logic it is right side up logic, it is a point well-made.

JESUS MOVES ON

Almost immediately after Jesus' baptism by John the Baptizer, and his month long experience of temptation in the wilderness, Jesus moved out of his family home in Nazareth and made his home in Capernaum by the sea (the Sea of Galilee) (Matt 4:12). Why he moved to Capernaum is not clear. Matthew says it's to fulfill Isaiah's prophesy that the Messiah was to come from the Land of Zebulun, land of Naphthali, the region where Capernaum is located, but elsewhere in all four gospels there is strong evidence that Jesus' family was solidly opposed to the direction he was about to take (see Matt 10:13;12:25; 13:57; Mark 3:31–34; 6:4; Luke 4:16–30; 11:17; 18:29; John 7:1–9). No one from his family, except possibly his mother, was in Jerusalem during his ministry prior to the Passover, his last supper, his betrayal, trial, conviction and crucifixion. John alone says that his mother, Mary, was at the foot of the cross, but her presence

A New Reality, New Rules

there is never mentioned by any of the other gospel writers, which would be incredulous if she were there and never even given a mention during Jesus' procession with the cross to the site of crucifixion, and especially two days later at the tomb when women, led by Mary Magdalene, go to the tomb to anoint his body on the day of resurrection. Certainly they would not have omitted her name from any of the appearances of Jesus to Mary Magdalene on the day of his resurrection, his appearance in the upper room the night of his resurrection, or his appearance to two disciples, who are never listed as among the twelve, walking to Emmaus after the resurrection. It was to Mary Magdalene, not his mother, that the risen Jesus appeared first (John 20: 11–18).

In any event, Jesus made his home in Capernaum, the home where Simon Peter's house was located, and there he began his ministry. Simon Peter's house in Capernaum has been positively identified by archaeologists, and is presumed to be the actual house where Jesus lived with Peter. The evidence is solid that the house is Peter's because around its walls was built an octagonal shrine in the very early years of the Christian era to preserve the site for pilgrims. On the inside stones of the house's wall was scratched the word *Petros* (Peter), and a cross. Inside the house first century commercial fishing equipment were found (hooks, net mending equipment, etc.).[4] It was in Capernaum where he called his first and most intimate disciples, Simon (later called Peter, "the rock" by Jesus), his brother Andrew, and James and his brother, John, all of them fishermen, who immediately followed him. From there Jesus began an intensive ministry throughout the Galilee region, teaching in their synagogues and proclaiming the good news of the kingdom (Matt 4:23), and curing every disease and sickness, including those who were afflicted with various diseases and pains, demoniacs, epileptics, and paralytics.

THE SHOCKING BEGINNING OF JESUS' TEACHING

Crowds began to flock to him, and he began to teach them:

> Blessed are you who are poor, for yours is the kingdom of God.
> Blessed are you who are hungry now, for you will be filled.
> Blessed are you who weep now, for you will laugh.
> Blessed are you when people hate you, and when they exclude you, revile you, and defame you on account of the Son of Man.

---

4. Strange and Shanks, "Where Jesus Stayed in Capernaum," 66.

Part Two: Moving Beyond Christian Folk Religion

> Rejoice in that day and leap for joy, for surely your reward is great in heaven. (Luke 6:20–23)

The word "blessed" (Gr. *makarios*, from which we get the English word "macarism" which means "happiness") can just as well be translated as happy. As Meyer so rightly points out, the heirs of the reign of God are not the good, but the miserable. Now the miserable as such are not irreligious, but this hardly alleviates the scandal of the macarisms. The point is that the heirs of the reign of God are the poor without qualification, not the deserving poor. They deserve nothing, yet salvation is theirs. Their virtue is merely to reveal God's goodness. Thus they show how it is that, in Jesus, God could offer salvation not only to non-observant people of the land (*'amme ha-arets*) but to the biblical sinners.[5]

The key point here, it seems to me, is that the poor's primary virtue is merely to reveal God's goodness. And then the antithesis:

> But woe to you who are rich, for you have received your consolation.
> Woe to you who are full now, for you will be hungry.
> Woe to you who are laughing now, for you will mourn and weep.
> Woe to you when all speak well of you,
> for that is what their ancestors did to the false prophets. (V. 24–26)

This a total shift in logic. The poor, the hungry, mourners, and persecutors can rejoice! But the rich, satiated, gleeful, and popular have already received their period of happiness. The human world seems turned upside-down. But that's the way it is when God rules. Meyer says that this

> rhetorical structure consisted, first in the setting up of a paradox (Happy the poor? the mourners? the hungry?), then in the resolving of it by showing the afflicted as those whom God had chosen as beneficiaries of his intervention. Happy the poor, the mourners, the hungry, for their time has come! The hour of great reversals has broken out! The theological savants of Israel, who bore the key of knowledge (Luke 11:52), had in Jesus' view blocked the way to the reign of God rather than opened it (Matt 23:12). He himself did just the opposite, opening the way wide first and foremost to the mass of the afflicted: Happy the poor, for the reign of God is (above all) for them![6]

---

5. Meyer, 131.
6. Ibid., 130.

A New Reality, New Rules

THE RIDDLES AND THE UPSIDE-DOWN LOGIC OF GOD

The great paradox of the kingdom had started. Its heirs were not the good but the miserable. The paradox was to continue throughout Jesus' ministry and became his primary teaching style. He spoke to his disciples, followers, and the public in general in what is commonly translated as parables (*parabole*, Gr.). But as we have already mentioned, Jesus did not speak in Greek. It is believed he commonly spoke in the *lingua franca* of the day, Aramaic. Garcia, in his excellent article "Jesus and the Meaning of the Parables," says that

> The Hebrew word [for parable] *mashal* and the Aramaic word *matla* can mean a short story, like those we call "parables," but can also mean a proverb, a figurative account, a conundrum, or a puzzle. So "to speak by means of parables" can mean "to speak through puzzles," or in an enigmatic language that is not understood. Therefore, Jesus' opening words in Mark 4:10 must be interpreted as follows: "To you has been given the mystery of the kingdom of God; for outsiders, instead, it is all an enigma, incomprehensible language."[7]

In addition to the parables there are numerous other sayings and riddles which cause great confusion for the average reader. In Jesus' teaching he said that "among those born of women no one has arisen greater than John the Baptist; yet the least in the kingdom of heaven is greater than he" (Matt 11:11), and "many who are first will be last and the last will be first" (Matt 19:30, 20:16; Mark 10:31; Luke 13:30), and "whoever wishes to be great among you must be your servant, and whoever wishes to be first among you must be your slave" (Matt 20:26–27; Mark 10:43–44; Luke 22:26–27). In the story of the rich man and the beggar Lazarus, it is Lazarus who is cradled and cared for in the afterlife by Abraham, while the rich man is tormented in flames (Luke 16:20–25). To understand Jesus, we must understand these riddles. The disciples wanted to know why he always spoke in riddles, and so asked him. Jesus answered, "To you it has been given to know the secrets of the kingdom of heaven, but to them it has not been given. For those who have, more will be given, and they will have an abundance; but from those who have nothing, even what they have will be taken away" (Matt 13:10–12). Jesus answers the question about riddles with yet another riddle. The abundance Jesus is talking about is the secrets of the kingdom of heaven,

---

7. Garcia, 2008.

Part Two: Moving Beyond Christian Folk Religion

not worldly goods. Those ignorant of the mysteries of the kingdom (the topsy-turvy logic of God) will become even more dumbfounded because his sayings will make no sense.

One of the early heresies the church faced, especially in the second century, was a movement within the church known as Gnosticism, the name of which is derived from the Greek word *gnosis*, which means knowledge. Gnostics believed that in the teachings of Jesus there were hidden messages, which Jesus explained to his closest disciples, but to no one else. They therefore speculated as to what those hidden messages might have been. They speculated that nothing Jesus said should be taken at face value, but considered a metaphor for something else: it had a hidden meaning. For the Gnostic, this became true for everything surrounding Jesus' life, his disciples, his teaching, his miracles, even the crucifixion and resurrection. Many of the writings by the Gnostics are spurious gospels written mostly in the second to fourth century. Gnosticism was declared heretical by Irenaeus in his best known book *Adversus Haereses* or *Against Heresies* written about 180. Most of the Gnostic works Irenaeus mentions had been lost to the world until a cache of documents, now known as *The Nag Hammadi Library*, were discovered accidently by farmers in 1945 near the village of Nag Hammadi along the east side of the Nile River in Egypt. Gnostic gospels included in the library are "The Gospel of Truth," "The Gospel of Thomas," "The Gospel of Philip," "The Gospel of the Egyptians," "The Gospel of Mary [Magdalene]." The Gospel of Thomas is the best known. Just a quick scan of these gospels will reveal that they have little or nothing in common with the canonical gospels. In the biblical gospels, all four are traveling the same path toward the crucifixion and resurrection. The Gnostic gospels, on the other hand, are laden with the speculated "secret" teachings of Jesus, all intent on sharing those secrets with their Gnostic audience.

The mysteries of the kingdom are not Gnostic revelations. They are the enigmatic teachings of a logic which seems upside-down from our own, "the first shall be last and the last shall be first," etc. Most strikingly, is the pattern that priority for entry into the kingdom of God goes to the underprivileged, the powerless, and the underclasses of society. They are the masses the world has left behind, mistreated, often forgotten, or pushed aside. They are the powerless people who have little or no say in the affairs of the world.

This, I believe, is why Jesus told Pilate, "My kingdom is not from this world . . . But as it is, my kingdom is not from here" (John 18:36).

This is not to suggest that the kingdom transcends the world, or is "other worldly," as is so often said, but that the kingdom is ruled outside the parameters of this world's rule. It is under the rule of Yahweh. He directs its every move. If it were within the parameter of the world's rule, human logic would assume that the event about to happen (Jesus' crucifixion) would be one of the greatest signs of divine failure ever seen. Jesus, along with his Father God, would be facing defeat by all the forces of evil. As it is, applying the upside-down logic of the riddle that "God's foolishness is wiser than human wisdom, and God's weakness is stronger than human strength" (1 Cor 1:25) means that what appears as God's weakness is more powerful than any human power. So it is with the cross. The cross, which appears, in human logic, to be the defeat of Jesus, is actually his greatest power. Paul said that his mission was "to proclaim the gospel, and not with eloquent wisdom, so that the cross of Christ might not be emptied of its power" (1 Cor 1:17). Jesus did not display his greatest power in his resurrection (that's what *our* logic tells us). His greatest power occurred on the cross. In fact the exact moment when the cross became the most powerful was when Jesus breathed his last and proclaimed, "It is finished." At the moment of his death, he snatched death away from the power of evil. It could no longer hold us captive to separate us from the love of God. Paul all but screamed it from the housetops,

> Death has been swallowed up in victory.
> Where, O death, is your victory?
> Where, O death, is your sting? (1 Cor 15:54–55, quoting Isa 25:8 from the LXX).

When Jesus told his disciples that "there are some standing here who will not taste death before they see the Son of Man coming in his kingdom" (Matt 16:28), he was not speaking of his Second Coming "on the clouds of heaven with power and great glory" (Matt 24:30), he was speaking of the power of the cross which all his disciples would witness. It was the moment of his greatest power. It was the moment when the Son of Man came into his kingdom. That is the most exceptional paradox of them all. What, for all intents and purposes appears as a spiral down to defeat, is, in fact, the moment of God's olympian display of power. It is a truth that is hard for the human mind to grasp, this upside-down logic of God. "God's foolishness is wiser than human wisdom, and God's weakness is stronger than human strength."

8

Opponents of Jesus

ACCORDING TO THE FIRST century Jewish historian Flavius Josephus in his book *The Jewish War*, "Among the Jews there are three schools of thought, whose adherents are called Pharisees, Sadducees, and Essenes respectively."[1] Only the first two of these groups appear in the New Testament. The Essenes are never mentioned, but the consensus of nearly all the scholars of the Dead Sea Scrolls is that the Essenes were an ascetic group who produced the scrolls in a community called Qumran, on the northwest shores of the Dead Sea. As we have already discussed, John the Baptizer may well have emerged from this group when he appeared out of the wilderness and baptized Jesus. It is entirely possible that when Jesus went into the wilderness during the month of his temptations he may have had at least a brief contact with some members of the group. Twice during Jesus' teachings he made references to precepts held by the Dead Sea ascetics. In his Sermon on the Mount in Matt 5:43 he said, "You have heard that it was said, 'You shall love your neighbor and hate your enemy.'" Nowhere in the Hebrew Scriptures is there any inference that one should "hate your enemy," but in *The Community Rule* (1QS), from the Dead Sea Scrolls, its adherents are instructed to "judge every man according to his spirit. He shall admit him in accordance with the cleanness of his hands and advance him in accordance with his understanding.

---

1. *Op cit*, 132.

And he shall love and hate likewise. "[2] On another occasion, reported by Luke in 14:1–6, Jesus was having dinner in the house of a leader of the Pharisees where, apparently, there were other Pharisees in attendance, and a man with dropsy was brought in, who was healed by Jesus. Nothing was said by the dinner guests, but Jesus broached the subject of what acts the Pharisees would approve doing on the Sabbath, "If one of you has a child or an ox that has fallen into a well, will you not immediately pull it out on the sabbath day?" And, according to Luke, they could not reply to this. The reason the Pharisees could not reply is because the subject had already been discussed at length in the literature and the consensus among the religious leaders were that such acts as saving a life on the Sabbath was indeed allowed. Therefore, Jesus and the Pharisees were in total agreement. But according to *The Damascus Document* (CD) the covenanters are instructed concerning what is permitted, or forbidden, to do on the Sabbath: "No man shall assist a beast to give birth on the Sabbath day. And if it should fall into a cistern or pit, he shall not lift it out on the Sabbath . . . But should any man fall into water or (fire), let him not be pulled out with the aid of a ladder or rope or (some such) utensil. "[3] The rescue of an animal on the Sabbath was forbidden even if the person relied on the animal for his well-being, but there was some leeway for the rescue of a person. The person could be pulled out of the well, or pit, if he or she was within an arm's reach, but not if a rope, or pole, or any other implement had to be used. The Essenes held a much more stringent interpretation of the Sabbath laws than the Pharisees. In both of these occasions Jesus was in agreement with the Pharisees, but was in opposition with the harsh interpretation of the Essenes.

All three of the groups mentioned by Josephus arose during the Hasmonean dynasty in 200–100 BC. That period in Israel's history was a brief respite when some autonomy seemed possible. Hellenistic influence was still strong with Greek being the language of the marketplace and commerce, and even the Hebrew Scriptures were now translated into Greek,[4] yet Israel was being controlled by the Hasmonean Jewish family, and would remain under control until the Romans intervened in 63 BC. Yet there was major turmoil because Israel was anything but united, and thus the schools of thought, each claiming it held the truth regarding

2. Vermes, *Dead Sea Scrolls*, 111.
3. Ibid., 142.
4. The Septuagint (LXX).

the Sabbath laws, the laws of purity, and how each of them were to be interpreted. In addition there were debates over how the dates of festivals were to be calculated. These issues divided the religious leaders into various camps, and these camps are clearly evident in the New Testament. The major groups mentioned in the NT are Sadducees, Pharisees, scribes, chief priests, and Herodians. The Herodians are only mentioned three times in the gospels (Matt 22:16; Mark 3:6 and 12:13). They were political partisans who were in favor of Herod Antipas, but also apparently had some religious leanings and sided with the Pharisees against some of Jesus' teachings. In each of the passages where they are mentioned, they are linked with the Pharisees.

THE SADDUCEES

The Sadducees were members of an aristocratic party of which very little is known other than what we read in the New Testament. When it came into existence and what its beginnings were is only open to speculation. It is generally agreed that it was certainly begun sometime after 200 BC and probably during the Hasmonean period from about 167–40 BC. The various disputes among scholars today concerning who the Sadducees were is largely the result of not finding one piece of writing composed by them. We have no direct evidence about them except that written by their opponents, almost always in the pejorative. The rabbinic literature, which dates from about the second century AD and later, was all produced by rabbis who traced their heritage back to the Pharisees who were ardent opponents of the Sadducees. In several places the name "Sadducees" has been inserted in place of the original "heretics" and Gentiles in the text. [5]

Of all the groups actively mentioned in the gospels, the Sadducees and the chief priest are the only groups complicit in the plot to execute Jesus. The only time Pharisees are mentioned as being involved at all in the activities leading up to his crucifixion occurs in John 18:3 where the chief priests and Pharisees are mentioned together as accompanying a detachment of the temple guard who arrive at Gethsemane to arrest Jesus. This is important because the decision to arrest Jesus was made by the religious ruling council in Jerusalem, the Sanhedrin, which had approximately 70 members and was composed of both Sadducees and Pharisees, with the Sadducees having the majority vote. Thus, for Jesus'

---

5. Saldarini, *Pharisees, Scribes and Sadducees*, 226.

arrest, members of both parties accompanied the temple guard to make the arrest, including the Pharisees. But John is alone in naming them accompanying the soldiers and guards. In Matthew, those accompanying the guards are the "chief priests and elders" (Matt 26:47); in Mark 14:43 it is the "chief priests, the scribes, and the elders." In Luke's version of the arrest, in 22:47, there is no mention of soldiers or guards at the outset and it says simply that "a crowd came" led by Judas Iscariot. However, a few verses later, in v. 52, Luke mentions the "chief priests, the officers of the temple police, and the elders who had come for him." There is no mention of the Pharisees involvement at all in the synoptic gospels—only the "chief priests, scribes, and the elders." I believe this triad were all Sadducees, a conclusion I make which will be explained below.

Not much is said about the Sadducees in the New Testament. They are only mentioned fourteen times by that name, and in Acts 5:17 they are called "the sect of the Sadducees." The term "chief priests" is mentioned sixty-three times, and in many cases they are mentioned being in the company of scribes. There is no disagreement, I think, that the term "chief priests" refers to the chief officiates in the temple.

As I've said, when the Sadducees came into existence is unknown. It appears, however, that they came to power during the Hasmonean rule of John (Jonathan) Hyrcanus (134–104 BC). He was the son of Simon Maccabeus, one of the five Maccabean brothers, and nephew of Jonathan Maccabeus. Jonathan Maccabeus was the first of the Hasmonean family to be appointed high priest, Hyrcanus father, Simon, was the second, followed by Hyrcanus as the third. Thus, the high priesthood was under the control of the entire Hasmonean family. They were the true aristocracy of Israel, and all future high priests would be drawn from the ruling class until the fall of Jerusalem and the destruction of the temple in 70 AD. Under the rule of high priest Hyrcanus (134 BC), a power struggle ensued between the Pharisees and the Sadducees, and Hyrcanus became a Sadducee and abolished Pharisaic rulings and made the Saducean statutes the standard for the interpretation of the law. Thus, Hyrcanus was the first high priest to rule under the moniker "Sadducee." The only other high priest specifically called a Sadducee was Ananus ben Ananus who, according to Josephus, was the high priest who stoned to death the leader of the Jerusalem church, James, the brother of Jesus. Though only two high priests are specifically called Sadducees, all of the intervening high priests were appointed from the aristocracy and a logical assumption has been made that they also were most likely Sadducees.

Part Two: Moving Beyond Christian Folk Religion

The origination of the name Sadducees (Heb. *Seduqim*; Gk. *Saddoukaioi*) is not known for certain, however, the majority consensus is that it is a derivation of the name of the high priest Zadok (Heb. *sadoq*, Gk. *sadok*) who served under King David in the tenth century BC. Ironically, the name Zadok is also a derivation from the Hebrew word *sadaq*, which means "just" or "righteous." All of these terms clearly describe what the Sadducees believed about themselves. They called themselves "Sons of Zadok" which was an attempt, apparently, to give them the semblance of being in the legitimate lineage of priests, even though a large part of the populace of Israel considered them illegitimate because they came to power within the Hasmonean family by appointment, rather than by the heritage of being in the lineage of Aaron as the law required. When Jonathan, the first Hasmonean to be appointed high priest in 153 BC, expelled and replaced the temple's legitimate high priest (his name is unknown), an uproar was caused throughout the priestly classes and a group of priests walked out of the temple in protest, never to return. They claimed that the priesthood had been corrupted. The group was led by a man who is known simply as the "Teacher of Righteousness," and may well have been the high priest so expelled. He and his group fled to the Dead Sea area and formed the ascetic group "Essenes," who also called themselves "the sons of Zadok" and produced the Dead Sea Scrolls. According to one of the scrolls, *The Damascus Document*, (CD, IV. 3–9):

> The Priests are the converts of Israel who departed from the land of Judah, and (the Levites are) those who joined them. The *sons of Zadok* are the elect of Israel, the men called by name who shall stand at the end of days . . . (They were the first men) of holiness whom God forgave, and who justified the righteous and condemned the wicked. And until the age is completed, according to the number of those years, all who enter after them shall do according to that interpretation of the Law in which the (men) were instructed.[6]

The covenanters believed themselves to be the legitimate priests and chief priests of the temple and often refer to themselves as "the elect," or "the elect of God." The chief priests were mostly Sadducees who ruled in the temple from the time of the walk out (about 150–152 BC) until the temple was destroyed by the Romans in AD 70. After 70 they simply disappear

---

6. Ibid., 132.

Opponents of Jesus

from the records. The high priest (the Hasmonean Jonathan) who seized power from the legitimate high priest is called in the Qumran literature

> the Wicked Priest, who was called by the name of truth when he first arose. But when he ruled over Israel his heart became proud, and he forsook God and betrayed the precepts for the sake of riches. He robbed and amassed the riches of the men of violence who rebelled against God, and he took the wealth of the peoples, heaping sinful iniquity upon himself. And he lived in the ways of abominations amidst every unclean defilement[7]. (*Commentary on Habakkuk* IQpHab).

Jonathan, the first "illegitimate" high priest is also called "the Liar," the "Man of Lies" or the "Spouter of Lies." These terms all appear in one of the most important documents among the Dead Sea Scrolls known as the *Commentary on Habakkuk* (IQpHab)[8]. It has been radiocarbon tested and dated to between 120 –5 BC. According to Vermes, "The Habakkuk Commentary is one of the main sources for the study of Qumran origins, as well as the Essene Bible exegesis and the sect's theology regarding prophecy."[9] At the end of Parchment Sheet VI and continuing to the beginning of Sheet VII of the *Commentary on Habakkuk* is the sect's interpretation of Habakkuk 2:1–2 (the biblical text is in italics):

> *I will take my stand to watch and will station myself upon my fortress. I will watch to see what He will say to me and how [He will answer] my complaint. And the Lord answered [and said to me, Write down the vision and make it plain] upon the tablets, that [he who reads] may read it speedily.*
> ... VII and God told Habakkuk to write down that which would happen to the final generation, but He did not make known to him when time would come to an end. And as for that which He said *That he who reads may read it speedily*: interpreted this concerns the Teacher of Righteousness, to whom God made known all the mysteries of the words of His servants the Prophets. [10]

Although a detailed study of the Qumran group is not possible in this book, it seems of interest to at least mention some influence which may,

---

7. Ibid., 513.

8 Cave 1 ("I"), Qumran ("Q"), *pesherim* ("p," Heb. for "interpretations" or "commentaries"), Hab (Habakkuk).

9. Ibid., 509.

10. Ibid., 512–13.

Part Two: Moving Beyond Christian Folk Religion

or may not, be present between the Essenes and the Sadducees. Lawrence Schiffman has said that some of the priests who fled with the Teacher of Righteousness may have been Sadducees who were part of the faction that eventually became the Dead Sea sect.[11] He has detected some elements of Saducean theology in a scroll fragment called 4QMMT, a designation for a Hebrew name best translated into English as *Some of the Works of the Torah*. Y. Sussman, in the essay "The History of the Halakha and the Dead Sea Scrolls," attached to the official edition of 4QMMT, agreed with the opinion that the theology expressed in 4QMMT is, at least partly, in agreement with Saducean theology. In that essay, Sussman writes:

> The priestly nobility were apparently not the only adherents of Saducean *halakha*[12]. The Saducean *halakha* mentioned in rabbinic literature was followed not only by the Saducean aristocrats of the other sources, but also by popular classes and fanatical religious sects, who even fought on its behalf. These sects waged a dual battle: a religious political struggle (ethical and social) against the priestly Saducean aristocracy, on the one hand, and a religious-*halakhic* struggle against the opponents of the strict Saducean tradition (i. e., the Pharisees), on the other. Only from the perspective of the Pharisees were all the opponents of Pharisaic tradition who followed similar *halakhic* practices included in the same category as those who deny the authoritative Pharisaic interpretation of the Torah's commandments. All these were termed Sadducees, regardless of whether they were Sadducees by virtue of their social and political status or only because of their *halakhic* tradition.[13] What he is saying
is that while there may be Saducean theology in some of the Dead Sea Scrolls, it does not necessarily mean that the members of the Qumran sect were Sadducees. Most scholars would agree with Sussman, and disagree with Schiffman. VanderKam summarizes this by saying,

> The fact that the Qumranites and the Sadducees agreed on some important *legal* views means only that they belonged to a similar legal tradition, apparently one noted for its literal and strict reading of the Torah. It is important to know this, but when one turns to the *theological* beliefs of the Qumran community and those assigned to the Sadducees by the ancient texts, one meets a number of fundamental contradictions. Take, for

---

11. *Reclaiming the Dead Sea Scrolls*, 75.
12. A collective body of religious laws for Jews.
13. *Op cit,* 191, in Qimron.

instance, the two doctrines ... predestination and the afterlife. Josephus says the Essenes and the Sadducees took opposing stands on predestination, with the Essenes attributing everything to fate and the Sadducees denying fate altogether. If the Qumran scrolls teach a strong predestination, they are clearly not Saducean in theology. Regarding the afterlife, we have noted the evidence from the scrolls for belief about survival after death, including a resurrection of the faithful. According to Acts 23:8, the "Sadducees say that there is no resurrection, no angel, or spirit, but the Pharisees acknowledge all three" (see also Mark 12:18) ... As a result, we may say that there are some agreements between Qumran texts and legal views of Sadducees, but disagreements on theological positions.[14]

According to Josephus, the Sadducees disbelieved in fate, and believed that "God is incapable of either committing sin or seeing it; they say that men are free to choose between good and evil, and each individual must decide which he will follow. The permanence of the soul, punishments in Hades, and rewards they deny utterly."[15] Thus they did not believe in life after death, heaven or hell, or in the resurrection of the dead. However his final analysis of the difference between the Pharisees and Sadducees is in their personalities, which he describes in this way, "Pharisees are friendly to one another and seek to promote concord with the general public, but Sadducees, even toward each other, show a more disagreeable spirit, and in their relations with men like themselves they are as harsh as they might be to foreigners."[16] In simple language, the Sadducees were plainly ill-mannered and ill-tempered. Apparently that was true because in none of the sources are there any indications that people of any stripe liked them, whereas, most sources indicate that the Pharisees were well liked, and listened to. Josephus, in his other main book, *Jewish Antiquities,* says that the Sadducees were only supported by the rich, and that people do not follow them, while the Pharisees were liked by the people.

It is everywhere acknowledged that the Sadducees were from the very highest echelons of society. As such they apparently worked closely to keep peace with Rome and maintain the status quo in this world, and had little interest in the next. When the Sadducees are mentioned in the New Testament, which is only fourteen times (the Pharisees are

---

14. VanderKam & Flint, *The Meaning of the Dead Sea Scrolls,* 251f.
15. *War,* 137–38.
16. Ibid., 138.

mentioned 104 times), they are never mentioned in conjunction with the chief priests, while the Pharisees are often in the company of the chief priests. The general assumption for that has been that the "chief priests" and the "Sadducees" are essentially synonymous terms. In fact, Josephus indicates that the Sadducees were drawn from that group and were Jewish leaders. This is, I believe, a valid assumption although some scholars dispute that. However, in rabbinic literature including the Mishnah (Yoma 1:5) and Sifra 81 a–b, the Sadducees are often mentioned as high priests or priests. In these documents the Sadducees are clearly in charge of the temple as a whole, yet "sages" often set the rules concerning the lighting of incense, which could only be lit after the high priest enters the Holy of Holies on the Day of Atonement (Yom Kippur). The Babylonian Talmud also tells the story of a high priest who fell dead after disobeying the rule. In the Talmud the "sages" are the Pharisees, and thus, although the Sadducees controlled the temple, they were following rules laid down by the Pharisees, who were not priests at all, but laity.[17]

Saldarini sums up his study of the Sadducees in this way:

> When the Hasmonean family became dominant in Jerusalem after the war against Antiochus IV and when Jonathan later became high priest and was succeeded by Simon and his descendants, the priestly class was thrown into confusion. Even before the war various factions had fought for control and the high priesthood had changed hands. In the Hasmonean takeover the traditional high priestly families lost power and influence. The Hasmoneans did not easily succeed in establishing power . . . In the Herodian period various priestly families had their members appointed high priest, with Herod choosing high priests who would enhance his power or at least not be a threat to it.[18]

The same can be said of the aristocracy as well, of which it is well attested that Sadducees were members. During the Greco-Roman period there were constant struggles for dominance. Thus the social and political fortunes of the governing class were complex and changing.

The Sadducees were the elite among the elite. Thus, they did not openly oppose the rule of their country by outsiders, and were content to let that be the status quo and to work within that framework. This is one of the contentions that made them unpopular with the common people. To them the Sadducees were endorsing the way of life imposed

17. Saldarini, 235.
18. Ibid., 307–8.

on them by the Greco-Roman rulers and their environment. In this the Sadducees were opposed also by the other religious parties of Pharisees and Essenes, both of whom advocated the overthrow of foreign domination and believed their faith set them apart from the people of the world, which constantly threatened to contaminate and destroy their faith. They were also violently opposed to Jesus and his followers because he threatened the temple in Jerusalem, which for them was *the* House of God, and also the seat of their power. And when Jesus proclaimed himself "the Son of Man," which they knew meant "heavenly high priest," he became their primary adversary threatening to assume the high priesthood for himself usurping all of their power. We'll see this develop in the chapters that follow, especially chapter 10.

THE PHARISEES

The Pharisees were a religious group and a school of thought among Jews which began during the Hasmonean dynasty in the mid-second century BC. They were a confronting lay group who challenged just about any belief which they suspected did not conform to traditional Jewish interpretations of the Torah law or its teaching. Thus their history was filled with debates with the Sadducees, with Jesus and his teaching, and even among members of their own group. Theirs was a give-and-take existence. However, just because they question a practice does not mean necessarily that they were opposed to another view, just that they wanted to determine whether a secondary view was justifiable. They also believed that they had been set apart for this task by God. The name Pharisee (Gk. *Pharisaios*) meant "separatist" in Greek. It was derived from the Hebrew *perushim*, meaning "set apart."

Beliefs

Primary to their beliefs was a covenant belief in the written Torah, as contained in the five books of Moses, the first five books of the Hebrew Bible. They also believed in oral tradition handed down from generation to generation which interpreted the meaning of the Torah. In addition to the Torah, they believed the scriptural word of God included the writings of the Prophets, and also the Writings of the Tanakh, as discussed above. The Tanakh consisted of the same writings included in the Protestant

Part Two: Moving Beyond Christian Folk Religion

OT, but reordered and with some books combined, so their scriptures contained twenty-four books instead of our thirty-nine, albeit the text is the same. This belief is in opposition to the Sadducees who believed only in the Torah. Though the prophets and writings are important, they were not included in the body of literature the Sadducees considered scripture.

Another prime belief is the belief in Wisdom. Wisdom is central to Jewish thought in general. Wisdom is the seeking after truth as God reveals it. In the Hebrew Bible there are a number of books classified as wisdom literature—Job, Psalms, Proverbs, and Ecclesiastes. Also important Jewish writings which are not included in the Hebrew Bible are the apocryphal books of The Wisdom of Solomon, and Sirach (a.k.a. "Ecclesiasticus" or "Ben Sirach").

A third belief is the belief that people have free will but God knows a person's ultimate destiny (predestination or fate). The Sadducees did not believe in fate, but did believe that humans have a free will to choose between good and evil.

Contrary to the Sadducees, the Pharisees believed in life after death achieved through the resurrection of the dead, and the entrance into the messianic age (the kingdom of God).

Practices

While the Sadducees functioned almost exclusively within the temple in Jerusalem, and nearly all of their encounters centered within the precincts of the temple, the Pharisees were more interested in teaching the common people total participation in the life emulating the high ideals of Jewish values and the desires of God. They emphasized social justice, belief in the brotherhood of mankind, and a faith in the redemption of the Jewish nation and, ultimately, humanity. Moreover, they believed that these ends would be achieved through *halakha* ("the walk," or "how to walk"), a corpus of laws derived from a close reading of sacred texts. This belief entailed both a commitment to relate religion to ordinary concerns and daily life, and a commitment to study and scholarly debate. Of the three religious parties most prominent during Jesus' life, the Sadducees, Pharisees and Essenes, the group Jesus most closely identified with in both beliefs and in practice were the Pharisees. Theologically they were very close to each other. Their primary disagreements centered on Sabbath observance, what was and was not considered proper behavior (i.e., who it was proper to dine with, talk with, and associate with), and how a person expressed his or her religion.

According to the writings of Josephus, there were approximately 6000 Pharisees throughout Palestine in the first century. Although most were probably in and around Jerusalem where the temple and the seat of Israel's power was located, there are numerous places in the gospels where they approach Jesus and question him in Galilee with his disciples in the north of Israel. They were often the primary teachers who interpreted the law and taught the common people the Jewish way of life, therefore they were almost anywhere there were synagogues to instruct the people. We know that Paul was also a Pharisee who lived in Tarsus, in Cilicia, a Roman Provence in Asia Minor (in modern day Turkey). We know of no other Pharisees, except Paul, in the diaspora at the time but that does not mean there were no others.

Many synagogues are known to have existed throughout the countries of the Jewish diaspora in the early centuries of the Christian era. The largest such synagogue was discovered in Sardis in western Asia Minor, in the territory of Lydia. Its ruins date from the fourth century, although it is known that the site was originally developed at least two centuries earlier. The size of the fourth century building measures 279 X 66 feet. More than 80 inscriptions were found during the excavations, mostly in Greek.[19] There was a Christian church in Sardis which is one of the seven churches of Revelation (1:11). Sardis was addressed with these words in Revelation 3:1–2, "To the angel of the church in Sardis write: These are the words of him who has the seven spirits and the seven stars: I know your works; you have a name of being alive, but you are dead. Wake up, and strengthen what remains and on the point of death." We do not know if this was one of synagogues visited by Paul, but it is not far from Smyrna (modern day Izmir) and Ephesus, both major cities of the ancient world, and we know that Paul spent more than two years in Ephesus (Acts 18:10), where there was a synagogue in which he taught for three months (Acts 18:19; 19:8). During his two year stay Paul went to all the residents of Asia, both Jews and Greeks and preached the word of the Lord (Acts 18:10). It is very likely, therefore, that Paul could have visited Sardis and taught in an earlier synagogue there as he always went to synagogues first, perhaps on the same site where the fourth century large synagogue was built (Acts 13:5; 14:1; 17:1, 10, 17; 18:19). One other synagogue in

---

19. Wilson, *Biblical Turkey*, 304.

Part Two: Moving Beyond Christian Folk Religion

Asia Minor has officially been discovered in Priene, a town again in the western territory of Lydia. It was discovered by a menorah carved into a panel alongside steps to a house, which was radically transformed into a place of worship in the late Roman period. The ruins of the synagogue date from the fourth through the seventh century,[20] but it is possible that there was also an earlier Jewish worship site there. More recent archaeological discoveries have also found evidences of synagogues at Korykos and 24 in the province of Cilicia, not far from Paul's hometown of Tarsus. In the necropolis at Korykos at least twelve epitaphs have been found of Jews buried there as well as two sarcophagi which display menorahs, a major Jewish symbol of the temple in Jerusalem.

The evidence of synagogues in the diaspora does not, of course, prove that there were Pharisees in those regions, but it seems likely there may have been, teaching and preaching in the synagogues there. Paul, always proudly proclaiming his Jewish heritage (Phil 3:5–6), did not reject his title as a Pharisee even after he converted to become a follower of Jesus. He said, I am "as to the law a Pharisee; as to zeal, a persecutor of the church; as to righteousness under the law, blameless" (v. 6; cf. Acts 23:6; 26:5). As a Pharisee he would have been given enthusiastic welcomes to any synagogue he visited, even after his conversion. Paul proudly admits this in 1 Corinthians 9:20: "To the Jews I became as a Jew, in order to win Jews. To those under the law I became as one under the law (though I myself am not under the law) so that I might win those under the law." As "one under the law" is most surely an indication that he entered the synagogues as a teaching Pharisee, which automatically gave him authority. The anger expressed against him in some synagogues may be interpreted as fury by members who began to consider him an impostor as he turned from traditional Jewish teachings to preaching about Christ.

We do not know precisely how the Pharisee sect came into existence or exactly when, only that it formed sometime in the second century BC and continued through the first century AD. After the temple was destroyed, along with Jerusalem, in 70, they accepted the fact that with the temple gone Judaism would have to change, and their understanding of the requirement to obey the tenets of the law would have to be revised. They could no longer practice sacrifices for the remission of sin and redemption. Following the disaster of losing their temple a process of reevaluation began, and discussions between them over the next thirty

20. Ibid., 260.

Opponents of Jesus

to fifty years began the process which we know of as Rabbinic Judaism today. No longer did they refer to themselves as Pharisees (separatists), but rather Rabbis (teachers).

We don't know how a man became a member of the Pharisees, or what qualifications made membership possible. No writings have surfaced which describe the process. The book of Acts tells us that Paul was trained to be a Pharisee by a leading Pharisee of his day, Gamaliel (Acts 22:3), but we are not told what qualifications Saul had for this training, or what the training entailed. Within the New Testament the Pharisees are generally portrayed as petty legalists, but they were surely more than that. Rabbinic literature often pictures them as a progressive party dedicated to making the Torah practicable for everyone.

The Pharisees were not priests, but a lay society who were passionate about the rules of the Torah and the law. They were marked by their high knowledge of all aspects of the law, their piety, and their unique ability to teach the traditional Jewish way of life. As such, they were immensely popular with the people. When Jesus was in the temple as a boy of 12 in Luke 2:41–51, he was undoubtedly listening and learning from the Pharisees. Following the event, Luke reports that as Jesus grew he increased in wisdom and in divine and human favor (v. 52). They were Israel's teachers and what the people knew and understood about their own faith and Judaism's laws and the Jewish way of life, they would have learned from the Pharisees.

Although the New Testament seems to paint the Pharisees as harsh opponents of Jesus, a closer look shows a different picture. Note that on several occasions he was invited to dinner by the Pharisees (Luke 7:36–50; 11:37–53; 14:1–24), and two Pharisees became his followers. Nicodemus in John 3, and Joseph of Arimathea, who with Nicodemus, took Jesus down from the cross (John 19:38–42) and laid him in Joseph's family tomb. On one occasion Nicodemus stood up before a crowd gathered to expect Jesus' arrest and spoke up defending him (John 7:50). In John 12:42 it is reported that many, even some of the authorities, believed in him. But because of the Pharisees they did not confess it, for fear that they would be put out of the synagogue. Nicodemus clearly might be so described because in John 3:1–2 he is called "a leader of the Jews" who came to him "by night." Also, in Acts 15:5, several Pharisees (possibly Nicodemus and Joseph of Arimathea were among them) are mentioned as members of the Jerusalem church. In addition, it needs to be mentioned that in Luke 19:39 some Pharisees warned Jesus to flee the area because

Part Two: Moving Beyond Christian Folk Religion

"Herod wants to kill you." To assume, therefore, that Jesus and the Pharisees were bitter enemies is a distorted picture of the facts. A common teaching method of the day was an interaction between teacher and pupil, or even between teacher and teacher, where the two would debate issues of importance. It was often in the form of one asking a question, and the other raising a debatable point, and both exchanging opposite sides of the issue (similar to today's individual who plays "devil's advocate"). Plato's *Republic* gives plenty examples of this kind of teaching technique. Many of the exchanges between Jesus and the Pharisees might fall into this kind of debate style, and not show animosity at all or may be simply question and answer (i.e., Matt 19:3; 22:41; Mark 2:16, 24; 7:5; 10:2; Luke 6:2; Luke 14:3; John 8:13). In the passage in John 9:13–17 Jesus has healed a blind man who was given his sight and Pharisees began to investigate the incident because it was on the Sabbath day, and the Pharisees began a debate among themselves (v. 16) and they were divided.

The Pharisee's House Divided

At this point I believe it is important to try to distinguish why there seems to be differences among the Pharisees and their reactions to Jesus. There are Pharisees who test him on Sabbath laws and legal implications. There are those who accuse him of "eating with tax collectors and sinners." In the NT it seems as though there is a constant stream of those who are asking him questions "to test him." At the same time, there are Pharisees who are secretly on his side, most notably Nicodemus (John 3) and Joseph of Arimathea. Then there are Pharisees who accompany the chief priests who come to arrest him (John 18:15). Yet there are Pharisees who become members of the Jerusalem church (Acts 15). Then, of course, there is Saul of Tarsus (after conversion known as the Apostle Paul) who is a Pharisee who was complicit in the murder of the first martyr of the church, Stephen (Acts 9), and it was Saul who was the first persecutor of the church (Acts 22:4; 26:11; 1 Cor 15:9; Gal 1:23). Why was there such a wide division among the Pharisees?

The answer lies in the fact that there were indeed two divergent groups, or "schools" of thought, among the Pharisees themselves. The leaders of those two schools were both roughly contemporary with Jesus. They were Hillel the Elder, ca. 60 BC—ca. AD 20, and Shammai the Elder, ca. 50 BC—ca. AD 30.

Hillel the Elder

One scholar calls Hillel "clearly the single most influential figure in postbiblical Jewish history."[21] He was a contemporary of both Herod the Great and Jesus, and was the leader of the Pharisees from 30 BC—AD 10. He was responsible for emphasizing leniency in the interpretation of the Scriptures, and opened the way for the poor, sinners, and Gentiles to learn the ways of God. He also taught that even the smallest activities are sacred when they are done for God.

He was the more popular of the two scholars and the most loved and admired leader the Pharisees ever had. Most likely those Pharisees who supported Jesus, or were lenient towards him, were influenced by Hillel. It seems that even Jesus may have felt his influence. It was Hillel who first taught the principle of the "Golden Rule" in his writings (*Sabb* 31a; cf. Matt 7:12) and that one should "Love and pursue peace" ('*Abot* 1:12; 2:8; cf. Matt 5:9), and also the view of divine judgement, known as "measure for measure" ('*Abot* 2:7; Matt 7:2).

Hillel's students formed, what became known as, the "Hillel School," under which Pharisees trained. Nicodemus and Joseph of Arimathea, as well as the Pharisees who warned Jesus that "Herod wants to kill you" (Luke 19:39), and those who became members of the Jerusalem church (Acts 15), were probably Hillel Pharisees.

Shammai the Elder

Shammai was a friend of Hillel's and also his friendly adversary. When Hillel was the president of the legal council (Sanhedrin), Shammai was his vice-president. He was far more stringent in his interpretation of the laws than Hillel. He was reputed to be a hothead, acerbic, and impatient. He was ultraconservative and afraid that if the Jews had too much contact with the Romans, the Jews would be weakened as a people, and thus maintained a strict interpretation of Jewish law, while Hillel had no such fear and had a more liberal view of law. Though Hillel's followers were far more numerous than Shammai's, Shammai's were probably much more vocal and more involved in the debates between the Pharisees and Jesus. It was probably also to Shammai's group that Jesus addressed the "seven woes" in Matthew 23.

---

21. Nunnally, "Hillel," *EDB*, 591.

Part Two: Moving Beyond Christian Folk Religion

Shammai's students formed the Shammai school of Pharisaism, who were probably the group who tested Jesus most on his interpretation of the laws concerning Sabbath observance and his eating with "tax collectors and sinners." The influence of Shammai on Saul of Tarsus is not certain, but may have precipitated his persecution of the early followers of Jesus. There is no indication that students of Hillel would seek to persecute any group in that manner. There is one rather humorous story about the two (no one can verify whether it is true or not) that illustrates their differences. Apparently Hillel was open to admitting proselytes into Judaism even when they made unreasonable demands. One such proselyte demanded that he be taught the whole Torah quickly "while standing on one foot." Hillel agreed and accepted him for conversion, while Shammai dismissed him as a person not serious enough about Judaism.

THE DEBATES

The common picture most people have of the relationship between Jesus and the Pharisees is that they were fiercely at odds with one another. Most notably were the debates between them on Sabbath observance. The Pharisees often questioned him on what is lawful or unlawful to do on the Sabbath. A major complaint many people had about the Pharisees was that they were such purists in their interpretation of the law that they subscribed to the belief that all people, even the common people should obey the strictest interpretation of the law which was required of only the priests. This was especially true regarding what could and could not be done on the Sabbath. This was often the reason behind the charge that Jesus disobeyed Sabbath laws. Consequently, because Pharisees apparently found such exchanges to be amusing for their guests, Jesus was sometimes invited to their homes for dinner, as mentioned above. These invitations included other guests as well, presumably other Pharisees and scribes. One such invitation was to the home of a leader of the Pharisees (Luke 14:1–24). It, like other confrontations with Pharisees, was dinner on the Sabbath. During dinner a man came in suffering from dropsy, a term no longer in use, but at the time signified that the person had fluid in the lower limbs. Never one to avoid conflict, Jesus actually began the confrontation by asking the scribes and Pharisees in attendance, "Is it lawful to cure people on the Sabbath, or not?" He was met with silence. It was not because he had stumped the group, but because they wanted to see what he would do, or listen to what else he had to say about what he would do, or had done. Jesus simply took the man and healed him, and the man left, cured. As with all of Jesus' healing miracles this one was a teaching moment about the renewal of mankind entering into the kingdom. But Jesus wanted to stay on topic and said, "If one of you has a child or an ox that has fallen into a well, will you not immediately pull it out on a sabbath day?" (Luke 14:5). Luke tells us that they could not reply to this. Again, it was not because the host and other invited guests were stumped, but because they already knew the answer to this question, and knew that Jesus probably knew it as well. The answer was "Yes, it is proper to help another human being on the Sabbath." In the gospels there are a number of instances of Jesus healing on the Sabbath such as the man with the withered hand, (Matt 12:9–14; Mark 3:1–6; Luke 6:6–1), the crippled woman (Luke 13:10–17), a crippled man by the pool at Beth-Zatha (John 5:2–18), and this man in Luke 14 with dropsy. None of these instances were violations of the Sabbath law. According to Sanders in *Jesus and Judaism*, the matter is quite simple: no work was performed. If Jesus had to remove a rock which was crushing a man's hand, there would have been a legal principle at issue: was the man's life in danger, or could the work have waited for the sun to set? But the laying on of hands (Luke 13:13) is not work.[22] In defense of his activities on the Sabbath, Jesus declares that the Sabbath was made for humankind, and not humankind for the Sabbath, and also that the Son of Man is lord even of the Sabbath (Mark 2:27–28). In John 7:14–24 there is the story of Jesus teaching in the temple and discussing the Mosaic Law with teachers of the law and he asks them, "You circumcise a man on the sabbath. If a man receives circumcision on the sabbath in order that the law of Moses may not be broken, are you angry with me because I healed a man's whole body on the sabbath? Do not judge by appearances, but judge with right judgment." (vv. 23–24).

These healing miracles raise a major question. Why did Jesus heal? Was it purely out of compassion? That is the common perception, and it is valid as far as it goes. Yes, Jesus healed because he loved people but he had a wider motive. He was beginning the renewal of the earth for the kingdom of God, which he was inaugurating. Healing was part of that renewal. Bodies were brought back to their pristine states. The blind could now see the beauty of God's creation: the mountains, the sea shore,

22. *Op cit*, 266.

Part Two: Moving Beyond Christian Folk Religion

the sky and the clouds, the golden sunsets. The crippled had new unfettered bodies—they could leap for joy, dance to the sound of music, walk in the sand, and play with their children. The deaf could hear the sounds of this world—the song of birds, the wind whistling through the trees, the water lapping at the shore, and the laughter of children. People with variable skin diseases, always referred to in the New Testament as leprosy, were now able to—live in peace without itches, flesh scaling off in pieces, and the misery of being shunned in the villages, or on the roadways, and again be allowed to live with their families, and, most important, have access to the synagogue and the temple where they could worship God, sacrifice to him, sing praises to him, and pray to him. Those with autism, mental illness, or retardation, could experience life with the same joys, pleasures, and ready access to everything the world has to offer. The possessed had their demons driven out, and were released from the terror that accompanied them wherever they went. Jesus was ushering in new world. It was the renewed Israel, and the pristine state of the world described as Eden in Genesis. This was more than compassion; it was the demonstration of what the kingdom of God was bringing to this world. These were the signs of the kingdom coming, not of his divinity, or that he was Israel's messiah. Before he even began his ministry, one of his temptations in the wilderness, you will recall, was to perform spectacular feats to prove who he was (Matt 4:6; Luke 4:9–11), but Jesus rejected all such demonstrations of proof (Luke 4:12). There was one time, however, when the reason he rejected that temptation became clear, and why it was often important that major healing miracles should be private affairs. It is in the story of the raising from death his friend Lazarus, who lived in the village of Bethany, just two miles from Jerusalem (John 11:1–44). The family there consisted of two sisters, Mary and Martha, and their brother, Lazarus. Jesus was so close to them that we are told Jesus wept upon learning of Lazarus' death. By the time Jesus arrived in Judea from the northern region of Galilee, his friend had already been dead four days. But Jesus allowed a crowd to remain and watch him as he shouted into the cave-tomb, "Lazarus, come out!" Following the miracle, a number of people in the crowd witnessing it spread the word to the chief priests (Sadducees) and leaders in Jerusalem and a plot began to kill Jesus (John 11:45–53). John ends the story by saying that Jesus therefore no longer walked about openly among the Jews, but went from there to a town called Ephraim in the region near the wilderness; and he remained there with the disciples (11:54–55). Ephraim was small village about fourteen miles north of Jerusalem, in the Judean hills. He sought privacy.

The most dramatic of Jesus' miracles was, of course, Jesus raising the dead as he had done with Lazarus. The first raising miracle, however, was the twelve year old daughter of Jairus, a leader of a synagogue somewhere along the shore of the Sea of Galilee, who begged Jesus to heal his little girl who is at the point of death (Mark 5:21–24, 35–43; cf. Matt 9:18–19, 23–26; Luke 8:40–42, 49–56). This story is important on several accounts. First, of course, is the restoring to health of the little girl. Upon entering the house Jesus is told the girl is already dead. We don't know if she is actually dead or not because Jesus tells the crowd there, "The child is not dead but sleeping" (v. 39), and they mock him for making such a ridiculous claim. They're certain she is dead. He then puts everyone outside the house except Jairus and his wife. When only Jesus and the family have privacy, he takes the girl's hand and says to her, *Tabitha cum* ("Little girl, get up"). It is one of the few Aramaic phrases we have from Jesus. Other Aramaic expressions used by Jesus and included in Mark are *Ephphatha* in 7:34 ("be opened"), *Abba* in 14:36 ("father"), and *Eloi, Eloi, lema sabachthani* in 15:35 ("My God, my God, why have you abandoned me?"). Immediately the little girl rises and begins to walk.

The second important thing to note is that in this story of healing, Jesus seeks privacy to perform the miracle. Privacy was important for Jesus on many occasions. In this case he ordered the family to tell no one about this healing (v. 43). Other examples of this desire for privacy are in Mark 6:31 where he tells his disciples to "Come away to a deserted place all by yourselves and rest a while." Wherever Jesus traveled, crowds rushed around him, and compelled him to teach (Mark 6:33–34) or to heal the local people (6:54–56). He often explained the meaning of his parables in private only to his disciples (Mark 4:34). And he often sought privacy for safety, as in the story of the raising of Lazarus above.

Jesus' encounters with the Pharisees were often, and some were very intense, but this does not mean all of his encounters were filled with hostility. As mentioned earlier, the Pharisee's standard of obedience to the law was equal to the obedience required of the temple priests, and not the level expected of those not of the priesthood. Therefore, they were requiring "burden" far greater than even God required of the common man. Is it any wonder that Jesus said, "Come to me, all you who are weary and heavy laden and I will give you rest . . . For my yoke is easy, and my burden is light" (Matt 11:28, 30)? He wasn't relieving them of the law, he

Part Two: Moving Beyond Christian Folk Religion

was just relieving them of the *excesses* of the law demanded by the overly pious.

As has been pointed out above, the Pharisees were not complicit in the plot to have Jesus killed. The plot was hatched and carried out by those who had a political stake in wanting to be rid of him.

Jesus was not the enemy of the religious, but of the politically powerful. The final condemnation came from the most assuredly Sadducee high priest, Caiaphas, who, when Jesus called himself "the Son of Man seated at the right hand of Power," understood the term Son of Man to be a reference to the heavenly high priest, and a direct threat to Caiaphas' own authority. It is on this reference that the high priest tore his clothes and called Jesus a blasphemer (Matt 26:65). Calling Jesus a blasphemer was not the real issue. The real issue with Caiaphas was one of power. Jesus had claimed to be seated at the right hand of Power (God) and thus was claiming power over any human high priest, dethroning him. He was also claiming to have been divinely sent, surely a blasphemous claim! The high priest proclaiming that Jesus had blasphemed justified his calling for Jesus' execution before the religious council, the Sanhedrin. Then the crowd, composed of a majority of Sadducees in the Sanhedrin, mocked him by spitting in his face, striking him, and slapping him, chanting "Prophesy to us, you Messiah! Who is it that struck you?" (Matt 26:67–68). The term Messiah, which Jesus never acknowledges publically, would be the title presented before the Roman governor, Pilate, as the reason they wanted Jesus' death. Messiah was understood as a title for the king of the Jews, which would then make him a threat to the power of Rome. And that would be the reason Pilate consented to the crucifixion. He wouldn't have cared at all if Jesus claimed to be a high priest. But the final decision *was* made by the Sadducean high priest, and presumably the Sanhedrin in general, which was composed of a ruling majority of Sadducees. How many Pharisees voted for the indictment or took part in the mocking of Jesus and his abuse, if any, is not known. In John 7:32 there is the statement that the chief priests and Pharisees sent temple police to arrest Jesus, but this is not connected to his final condemnation, and is the only passage where the Pharisees are linked with the chief priests (most likely Sadducees) in any plot to place Jesus under arrest. The only other reference to chief priests and the Pharisees is in Matthew 27:62 where, after the crucifixion, a contingent of both chief priests and Pharisees, probably as representatives of the Sanhedrin, go to Pilate to warn him that Jesus had prophesied his resurrection. These passages in

Opponents of Jesus

no way confirm any complicity on the part of the Pharisees in seeking his death. Even the Matthew 27 citation does not necessarily suggest that the Pharisees accompanying the chief priests were in agreement with the purpose of the visit. They were only representatives of the members of the Sanhedrin, although it is possible that there were a number of Pharisees siding with the Sadducees. But if that were so, it was an unusual coalition as the history of the Pharisees and the Sadducees was one of divisiveness between them. Rarely did they ever agree on anything. I see no evidence that Pharisees ever sought the death of Jesus, even though his relations with them seemed quite contentious. We will explore that in more detail when we compare Jesus' lack of piety, with the high Torah piety of the Pharisees.

SCRIBES

The third major group among the religious parties was the scribes. Very often they are mentioned along with the Sadducees, the Pharisees, or the chief priests (Sadducees). Apparently the scribes were the Torah legal experts who advised the Pharisees or the Sadducees on legal matters relating to Torah law. The Essenes, who are not mentioned by name in the New Testament, had their own scribes who copied their sacred texts, and apparently advised them. Because both Sadducees and Pharisees are often mentioned as being in the company of scribes, each party apparently had their own scribal members.

Scribes were the legal experts (lawyers) for their respective group. Occasionally they are simply referred to as lawyers in the New Testament (Matt 22:35; Luke 7:30; 10:25; 11:45, 46, 52; 14:3). Because of their knowledge of sacred texts they were highly respected as the ones to turn to for interpretation of the law. Another primary task of the scribe was as a secretary or copyist. Apparently all of Paul's letters were dictated to scribes, one of whom was named Tertius, rather than writing them himself (Rom 16:22). There is evidence that the reason Paul did not write his letters himself was that his eyesight was so bad he had trouble seeing and therefore would close his epistles with simply a personal greeting written in larger than usual letters (Gal 6:11; 1 Cor 16:21; Col 4:18; 2 Thess 3:17). Most likely Paul was almost blind during most of his travels and this may be the "thorn in the flesh" for which he prayed three times to have taken away (2 Cor 12:7–8), but it was not to be.

Part Two: Moving Beyond Christian Folk Religion

As copyists, the scribes were the most literate of the people of Israel, and they are the ones who so carefully and meticulously preserved letter by letter all of the ancient literature, including the sacred writings we have included in our Bibles, as well as all the wisdom of the ancients. This activity went on century after century until around 1439 when Johann Gutenberg, of Mainz, Germany, invented movable type for a screw type printing press. In 1455 he printed his beautiful copy of the Gutenberg Bible, of which 48 copies are known to survive, two of which are in the British Museum. They originally sold for 30 florins, which was roughly three years wages for the average clerk.

Without the scribes, however, there would have been no text to print. Thus the scribes are owed an immense debt of gratitude by the whole world. In addition to merely being copyists, many were also artistic calligraphers whose copies are often considered priceless works of art.

There is no finer praise for the scribe than that recorded in the apocryphal book of Sirach (38:34b—39:11). It is worth quoting in its entirety:

> How different the one who devotes himself to the study of the law of the Most High!
> He seeks out the wisdom of the ancients, and is concerned with prophecies;
> he preserves the sayings of the famous and penetrates the subtleties of parables;
> he seeks out the hidden meanings of proverbs
> and is at home with the obscurities of parables.
> He serves among the great and appears before rulers;
> he travels in foreign lands and learns what is good and evil in the human lot.
> He sets his heart to rise early to seek the Lord who made him, and to petition the Most High;
> he opens his mouth in prayer and asks pardon for his sins.
> If the great Lord is willing, he will be filled with the spirit of understanding;
> he will pour forth words of wisdom of his own
> and give thanks to the Lord in prayer.
> The Lord will direct his counsel and knowledge, as he meditates on his mysteries.
> He will show the wisdom of what he has learned,
> and will glory in the law of the Lord's covenant.
> Many will praise his understanding; it will never be blotted out.
> His memory will not disappear, and his name will live through all generations.

Opponents of Jesus

> Nations will speak of his wisdom, and the congregation will
> proclaim his praise.
> If he lives long, he will leave a name greater than a thousand,
> and if he goes to rest, it is enough for him.

It is hardly possible to outdo this hymn of praise. Because the scribe is usually portrayed in the New Testament as being in opposition to Jesus, it is necessary to put that into perspective. Yes, some were surely enemies, but what they contributed to the welfare of the world can never be diminished. Without them we would have lost the wisdom of the world behind them. There would be no story of Israel, except stories passed on orally; there would be no gospels or letters by Paul, or any of the other books of the New Testament. We would have no theology, philosophy, or science. Our world would simply be illiterate and primitive.

CONCLUSION

There were many forces at work in Israel in the first century. Josephus, in his *Antiquities of the Jews*, speaks of four philosophies, Sadducees, Pharisees, Essenes, and a forth philosophy, which can best be called "revolutionary." This latter category includes violent political parties intent on driving out any and all foreign interveners, Romans, Greeks, or whatever power held them under their yoke. Two of the most well-known were the party of Zealots, of which one of Jesus' named disciples, Simon (not Simon Peter), was a member (Matt 10:4; Mark 3:18; Luke 6:15; Acts 1:13), and the *sicarii*, which were a group of terrorist assassins, who carried small knives under their clothes to quickly assassinate those who were complicit, or believed to be complicit, with the occupiers. Josephus, in his *Jewish War* attributes the Jewish war as being started by the *sicarii*. This was the world in which Jesus was born, and to which he proclaimed the coming of the kingdom of God. In addition there many others that were strictly political parties and most are not mentioned in our literature. Only one such party mentioned in the New Testament is the Herodians, mentioned earlier.

Of the three major sectarian parties, the Essenes are never mentioned. Even so, Josephus spends a great deal of his time describing them in his *Jewish War*, and it is the group most scholars believe was responsible for the Dead Sea Scrolls, although the scrolls never call their authors by the name "Essene," but rather "Sons of Zadok," "Sons of Light," or "the elect. " It is the

Part Two: Moving Beyond Christian Folk Religion

Pharisees which command the most attention, and are often pictured in a negative light in the NT, although I believe Jesus had a closer attachment to them than is often thought. Their beliefs were much closer to his than any of the others, except for their outward display of piety and their sometimes harsh interpretations of the law—ritual purity, Sabbath observance, etc. It has even been suggested by some that Jesus leaned more toward Pharisaic thought than any other group within Israel. Now it is time to turn to the issue of piety, which we will do in the next chapter.

9

Quiet Piety

THERE IS A REMARKABLE story in the Hebrew Bible about the prophet Elijah who is led by "an angel of Yahweh" into the wilderness to "Horeb the mount of God" where he spent a night in a cave there:

> Then the word of Yahweh came to him, saying, 'What are you doing here, Elijah?' He answered, 'I have been very zealous for Yahweh, the God of hosts; for the Israelites have forsaken your covenant, thrown down your altars, and killed your prophets with the sword. I alone am left, and they are seeking my life, to take it away.'
>
> He said, 'Go out and stand on the mountain before Yahweh, for Yahweh is about to pass by.' Now there was a great wind, so strong that it was splitting mountains and breaking rocks in pieces before Yahweh, but Yahweh was not in the wind; and after the wind an earthquake, but Yahweh was not in the earthquake; and after the earthquake a fire, but Yahweh was not in the fire; and after the fire a sound of sheer silence. (1 Kgs 19:9–12)

Amid the din of the world's voices, each vying for our attention, calling us this way or that in our lives, sometimes the answer comes to us in "sheer silence." Churches try to get our attention by shouting out to us that they are a "Bible believing church," or that they are an "all inclusive church, welcoming everyone," or that they preach only "the Word of God." Relative strangers approach us and ask us, "Have you taken Jesus as your personal Savior?" Billboards scream out to us that "Jesus saves,"

Part Two: Moving Beyond Christian Folk Religion

or "He is coming again soon." People are endlessly "witnessing" for their faith and want you to respond to them in *their* faith words. This is what is known as "piety." People are doing what they believe God wants them to do. It is their call to "evangelize" the world. After all, Jesus said, "Go therefore and make disciples of all nations, baptizing them in the name of the Father and of the Son and of the Holy Spirit, and teaching them to obey everything that I have commanded you. And remember, I am with you always, to the end of the age" (Matt 28:19–20).

Piety is, by definition, doing what we believe God wants us to do. It is the sign of religion, faith, and spirituality. Piety can be either genuine, which comes from a deep spirituality, out of profound reverence and devotion or it can be false, where piety is exhibited for a person's own sake. False piety is intended to make the pious person feel more spiritual and religious than he or she really is. Thus, it is hoped, the person will win favor or forgiveness from God. It is almost impossible for someone else to know which is which. When we kneel for prayer, is it out of deep reverence for God, or simply because that's what we think God wants us to do, or because others expect us to do it? In 1963 there was a small book by an Anglican bishop, John A.T. Robinson, which caused a firestorm of controversy. Its title was *Honest to God*. The main theme of the book was that God is not a "Being" "out there" somewhere, or "up there" in his heaven. Robinson said he is not transcendent in the sense that he is someplace else, but rather that he is right here, around us and in us. When it was published he had his critics who called him an "atheist," or a "heretic," and some voices were even calling for an ecclesiastical trial and removal from office. The great shock to some was that Robinson was not just parroting the words handed down generation by generation from doctrines and dogmas the church had long before settled on. It was a new vocabulary, using new ways of expressing the "shocking" suggestion that God is far more than someone's idea of God floating around in his heaven monitoring the affairs of mankind. It has been a long time since I have read this book, and somewhere along the line I have lost my copy, or "loaned" it to someone, but I remember wondering what all the fuss was about. He was, of course, challenging the way we think, but I thought that was a good thing. In the early 1960s "new" expressions of faith, as daring as Robinson's, was simply not done, especially from a bishop of a mainline church. A bishop was expected to reaffirm age-old doctrines and confirm church theology and teaching. He was expected to simply parrot "that old time religion" handed down from generation to generation. Today *Honest to God* is back in print, published in 2003 on the 40th Anniversary of its first appearance. The original edition had less than 150 pages, but a book which followed it, called *The Honest to God Debate*, documenting the firestorm surrounding it was twice as thick. I still remember some of the points Robinson made, and which I thought, at the time, were brilliant. As I remember it, one suggestion he advocated was that the churches call a moratorium on prayer for an unspecified period of time. He suggested churches stop offering prayers, for anything. Jaws dropped around the world at such a suggestion. It went against the grain of common faith and the Bible, where in 1 Timothy 5:17 we are told to "Pray without ceasing"! But then Robinson clarified that by explaining that the "moratorium" should continue until "we are *driven* to our knees in prayer." In other words, we should step back from our piety until we cannot stand it any longer and we absolutely, positively, *must* fall down in prayer. Kneeling for prayer, or folding our hands in prayer, or bowing our heads in prayer, and closing our eyes for prayer—these are actions we have been taught are appropriate for prayer—it is what is done! These are acts of piety, as are raising our eyes and hands to heaven, speaking in tongues, dancing sacred dance, crossing ourselves, and genuflexing. All these actions are culture bound and external signs of spirituality, and they will vary with different cultures, different denominations, and different faiths. In Islam the faithful kneel and bow their forehead to the ground in prayer. In Eastern Orthodox churches the faithful often lay prostrate before God. In Hinduism the faithful are instructed in the appropriate positions for various kinds of prayer, and what benefits the positions give the worshipers. Piety is as much a part of our worship as reading scripture, attending worship services. Piety determines how our worship service is structured—when we stand, when we kneel (or if we do), when the sermon or homily will be given, what songs we sing, how formal or informal the service will be, what the "appropriate" dress is for worship, the actions and dress of the clergy and his or her assistants during worship, the actions and dress of the choir, how music is accompanied (if at all), how communion is served and received, how baptism is done and how old the person baptized is, etc. I have known of members who have actually quit a congregation because something was changed. In one case a family left because the American flag was removed from the chancel, and in another case a family left because some in attendance were not dressing appropriately—"not like we're used to seeing"! I know of one pastor of a rural congregation who one Sunday appeared before the altar not wearing his usual robes, but rather wearing country overalls and a plaid shirt, and he announced to the congregation, "I have heard many farmers making the excuse that they don't come to church because the service is held too soon after doing the Sunday morning chores, and there isn't time to change into 'proper' Sunday clothes. I'm here to tell you we don't care what you wear to church. Just come!" Then he began the service dressed in overalls. You can search the New Testament from page one in Matthew to the last page in Revelation and there are no definitive answers on how to dress or "properly" worship. Yet denomination has fought with denomination for centuries over these issues. Each denomination professes adamantly that they're right, while the others are either partly right, or totally wrong. Thus the primary reason for 9000+ denominations worldwide discussed earlier, each claiming to hold the truth. Now these debates are almost always about acts of piety—what is right action, and what is proper, in the worship of God and Jesus the Messiah, and often they trump even doctrines of faith, or church dogma. All of this occurs despite the prayer of Jesus on the night before his death, where he "looked up to heaven" and pleaded with God, saying, "Holy Father, protect them in your name that you have given me, so that they may be one, as we are one" (John 17:11). Obviously it was a petition that never saw the light of day. Just a few years later Paul screamed at the Corinthians:

> I appeal to you, brothers and sisters, by the name of our Lord Jesus Christ, that all of you be in agreement and that there be no divisions among you, but that you be united in the same mind and the same purpose. For it has been reported to me by Cloe's people that there are quarrels among you, my brothers and sisters. What I mean is that each of you says, "I belong to Paul," or "I belong to Apollos," or "I belong to Cephas," or "I belong to Christ." Has Christ been divided?" Was Paul crucified for you? Or were you baptized in the name of Paul? (1 Cor 1:10–13)

How different it is in the Hebrew Scriptures where in the books of the Torah the garments of the priests and high priest are carefully described, and the furniture of the temple meticulously ordered, and the actions of the priests given.

In Jesus' day the religious elite of Israel (Sadducees, Pharisees, and their scribes) were highly pious, and openly so. In Matthew 23 Jesus, addressing the crowds and his disciples, says to them:

> The scribes and the Pharisees sit on Moses' seat; therefore do whatever they teach you and follow it; but do not do as they do, for they do not practice what they teach. They tie up heavy burdens, hard to bear, and lay them on the shoulders of others;

but they themselves are unwilling to lift a finger to move them. They do all their deeds to be seen by others; for they make their phylacteries broad and their fringes long. (Matt 23:2–5)

"Phylacteries" (Heb: *tephillin*) were two small leather bound boxes each of which contained four parchment pieces inscribed with biblical commandments (Exod 13:1–10, 11–16; Deut 6:4–9; 11:13–21). One of these *tephillin* was bound with a leather strap on the left arm, and the other on the forehead. This was done as part of the prayer ritual. "Fringes" were the hems along the bottom of a garment. These hems had blue twisted threads formed like tassels at the four corners of a garment, which was a reminder to obey the commandments "and do not follow the lust of your own heart and your own eyes" (Num 15:37–40). We do not know if Jesus ever wore phylacteries during prayer, but he apparently had the blue fringe tassels on the four corners of his garment, because in Matthew there are two times when people touched Jesus' fringes, seeking to be healed. The first was a woman who had been bleeding for twelve years (probably a continual menstrual flow). She is reported to have said to herself, "If I only touch his cloak, I will be made well." For her, just a touch of a fringe would have magical power to heal her. And, indeed, she was healed. Jesus' response to her was, "Take heart, daughter, your faith has made you well" (Matt 9:21–22; cf. Mark 5:25–34). Jesus wanted to assure her that it was not the magic of the fringe, but her faith that made her well. Mark's version of the story adds a detail Matthew omits. In it, when the woman touches Jesus' clothes he becomes "aware that power had gone from him, and rather curtly, I think, asked, "Who touched my clothes?" I say "curtly" because remember the temptation in the wilderness that suggested Jesus throw himself down "from the pinnacle of the temple" and that angels wouldn't let him be harmed? This was the temptation to perform magic, and people often believed in magic. Compare, for instance, the story of Simon, the Samaritan magician, in Acts 8 when people who saw his magic believed that "This man is the power of God that is called Great" in v. 10. Jesus had rejected the temptation to perform feats of magic, and in this case was disturbed that someone took power from him without his knowledge and permission. Jesus turned and scouted the crowd seeking who might have done such a thing. "But the woman, knowing what had happened to her [she was indeed healed], came in fear and trembling, fell down before him, and told him the whole truth" (v. 35). Then Jesus' response to her was

Part Two: Moving Beyond Christian Folk Religion

essentially the same as in Matthew, "Daughter, your *faith* has made you well; go in peace, and be healed of your disease."

This healing of the hemorrhage was important because a person in the process of menstruation was considered "unclean," or ritually impure, by Jewish law and would preclude her being able to enter the temple for worship. So her healing was not just curing her body, but was for the benefit of healing her soul. She would once again have access to the public worship of God.

The other Matthew passage is in 14:36 where, on the coastal plain Gennesaret on the northeast side of the Sea of Galilee, crowds brought their sick to Jesus begging him "that they might just touch even the fringe of his cloak" and all who did so were healed. Again, this is also an act of faith, not magic.

These two instances raise a very important question: what is the relationship of "faith" to "belief"? In both these cases it is apparent that people believed that the fringes of Jesus' garment held some kind of magic power in their own right. It was clear to Jesus that this *was* the common belief of those who approached him and touched him, yet Jesus called it "faith." It was called "faith," even though the belief in magic was erroneous. It seems that for Jesus "faith" goes much deeper than "belief." It is not so important that the belief is right, as long as the heart is right. These people believed that, somehow, and they might not even have understood how it would happen, whether by magic or the hand of God, but only that they would be healed by just a touch. It was enough. In Matthew 8:5 a noncommissioned officer of the Roman army, a centurion, approaches Jesus and asks him to heal his servant, and without even going to his home, Jesus heals the servant from afar and then declares, "Truly I tell you, in no one in Israel have I found such faith" (v. 10). This man was a Roman pagan, yet Jesus praises him for his faith! Not a word is mentioned about his paganism, his idolatry, the temple prostitutes in Roman temples, the temple orgies, just praise for his faith. But, surprisingly, Jesus went beyond a word of praise. He tells those who witness this interaction with the centurion, "Truly, I tell you, many will come from east and west and will eat with Abraham and Isaac and Jacob in the kingdom of heaven, while the heirs of the kingdom will be thrown into outer darkness, where there will be weeping and gnashing of teeth" (vv. 10–12). Is he suggesting that faith, coming from the heart, supplants erroneous belief? Is he suggesting that even correct belief in God, in himself, and in all the traditions of Israel, the incarnation, and beyond, and all the piety of the religious life, unless it comes from the depths of the heart, are not as important as simply falling down before him and pleading for mercy? I think that's what he is saying. I don't hear a demand for "conversion" in this, or a "change of heart" in this, or that this person or that person must first "take Jesus Christ as their personal savior." All I hear is the plea for mercy.

The prophet Isaiah (29:13–14), speaking of the people of God, the people of the covenant warns this:

> The Lord said:
> Because these people draw near with their mouths
> and honor me with their lips,
> while their hearts are far from me,
> and their worship of me is a human commandment learned by
> rote;
> so I will again do amazing things with these people,
> shocking and amazing.
> The wisdom of their wise shall perish,
> and the discernment of the discerning shall be hidden.

Another time a Canaanite woman shouted out to Jesus, "Have mercy on me Lord, Son of David, my daughter is tormented by a demon" (Matt 15:22–28). This time Jesus did not respond to her and his disciples' pleaded with him to "send her away." After some discussion by Jesus that his mission was only to the "house of Israel," she came, knelt before him and begged him, "Lord help me!" Jesus' final response to her was "'Woman, *great is your faith* let it be done for you as you wish.' And her daughter was healed instantly." There was no comment by Jesus that her religious faith was not right. He doesn't argue religious belief with her that she must change to Yahwism, have her male children circumcised, and then come and see him about an exorcism for her daughter. The woman is a pagan pleading for mercy from Jesus, yet her religion still includes the storm god *Ba'al Hadad*, mentioned so often in the Hebrew Bible (fifty-seven times) from Numbers through Zephaniah, and even warned against by Paul in Rom 11:4. And that's not all: her Canaanite religion had a whole pantheon of at least twenty-six gods and goddesses, and practiced many other peculiarities, such as the Cult of the Dead, or a strange mythology of how the universe was created. Jesus made no mention of any of this, only his praise that "Great is your faith!" Her faith was that Jesus could, and would, heal her daughter. And he obliged immediately.

Once again, the strange blessings of Jesus jump out at us. They don't match any of our sense of "rightness": "Blessed are the poor," they'll see

Part Two: Moving Beyond Christian Folk Religion

God; "Blesses are the hungry," they'll be fed; "Blessed are those who weep," they'll laugh; "Blessed are those who are hated, and excluded," their reward is great in heaven. But then Jesus dares to go on: "Woe to the rich," they've already received their reward; "Woe to the full now," they're going to go hungry; "Woe to the happy," for they're going to weep; "Woe to the popular," for they're just like the false prophets (a paraphrase of the Luken beatitudes in Luke 6:20–26). Once again we see what seems to be a reverse logic on the part of God. To be one of the blessed you must live a miserable life, or so it would appear, at least as far as the Beatitudes seem to suggest. I remember once, while an Air Force chaplain, a member of a congregation came to me and proudly announced, "The Lord has blessed us with a new Mercedes!" People constantly speak of being blessed when something good happens in their lives. Indeed, we are often blessed when we experience good events and in the Hebrew Bible especially God bestows blessings on individuals (Job 42:12), groups (as in Exod 12:29) and nations and particularly Israel (Jer 4:2; Deut 26:15), but these are blessings of those who are in a covenantal relationship with God.[1] When this understanding is applied to the Beatitudes it means that God has made a unique covenant with the underclasses of society and has placed them into his loving care. It does not necessarily mean that those in the upper classes are not blessed, but that their possessions are not the *sign* of a blessing. Jesus makes it abundantly clear that those with possessions are always at risk of prizing their possessions more than their heavenly Father (Matt 6:24; 13:22; 19:23, 24; Mark 4:19; 10:23–25; Luke 1:53; 8:14; 16:13; 18:24–25). This makes them very vulnerable to the woes in Luke 6:20–26.

Here again we see this strange logic of the Almighty, where "the first shall be last and the last shall be first," and again the riddle:

> I bring low the high tree,
> I make high the low tree;
> I dry up the green tree
> and make the dry tree flourish.
> I Yahweh have spoken; I will accomplish it. (Ezek 17:24)

Today a popular form of Christianity has been dubbed "The Prosperity Gospel," the theme of which is that God wants us to have many material things and achieve wealth. One retired minister in our town was pastor of the largest church in the city. His church was packed to overflowing Sunday

---

1. Magdalene, "Bless, Blessing," *EDB*, 192.

Quiet Piety

after Sunday. After he retired he opened a furniture store, which advertises regularly on T.V. The commercials have the retired minister's "voice over" and at the end of every commercial closing the ad with this saying, "We pray that God will bless you richly," and that's the basic theme of "The Prosperity Gospel." The motive behind such "good news," of course, is that it's what most people want to hear. After all, didn't Jesus say, "Give, and it will be given to you. A good measure, pressed down, shaken together, running over, will be put into your lap" (Luke 6:38)? Yes, he said that, but look at the verse in its context. The whole first sentence is, "Forgive, and you will be forgiven; give, and it will be given to you" (vv. 37b–38). The sentence is about forgiveness, not material goods! If you "forgive" you'll be forgiven, and if you forgive more, forgiveness will be heaped upon *you*. The saying has nothing to do with wealth or poverty. But the Hebrew Bible *and* Jesus have plenty to say about the dire consequences of wealth based on greed, and those who take no responsibility to help those who are in need! Jesus saw it everywhere he went, and he was appalled.

He was also appalled at the religious elite and their pious ways, yet who rarely cared for the underclasses of society, whether they are in poverty, or disabled, or ill. Their priority was to "please" God, as though God needed "pleasing," or needed anything, for that matter.

It is time, therefore, to explore the piety of the Pharisees and compare it to that of Jesus. The woes of Matt 23—"Woe to you scribes, Pharisees, hypocrites." Appearances were a leading issue between the Pharisees and Jesus. It is worth quoting the entire section of "woes." He begins this remarkable series with again the "upside down logic" of the kingdom:

> The greatest among you will be your servant. All who exalt themselves will be humbled, and all who humble themselves will be exalted.
>
> But woe to you, scribes and Pharisees, hypocrites! For you lock people out of the kingdom of heaven. For you do not go in yourselves, and when others are going in, you stop them. Woe to you, scribes and Pharisees, hypocrites! For you cross sea and land to make a single new convert, and you make the new covert twice as much a child of hell as yourselves.
>
> Woe to you, blind guides, who say, "Whoever swears by the sanctuary is bound by nothing, but whoever swears by the gold of the sanctuary is bound by an oath." You blind fools! For which is greater, the gold or the sanctuary that has made the gold sacred? And you say, "Whoever swears by the altar is bound by nothing, but whoever swears by the gift that is on the altar is

Part Two: Moving Beyond Christian Folk Religion

> bound by the oath." How blind you are! For which is greater, the gift or the altar that makes the gift sacred? So whoever swears by the altar, swears by it and everything on it; and whoever swears by the sanctuary, swears by it and by the one who dwells in it[2]; and whoever swears by heaven, swears by the throne of God and by the one who is seated upon it.
>
> Woe to you, scribes and Pharisees, hypocrites! For you tithe mint, dill, and cummin, and have neglected the weightier matters of the law; justice and mercy and faith. It is these you ought to have practiced without neglecting the others. You blind guides! You strain out a gnat and swallow a camel!
>
> Woe to you, scribes and Pharisees, hypocrites! For you clean the outside of the cup and of the plate, but inside they are full of greed and self-indulgence. You blind Pharisee! First clean the inside of the cup, so that the outside also may become clean.
>
> Woe to you scribes, Pharisees, hypocrites! For you are like whitewashed tombs, which on the outside look beautiful, but inside they are full of the bones of the dead and of all kinds of filth. So you also on the outside look righteous to others, but inside you are full of hypocrisy and lawlessness.
>
> Woe to you, scribes and Pharisees, hypocrites! For you build the tombs of the prophets and decorate the graves of the righteous, and you say, 'If we had lived in the days of our ancestors, we would not have taken part with them in shedding the blood of the prophets.' Thus you testify against yourselves that you are descendants of those who murdered the prophets. (Matt 23:11–31)

Yes, it is a long passage, but read again the last paragraph. It is one of the clearest examples of how relevant Jesus' sayings are for today. These "woes" are not just aimed at a long ago disappeared religious group from the first century! They are aimed at the religious elite of every age. And I don't just mean the clergy, or scholars, but anyone of faith. In 2011 I was struck full face with this last paragraph. When my wife and I were traveling in Israel, we visited the *Yad Vashem* (The Holocaust History Museum) in Jerusalem. It is a very moving and emotional experience. I have read, and researched the holocaust for more than fifty-five years, five years of which I lived in Germany while stationed there as an Air Force GI in the mid-fifties, and as a chaplain in 1981–1983. I remember attending the first German movie ever made about the Hitler

---

2. The "sanctuary," of course is the temple, and "the one who dwells in it" is God—in the Holy of Holies as we learned earlier.

years. The movie was titled *Until Five Minutes to Twelve*. I went to it in 1954 with a GI friend of German heritage, who spoke German fluently, and translated the German language of the film for me. The movie had the German audience in tears, and some people could not even remain for the whole thing because it was so direct and shocking, and included details about the holocaust. I've read the play *The Diary of Ann Frank*, seen the movie, and read the book on which it was based, *The Diary of a Young Girl*. I've been to Ann Frank's house in Amsterdam twice. And I've read so much more. So before going into the Holocaust Museum, I knew a lot about the holocaust. But as I walked through, and saw the thousands of pictures, I had to pick up the pace because it was wearing on me emotionally, and suddenly I stopped in front of one picture which showed one of the German hierarchy who helped engineer "the final solution." His name, though not being the same individual, was identical to a name I knew well, "Dr. Martin Luther." Of course he was not the reformer of the sixteenth century, but a Nazi officer of the 1940s. This "Dr. Martin Luther" represented the Foreign Ministry at the Wannsee Conference, which was convened in order to work out the details of the "Final Solution to the Jewish Question." I immediately broke into tears. I am a Lutheran clergyman, and I felt the weight of the terrible event squarely on my head and shoulders. Our wonderful Israeli guide, Ran Tzabar, put his arm around my shoulder and said, "Ed, you're not responsible." It was a great comfort, but it only eased the pain a little. Oh? Read again what Jesus said, "You say, 'If we had lived in the days of our ancestors, we would not have taken part with them in shedding the blood of the prophets.' Thus you testify against yourselves that you are descendants of those who murdered the prophets" (v. 30).

I cannot be convinced that these "woes" pertain just to the Pharisees. Once, when I told some people that these are aimed right at us, they became very angry at me. Oh, yes, they are! Read the whole section over and over again and if you don't see yourself reflected in them, you *are* a "blind guide."

These verses are Jesus' most devastating criticisms of piety. As I've said, piety is an attempt to show God how religious, or faithful we are. Yes, they display reverence, but Yahweh has said over and over again in the Hebrew Scriptures, and Jesus has shown time and time again, that God does not need a public display of obeisance to indicate our level of faith:

Part Two: Moving Beyond Christian Folk Religion

> I hate, I despise your festivals,
> and I take no delight in your solemn assemblies.
> Even though you offer me your burnt offering and grain offerings,
> I will not accept them; . . .
> Take away from me the noise of your songs;
> I will not listen to the melody of your harps,
> But let justice roll down like waters,
> and righteousness like an ever-flowing stream. (Amos 5:21–24)

Early on Jesus revealed that he was neither ascetic, nor pious. Speaking of the Baptizer, Jesus declares that John "came neither eating nor drinking, and they say, 'He has a demon'; the Son of Man came eating and drinking, and they say, 'Look, a glutton and a drunkard, a friend of tax collectors and sinners!' Yet wisdom is vindicated by her deeds" (Matt 11:18–19). John, an ascetic, regularly fasted and was accused of being possessed, while Jesus, on the other hand, was just the opposite, he loved to dine with others, eating and drinking wine, and because his eating companions often included persons of lesser status than those who judged him, they called him a drunkard and a glutton who dines with the riffraff of society—"tax collectors and sinners."

In the Sermon on the Mount Jesus told his hearers, "Unless your righteousness exceeds that of the scribes and Pharisees, you will never enter the kingdom of heaven" (Matt 5:20). Of course to reach those standards is impossible, however, Jesus was affirming something that he implies throughout his ministry, and that is that piety is not the sign of righteousness, as he expresses in the well-known parable of the Pharisee and the tax collector. He told it "to some who trusted in themselves that they were righteous and regarded others with contempt" (Luke 18:9–14). These "some," who considered themselves "righteous," were probably not Pharisees or they would have been identified as such, but rather some of the other pious people who surrounded him:

> Two men went up to the temple to pray, one a Pharisee and the other a tax collector. The Pharisee, standing by himself, was praying thus, 'God, I thank you that I am not like other people; thieves, rogues, adulterers, or even like this tax collector. I fast twice a week; I give a tenth of all my income.' But the tax collector, standing far off, would not even look up to heaven, but was beating his breast and saying, 'God, be merciful to me, a sinner!' I tell you, this man went down to his home justified rather than the other; for all who exalt themselves will be humbled, but all who humble themselves will be exalted.

Quiet Piety

Both of these men were pious, but note the differences between them. The Pharisee, stands aside "by himself" and prays (the KJV says that he "prayed thus *with himself*"—an interesting choice of words), while the tax collector, also standing "would not even look up to heaven." This last additional phrase describing the tax collector implies that the Pharisee *was* looking heavenward. The contrast in posture is markedly different. The Pharisee was praying in the expected posture for prayer, while the tax collector simply couldn't. The Pharisee's prayer was a prayer informing God of his righteousness before heaven and of his status within the religious community. The tax collector was, instead, full of remorse, pleading for forgiveness. This does not necessarily mean that the tax collector was wicked, but that he was a sinner in the eyes of God, just as everyone sins. These are stark images of genuine piety (the tax collector) who stands before God simply as he is, seeking forgiveness and redemption for his failure to live up to God's standard, while the Pharisee, who's piety is false (even though its display is "proper") is proudly reminding God that he *does* live up to the standard required of such a "spiritual" man.

There is no better illustration in scripture of the marked contrast between the two types of piety. There is no indication that Jesus was ever anti-Pharisee, but there is every indication that the external show of piety because it's "proper," or "expected" is not acceptable in God's eyes. The extreme conservatism of the religious elite was not what God wanted. In a few minutes we're going to see how the relatively liberal actions of Jesus trump those of the religious elite. But first it is important that we turn again to the Hebrew Bible where piety is harshly criticized because it often does not come from the heart. Piety is a major theme in the writings of the prophets. Perhaps the most telling of the passages is in Amos 5:18–24 where Yahweh asks why Israel is so desirous for "the day of Yahweh" to come (compare this with the modern high expectation of the conservative right for the Second Coming of Christ). God tells Amos that the "day of Yahweh," will be a day of judgment that "is darkness, not light" and there is only "gloom with no brightness in it." He goes on then and declares the passage I just quoted above before the parable of the Pharisee and tax collector. Look again at that passage.

The prophet Amos says that worship, in whatever form, is not acceptable, and will not even be heard, unless it is accompanied by justice and righteousness. The prescription for justice and righteousness is in the summary of the law as given by Jesus when he was asked what the greatest commandment is, and he replied, "'You shall love the Lord your God with all your heart, and with all your soul, and with all your mind.' This is the greatest and first commandment. And the second is like it: 'You shall love your neighbor as yourself.' On these two commandments hang all the law and the prophets" (Matt 22:36–40; Mark 12:30–31; Luke 10:27; cf. John 13:34; 15:12). The Pharisee in the above parable obviously did not abide by the second great commandment to "love your neighbor as yourself," while the tax collector obviously obeyed the first great commandment to love God with his heart, soul, and mind. He loved him so much he could not even look heavenward, but cast his eyes downward and pled for mercy.

The same theme, spoken by Amos against the empty piety of their worship, is echoed by the prophet Micah, a near contemporary of Amos (eighth century BC):

> With what shall I come before Yahweh,
> and bow myself before God on high?
> Shall I come before him with burnt offerings, with calves a year old?
> Will Yahweh be pleased with thousands of rams,
> with ten thousands of rivers of oil?
> Shall I give my firstborn for my transgression,
> the fruit of my body for the sin of my soul?
> He has told you, O mortal, what is good;
> and what does Yahweh require of you
> but to do justice, and to love kindness,
> and to walk humbly with your God? (Micah 6:6–8)

This second example could well be the prayer of the tax collector in the parable. How can he even appear before God? There is nothing he can do for the sins of his soul except plead for mercy. But the answer of what is acceptable above any act of piety is this: "to do justice, and to love kindness and to walk humbly with your God." With downcast eyes, and thumping his chest begging for mercy, there is no better description of someone who walks "humbly" with his God than the tax collector. It is for this reason more than any other that Jesus said "this man went down to his home justified rather than the other." Here "justified" (Gk. *dikaioo*) is synonymous with "righteous" (*dikaios*).

JESUS' PRAYERS IN SECRET

One of the most baffling characteristics noted in Jesus' non-pietistic style is the fact that he suggested we must do many things "in secret." For instance, in the Sermon on the Mount he advises his hearers that when they

> give alms, do not sound a trumpet before you, as the hypocrites do in the synagogues and in the streets (this may well be a hyperbole to make a point, rather than an actual practice), so that they may be praised by others. Truly I tell you, they have received their reward. But when you give alms, do not let your left hand know what your right hand is doing, so that your alms may be done in secret; and your Father who sees in secret will reward you.
>
> And whenever you pray, do not be like the hypocrites; for they love to stand and pray in the synagogues and at the street corners, so that they may be seen by others. Truly I tell you, they have received their reward. But whenever you pray, go into your room and shut the door and pray to your Father who is in secret; and your Father who sees in secret will reward you. (Matt 6:2–6)

One of the largest Christian relief organizations in the world is Lutheran World Relief. They have a policy that goods delivered to the organization for distribution worldwide must not have any religious symbols of any sort, such as crosses, or bible verses, or the popular Christian symbol of the outline of a fish, or symbols of the trinity, etc. One time a lady asked me why, when women make quilts for LWR they can't have any symbols on them. The answer is that Christian relief organizations should be exactly that, for relief, not for conversion. A quilt with a cross on it might seem harmless for the giver, but offensive to a Muslim who is receiving it because he or she is simply cold and needs a blanket. This is simple relief, not evangelization. This is the "secret" Jesus is talking about.

There is no record of Jesus ever praying in public. He taught his hearers *how* to pray such as when he gave "the Our Father" as an example of prayer. But it was not Jesus' own prayer (to call it "The Lord's Prayer" is really a misnomer), it was the Disciple's Prayer, because it was given to them. Jesus always sought privacy when he prayed, as explained in Mark 1:35, "In the morning, while it was still very dark, he got up and went out to a deserted place, and there he prayed." He found such a "deserted place" that Simon Peter, along with other disciples, had to go searching for him (v. 36). At another time, after numerous healings, crowds

Part Two: Moving Beyond Christian Folk Religion

gathered around him to be cured, "but he would withdraw to deserted places and pray" (Luke 5:16).

There is one occasion in which Jesus utters a "somewhat" prayer in Matthew 11:25 and Luke 10:21–22 but it is really a declaration of thanksgiving to God rather than a prayer. In neither Matthew nor Luke is it called a prayer. In both cases the gospel writer says simply that "Jesus said." This is the declaration: "I thank you, Father, Lord of heaven and earth, because you have hidden these things from the wise and intelligent and revealed them to infants . . ." Note the phrase "you have *hidden* these things." There is much about the kingdom of God which has been hidden via the riddles of so many of Jesus' parables, the reason he healed, etc. In Mark 4:33–34 we are told that the parables were mainly riddles, "With many such parables he spoke the word to them, as they were able to hear it; he did not speak to them except in parables, but he explained everything *in private* to his disciples." Similarly, in Luke 10:23–24, in "turning to the disciples, Jesus' said to them privately, 'Blessed are the eyes that see what you see! For I tell you that many prophets and kings desired to see what you see, but did not see it, and to hear what you hear, but did not hear it.'"

At his last supper, Jesus told Simon Peter, "I have prayed for you (obviously in secret) that your own faith may not fail" (Luke 22:32), and this was the night before Peter denied three times even knowing who Jesus was! In John's chapter 17 Jesus' prayer, often called "The High Priestly Prayer," is the longest of Jesus' prayers ever recorded, but it was in the midst of the intimate last meal with his disciples, presumably *all* his disciples, not just the twelve. There were probably a good number of women there: Mary Magdalene, Joanna, Susanna, and many others (cf. Luke 8:1–3). There was probably a cadre of men also there, who were disciples in addition to the twelve. The "Upper Room" was most likely full for this great Passover feast. Most of them likely witnessed the crucifixion—the notable absences were most of the twelve. Judas Iscariot had withdrawn and committed suicide, and, of course, was not there. Only the "disciple whom he loved" was at the foot of the cross (John 19:26). We don't know who that was. It is a long held mystery never adequately solved. It is assumed that he was one of the twelve, but we don't even know that for sure.

Jesus' most grievous prayer was the prayer in Gethsemane. It should be noted that the gospels at no time call it the "Garden of Gethsemane." The synoptic gospels simply refer to it as a "place called Gethsemane" (Matt 26:36; Mark 14:32), or as Luke says he went, "as was his custom, to the Mount of Olives; and the disciples followed him. When he reached

Quiet Piety

the place . . . he withdrew from them about a stone's throw, knelt down, and prayed" (22:39–41). John just says that "he went out with his disciples across the Kidron valley to a place where there was a garden (Gk. *kepos*), which he and his disciples entered" (18:1). The Mount of Olives is a cultivated land of olive trees (a *kepos*), not a garden of fruits and vegetables, and is legitimately called a *kepos*. Below the Mount of Olives is a cave which once held an olive press, and the word "Gethsemane" means "olive press." Its location has been authenticated by archaeologists[3] and today under a prominent sign, reading "Gethsemane," is the entrance to that cave. Inside a worship site has been established where pilgrims from around the world go to worship. Joan Taylor in her excellent article, "The Garden of Gethsemane," says that "the Cave of Gethsemane . . . is very probably the genuine Biblical site—the location of Jesus' arrest."[4] It is believed by scholars today that Jesus and his disciples probably rented the cave with its olive press as a place to sleep out of sight and hearing of the crowds of pilgrims swarming through Jerusalem during the Passover season. Passover was a time when Jerusalem was so overcrowded with pilgrims any place where lodgers could stay was used. Many of the poorer slept on the streets, and in graveyards, such as the one at the base of the Mount of Olives, and a cave would be highly sought out for lodging as it protected pilgrims from the weather, and also could be guarded as protection against roving bandits and wild animals. Even today hyenas have been seen among the grave stones below the Mount of Olives by archaeologists working there. We know that Peter was armed with a sword while keeping watch (John 18:10; cf. Mark 14:47). The Gethsemane cave is now most certainly the "place called Gethsemane" where Jesus withdrew "about a stone's throw" from his most intimate threesome, Peter, James and John, whom he asked to stand guard for him while he prayed. They apparently blocked the entrance to the cave, giving him his private time. The prayer vigil lasted for an extended period, but more than an hour, yet the prayer is his shortest prayer ever recorded, "My Father, if it is possible, let this cup pass from me; yet not what I want but what you want" (Matt 26:39). Twice during his time of prayer he came back and found his most trusted friends sleeping and he chastised them for it. Three times he repeated that prayer, but the rest of the time he was listening for the reply. When he heard it (the answer of God was a definite "no") the prayer time was over. But it was in secret.

3. Taylor, "The Garden of Gethsemane," 116–27.
4. Ibid., 116.

Part Two: Moving Beyond Christian Folk Religion

On many occasions I have told classes that it is my policy never to pray in public places, even before meals in restaurants, because of Jesus' stern warning *not* to pray in public "so that they may be seen by others." Every time I have told others that, they are shocked. Their usual response is that Jesus was only talking about the "self-righteous," not the devout who simply want to give God thanks. Isn't that always the way it is? Jesus' criticism must be aimed at "those other people because *I'm* doing it out of my great devotion." And Jesus, as forceful as he is, could never be taking about *us*! But Jesus' actions tell otherwise. His example is one of private, and secret, prayer. He does not forbid us from giving thanks, but it is done "in secret" with no outward sign that it a prayer is even being said. Yes, I pray before meals with my family—at home. I also thank God for my meal in public, but with no outward sign that I am doing so.

We often say that we are "blessing the food" before the meal, but nowhere in scriptures is a "blessing" a prayer. Our prayers before meals are usually true prayers, giving thanks for the food, and praying that it will provide substance for your bodies that we might have the strength to serve God. A blessing, on the other hand, is a dedication of something to God, pronouncing God's blessing on it. When Jesus miraculously fed the multitude (Matt 14:13–21; Mark 6:30–44; Luke 9:10–17; John 6:1–13; cf. Mark 8:1–10) he "looked up to heaven, and blessed and broke the loaves" (Matt 14:19), but this was pronouncing a blessing of dedication to God, not a prayer. In fact, immediately following the feeding he got into a boat and crossed the Sea of Galilee to the other side, "and after he had *dismissed the crowds*, he went up the mountain by himself to pray" (Matt 14:23), and he remained there alone into the night.

JESUS ORDERS HIS HEALINGS BE KEPT SECRET

In Matthew (12:9–21) Jesus heals a man with a withered hand on the Sabbath, but when the healing was completed, some Pharisees took offense that it was performed on the Sabbath day, and in a synagogue at that. And, Matthew says, "The Pharisees went out and conspired against him, how to destroy him." Matthew then goes on to say that "when Jesus became aware of this, he departed. Many crowds followed him, and he cured all of them, and *he ordered them not to make him known* [italics mine]. This was to fulfill what had been spoken through the prophet Isaiah:[5]

---

5. 42:1–4, 9

> Here is my servant, whom I have chosen,
> my beloved with whom my soul is well pleased.
> I will put my Spirit upon him, and he will proclaim justice to
> the Gentiles.
> He will not wrangle or cry aloud, nor will anyone hear his voice
> in the streets.
> He will not break a bruised reed or quench a smoldering wick
> until he brings justice to victory.
> And in his name the Gentiles will hope."

This is exactly the opposite of what the religious elite did. The Sadducees, Pharisees, and the scribes were proud of their piety. They wanted the whole of Israel to see how religious and righteous they were. The vast majority of Israel's population were peasantry or of the artisan class. Jesus being a skilled *tekton*, a builder, he was a member of the artisan class, but just a small step above a peasant, barely able to eke out a living for himself. The members of these lower classes could not afford to be pious. They could not afford, for instance, the "luxury" of doing nothing on the Sabbath, as the religious elite were all too obliging to point out, i.e., they were the "sinners" so often denigrated by the scribes and Pharisees accusing Jesus of eating "with tax collectors and sinners," which included all of his twelve disciples. Matthew was a tax collector. The rest were artisans (the four fishermen), peasants, or perhaps even terrorists. In comparing his "non-pious" demeanor with that of the religious elite, he told his followers: "Come to me, all you that are weary and are carrying heavy burdens and I will give you rest. Take my yoke upon you, and *learn from me* [italics mine]; for I am gentile and humble at heart, and you will find rest for your souls. For my yoke is easy, and my burden is light" (Matt 10:28–30).

In healing on the Sabbath Jesus illustrated just how pragmatic he was. In Matt 12:1–8, Jesus' disciples began to pluck grains of wheat on the Sabbath because they were hungry, and the Pharisees called them on it, but then Jesus tells them how King David, when he was hungry, actually entered the temple and ate "the bread of the Presence" there, which was only to be eaten by the priests! He also reminded them that temple priests constantly break the Sabbath laws when they conduct sacrifices on the Sabbath, yet *they* are guiltless! And in Mark's version of the story (2:27), he reminds his detractors that "the sabbath was made for humankind, and not humankind for the sabbath."

Because of incidents like the one above, many of Jesus' healings were to remain private affairs between Jesus and the person cured. In Matthew

9:30, after he had restored the sight of two blind men, he "sternly ordered them, 'See that no one knows of this,'" but as would usually happen, "they went away and spread the news about him throughout the district" (v. 31). In Mark 1:40–45 (see also its parallel in Luke 5:12–15) he healed a leper (a common biblical term used for just about anyone with a skin disease of any kind) who begged him for healing, and with just a touch of his hand was made clean. Being "unclean" had nothing to do with hygiene, but was the classification for those who are ritually "unclean" by Jewish law, and being declared "unclean" meant that they did not have access to the temple, or even the synagogues. Thus, they were cut off from the worship of God, the very thing Jesus accused the Pharisees of doing when he told them they "lock people out of the kingdom of heaven [God]" (Matt 23:13). When the man with a skin disease was healed Jesus "sternly" warned him, "See that you say nothing to anyone; but go, show yourself to the priest [so the priest could certify the healing], and offer for your cleansing what Moses commanded," but again the man "went out and began to proclaim it freely, and to spread the word, so that Jesus could no longer go into a town openly, but stayed out in the country; and people came to him from every quarter." Note this massive rush of people to Jesus despite his order to "say nothing to anyone." In Luke's version in verses 15–16 he also adds that the crowd was so large "to hear him and to be cured of their diseases" that "he would withdraw to deserted places and pray." This seems to indicate that not everyone who came to him to be healed was necessarily cured by him. Luke implies that at times he needed solitude in "deserted places" to pray.

Jesus' request for anonymity is in keeping with his desire not to be deluged by people seeking healing, giving further credence to the belief that his healing miracles where not performed simply out of his compassion for the victims of disease, but had a much more profound reason. He was beginning the renewal of the earth and mankind as the kingdom of God is inaugurated:

> The blind receive their sight,
> the lame walk,
> the lepers are cleansed,
> the dead are raised,
> and the poor have good news brought to them. (Matt 11:4–5)

In John's gospel (5:1–16) there is another story of Jesus healing a man lying by the pool called Bethzatha, where there "lay many invalids–blind,

Quiet Piety

lame, and paralyzed." One man who lay with the sick, we are told, had been ill for thirty-eight years. The man could find no one who would pick him up and put him in the pool, hoping the healing waters of the *Miq'vah* might heal him. With that Jesus said to him, "Stand up, take your mat and walk" (v. 7) and the man was immediately cured. But then, a curious thing happened, Jesus just simply walked through the crowd and disappeared from sight, and the man had no idea who he was. Later, Jesus came up to him in the temple and identified himself as the healer. In this case, Jesus healed one man among the "many invalids," but did not warn him not to tell anyone about the healing, but simply walked away through the crowd, anonymously. The man apparently knew to go to the priest in the temple to be certified that he was "clean," and that's where Jesus met him and revealed himself to him.

Jesus had a mission, and he kept to that mission. He was not one whose religion was easily recognized by acts of piety, special clothing, preaching on the street, or praying before the masses. He kept fairly private, yet his fame spread like wildfire, especially his healing miracles. He did not shout warnings like John the Baptizer, or many of the earlier prophets of ancient Israel, but rather stood with his feet firmly grounded. God was not an "idea" for him, but a deep relationship. That deep relationship was so intense he could even scream out in agony from the cross, "My God, my God, why have you abandoned me?" He was never afraid of offending his Father who sent him, or even those who heard him cry out. He also never felt he had to go through proper religious rituals or actions to gain God's favor or the people around him. The laws of God were not legal loads which became burdens too heavy for people to bear. They were part of a lifestyle which simply was lived for a relationship with God. However, simple non-piety *was* offensive to the religious elite, although it was not the primary cause of the plot to murder him. It is now time to consider that plot.

10

Power and Glory

IF YOU WERE TO ask most Christians what Jesus meant when he declared that the Son of Man will come "on the clouds of heaven with power and great glory" (Matt 24:30; Mark 13:26; 14:62) they would respond that he is speaking of his Second Coming, but they would only be partly right. The power and glory of the Son of Man was witnessed long before the *Parousia* (Gr. which means "return"), or Second Coming, an event sometime in the future. At another time Jesus told his hearers that the Son of Man will come "in the glory of his Father" and that "there are some standing here who will not taste death until they see that the kingdom of God has come with power" (Matt 8:38–9:1). Clearly the coming of the Son of Man and the inauguration of the kingdom coming "with power" were immanent events which all humankind would witness within their lifetime. It is those events to which we now turn our attention.

THE JOURNEY "UP" TO JERUSALEM

Most of Jesus' ministry was conducted near or around the Sea of Galilee, which is in the north of Palestine, and for a while he took his disciples even farther north to areas that are today in southern Lebanon. But Luke (9:51; cf. Matt 20:18; Mark 10:33) tells us that there came a point when "he set his face to go to Jerusalem." With that determination they began their journey to the south, about 85 miles, almost a week's journey, toward Judea, and the capital city, Jerusalem. It was a necessary trip because only it would satisfy the journey that culminates the ministry of the Son of Man. It was the journey to his ultimate destination, the temple situated high on Temple Mount. The temple was the House of God. It was the dwelling place and the throne room of Yahweh, God of creation, and God of Israel, God of Abraham, Isaac and Jacob. It was also the primary destination of the Son of Man, the heavenly High Priest, who was the intermediary between Yahweh and his people. The High Priest Son of Man would there present the ultimate sacrifice for the sins of all people, living and dead, both now and forever. And so Jesus and his followers trudged southward and "up" to Jerusalem, through the region of Samaria, and on into Judea "because it is impossible for a prophet to be killed outside of Jerusalem" (Luke 13:33). And as they came within sight of the great city, with its gleaming marble temple dominating the city, Jesus wept at the sight and lamented, "Jerusalem, Jerusalem, the city that kills the prophets and stones those who were sent to it! How often have I desired to gather your children together as a hen gathers her brood under her wings, and you were not willing!" (Luke 13:34). N.T. Wright paints a clear picture of the scene when he tells us that if "we study the city-plan of ancient Jerusalem, the significance of the Temple stands out at once, since it occupies a phenomenally large portion (about 25%) of the entire city ... It was not so much a city with a temple in it; more like a temple with a small city around it."[1]

It was the destination the Son of Man had to make from the very beginning. Everything else was a prelude to this moment. It would be the climax of the story of Israel.[2] Jesus had all along told his disciples that this moment would come (Matt 16:21; 17:22–23; 20:17–19; Mark 10:33–34; Luke 18:31–34), and at last it had. And so he rode on the back of a donkey into Jerusalem, and his destination.

There are just two times when Jesus was hailed as king by the people of Israel. One, recorded in the gospel of John (6:15), is after Jesus had fed a multitude of "about five thousand" and Jesus knew that the people wanted to "come and take him by force to make him a king," so, we are told, "he withdrew again to the mountain *by himself*" (Italics mine). It is just one more example of Jesus walking away from accolades and seeking

---

1. *The New Testament and the People of God*, 225.
2. Wright, *How God Became King*, 83.

Part Two: Moving Beyond Christian Folk Religion

the solitude of privacy. The second occasion, recorded in all of the synoptic gospels, is this entry into Jerusalem, usually called a "triumphal" entrance. For this brief event he was seated on a donkey just five days before he was crucified (Matt 21:1–11; Mark 11:1–10; Luke 19:28–38). It was the week before the Feast of the Passover, when Jerusalem swelled from about 60,000 people to an estimated 250,000. The pilgrims came from Jesus' own district of Galilee to the north and from cities across northern Africa. We know of a man named Simon, from Cyrene, the capital of the North African Roman provenance of Cyrenaica (modern day Libya), who carried his cross for him (Matt 27:32). And certainly there were many others who came from all over the region, and perhaps as far away as Rome. Undoubtedly there were many from Alexandria, Egypt, a center where many Jewish theologians and philosophers resided. Other pilgrims must have come from towns and villages in the northern provenances of Syria, and towns all across Asia Minor (modern Turkey), where Saul (later Paul) was raised. Many towns there have shown evidences of first century Jewish presence besides the town of Tarsus, Paul's home town.

Every inn and dwelling place in Jerusalem was full during Passover. The festival began on *Shabbat,* the Sabbath, that year. The date of Passover always fell on Nisan 14, according to the Jewish calendar, and in the year 30, its equivalent on our calendar is April 8. Most of the pilgrims arrived a full week before that date. Jesus was crucified on Friday, the day before the Festival of Passover, or April 7, 30. The reason for the early arrival of the pilgrims was: (1) so the pilgrims could find a place to lodge; and (2) they could visit the *Miqva'ot,* baths where Jews could immerse themselves to maintain and/or gain ritual purity, in accordance with religious customs and biblical law. During Jesus' day there were a number of public *Miqva'ot* in Jerusalem: the pools of Siloam (Luke 13:4; John 9:7–11), and Bethzatha (John 5:2, also called Bethesda in some translations). Other pools in Jerusalem, mentioned by the first century Jewish historian, Josephus, are the Amygdalon pool (Tower Pool), near the Jaffa Gate, the Serpent's pool, also near the Jaffa Gate, and the Struthion pool, at the northwest corner of Temple Mount. Another pool, simply called the pool of Israel lay at the eastern end of the northern wall of the Temple Mount. There were no shortage of water installations to accommodate the vast crowds visiting the city during religious festivals, such as Passover and the High Holy Days (the "Days of Awe" in Hebrew) of Rosh Hashanah (Jewish New Year: September/October) and Yom Kippur (the Day of Atonement). The High Holy Days also include the ten days between these last two holidays and are known

Power and Glory

as The Days of Remembrance. Although the Bible does not record Jesus' undergoing his own purification prior to Passover, it is certain that he did so. While not attaining the piety of the scribes, Pharisees and Sadducees, he was a devout Jew who obeyed the letter of the law and would certainly have followed the customs expected before the great festival. There is also no mention in any of the gospels at any time that Jesus' own purity was questioned before entering the temple.

As he drew near the "Golden Gate," on the eastern city wall leading to the temple area, news spread of his arrival, possibly caused by the cheering and shouting of his own disciples. And crowds joined them and led him into Jerusalem shouting (according to Luke 1:38):

> Blessed is the king who comes in the name of the Lord!
> Peace in heaven, and glory in the highest heaven!

This version in Luke of the crowd's shouts echo his version of the angel multitude praising God at Jesus' birth and saying (2:14):

> Glory to God in the highest heaven,
> and on earth among those whom he favors!

It is also quite different from Matthew's version in 21:9:

> Hosanna to the Son of David!
> Blessed is the one who comes in the name of the Lord!
> Hosanna in the highest heaven!

And Mark's version is still another variance (11:9–10):

> Hosanna!
> Blessed is the one who comes in the name of the Lord!
> Blessed is the coming kingdom of our ancestor David!
> Hosanna in the highest heaven!

According to Matthew's account this was to fulfill Zechariah's prophecy (9:9), made about five centuries earlier, who wrote:

> Lo, your king comes to you;
> triumphant and victorious is he,
> humble and riding on a donkey, on a colt, the foal of a donkey.

"Your king," in Zechariah's prophecy, is rendered into "Son of David" by the shouting crowds preceding Jesus as he rode through the gate of Jerusalem's walled city and into the capital city. It is the only time Jesus did not stop the crowds from their exuberance proclaiming him king (Luke

19:39–40). Earlier in John 1:49 Jesus is called "the King of Israel" by Nathaniel, but Jesus dismisses the declaration without responding to it.

During Jesus' trial before Pilate he is accused of *claiming* to be the king of the Jews (which was false), and Jesus never responded to those charges. When Pilate finished interrogating him he presented him to the mob, saying, "Here is your King!" (John 19:14). This time the crowd was angry, and instead of shouting "hosannas," the shouts changed to, "Away with him! Away with him! Crucify him! . . . We have no king but the emperor!" (John 19:15).

This scene of the king coming to town sets the stage for the culmination of Jesus' actual inauguration of the kingdom of God. Jesus never claimed himself to be king. The kingdom of God is *God's* reign. Yahweh, the one true creator God, is monarch of the kingdom over which he reigns. As we have seen above in our study of Jesus as the Son of Man, which he *did* claim for his title, he was claiming to be the "Priest Messiah." It was the primary Messiah of the two Messiahs hoped for in the Dead Sea Scrolls—the Messiah of Aaron (the Priest Messiah) and the Messiah of Israel (the King Messiah). He is the redeemer, forgiver, savior, and intermediary between his Father God and humankind. This is why, just after entering the city, he went, without stopping, into the temple. The temple was the "House of God," where God dwelt with his people. That would be the primary destination for the Son of Man, the Heavenly High Priest.

JESUS IN THE TEMPLE

The temple was unlike any other temple in the ancient world. There was only one temple in Palestine, and it was for the Jews anywhere in the world, and that was located in Jerusalem. It was not the "House of God" in the sense that Christians call their churches that. It was far more than a religious building of worship. The temple in Jerusalem was the center of life for all the Jewish people, wherever they may be. It was the place "where heaven and earth themselves interconnected and overlapped."[3] It was also the power base of Yahweh God, and where his throne was located, in the inner sanctum of the Holy of Holies. That part of the temple no one could *ever* enter, except for one person, the high priest, and that was only on the Day of Atonement, when the high priest would enter the Holy of Holies with the blood of sacrifice for the whole nation. He brought the

3. Ibid., 235–36.

blood in, along with an incense pot letting off clouds of smoke to shield him from the glory of God's presence. In the Hebrew Bible there are stories of people dying because they were caught in brightness of that glory. People always tried to hide themselves from that awe-filled presence. In the Garden of Eden, we are told, Adam and Eve, following their falling to temptation, "heard the sound of Yahweh walking in the garden at the time of the evening breeze, and the man and his wife hid themselves from the presence of Yahweh among the trees of the garden" (Gen 3:8). When Yahweh revealed himself to Moses and identified himself as the God of Abraham, the God of Isaac, and the God of Jacob, "Moses hid his face, for he was afraid to look at God" (Exod 3:6). When the "ark of the testimony" (a.k.a.: "Ark of the Covenant") was made Moses was told that it must be covered by a screen (Exod 40:3), and when it was installed in the tabernacle (the "tent of meeting" which was a temporary "temple" to be used until a permanent house could be built for Yahweh by King Solomon, some 300 years later) a golden altar for incense was to be placed in front of it, and further screened at the entrance of the tabernacle (Exod 40:5). This was such a sacred shrine, it struck fear into the hearts of the enemies of the Israelites. When they were at war with the Philistines the elders of Israel said, "'Let us bring the ark of the covenant of Yahweh here from Shiloh, so that [Yahweh] may come among us and save us from the power of our enemies.' So the people sent to Shiloh, and brought from there the ark of the covenant of Yahweh of hosts, who is enthroned on the cherubim" (1 Sam 4:3–4). When the ark arrives the scene is electric:

> When the ark of the covenant of Yahweh came into the camp, all Israel gave a mighty shout, so that the earth resounded. When the Philistines heard the noise of the shouting, they said, "What does this great shouting in the camp of the Hebrews mean?" When they learned that the ark of Yahweh had come into camp, the Philistines were afraid; for they said, "Gods have come into the camp." They also said, "Woe to us! For nothing like this has happened before. Woe to us! Who can deliver us from the power of these mighty gods?

The ark was considered such a powerful symbol for Israel, its presence almost became synonymous with Yahweh himself. According to Numbers 10:34–35, when the ark was transported (there were rings on each side through which poles were strung for carrying), and the ark was lifted from the ground, Moses would say, "Arise, O Yahweh," and when it would be set down, he would say, "Return, O Yahweh." It was so sacred

Part Two: Moving Beyond Christian Folk Religion

that even inadvertently touching it, to prevent it from falling, could spell death. As the ark was being moved toward Jerusalem by David, it was being transported in a cart, driven by men named Uzzah and Ahio. David and his entire house were celebrating its arrival by dancing and singing, and playing lyres, harps and tambourines. It was a great festival celebration, but then the oxen pulling the cart shook and the ark became unstable, and Uzzah reached out his hand to steady it, but "the anger of Yahweh was kindled against Uzzah; and God struck him there because he reached out his hand to the ark; and he died there beside the ark of God" (2 Sam 6:1–7). David was so frightened by the incident he was afraid to accompany it any further and brought it into a family's house, where it remained for three months. After David learned that the family in whose house it resided received blessings for having it, David decided to bring the ark the rest of the way into "the city of David" (an ancient name for Jerusalem) and set it in place, inside a tent, and he offered sacrifices before it (2 Sam 6:8–19).

When Jesus came into Jerusalem, the original Ark of the Covenant was no longer there. It had disappeared almost 600 years before, when Judea lost its war with the Babylonians, and the elite of its citizenry were taken into exile in Babylonia in 586 BC. But it was still the temple of God, and his dwelling place, with or without the original ark. The temple was, after all, as Wright has said, "the place where heaven and earth themselves interconnected and overlapped"[4] (i.e., it is where heaven and earth meet). Ark or no ark, Yahweh God is there! And Jesus was on his way to meet him there.

When Jesus entered the temple, he did so through the Royal Portico on the south side of the temple complex. It was a beautiful covered portico which was magnificent in its own right. The ceiling was over 50 Roman[5] feet high, held up by 162 columns, and the structure was 600 Roman feet long, which Josephus says was "the largest known in the east at the time." According to Hershel Shanks, the Royal Portico was used for "ad hoc meetings of citizens, settlements of disputes, negotiations of all kinds, banking transactions where Jews from the diaspora exchanged foreign currencies for local ones, payment of the annual half-shekel contributions to the Temple, religious harangues, sales of animals for sacrifice and grain for

---

4. Ibid.

5 The Roman foot was just slightly shorter than an English foot.

meal-offerings."[6] It was here that Jesus encountered the money changers exchanging Roman currency from many different Roman provenances for acceptable temple coinage. Roman coins had an image of the emperor of Rome on its obverse which violated Jewish law where no images of either humans or animals were allowed. Temple currency consisted of Jewish coins with no such depiction. The merchants were also selling sacrificial animals which had been inspected by temple officials and certified to be unblemished and free of any defect which would make them unacceptable for sacrifice. These were legitimate business dealings, serving the needs of long distant travelers who would be unable to bring unblemished sacrifices, and non-acceptable Roman coins to pay the temple tax, or alms for the poor, or other offerings. Jesus' famous attack on these merchants was not because of his disapproval of commercialism within the temple grounds. This area was located well outside of the temple sanctuary. The merchants were not in "the House of God" proper. His attack on them had a far more significant symbolic meaning.

Turning the tables and releasing many of the sacrificial animals (Matt 21:12–27; Mark 11:15; Luke 19:45–46; John 2:13–17) was the symbolic act of the "new" High Priest, Son of Man, overturning the old temple itself, which had been "made with hands," and tearing it down brick by brick, to make ready for a "new" temple, not made with hands in a "new" Jerusalem. It would be a temple ruled by Yahweh himself, and managed by the Son of Man, the heavenly High Priest. It was the dawning of a new day. Jesus, quoting passages from Jeremiah 7:11 and Isaiah 56:7 and declaring, "My house shall be called a house of prayer; but you are making it a den of robbers", was a condemnation of the entire temple cult: its high priest, its chief priests (Sadducees), and its daily functions. Ever since the Hasmonean dynasty in the mid-second century BC the temple had been occupied by high priests and chief priests appointed from the aristocracy and therefore not considered legitimate occupants of the positions. Therefore their functions, rituals, and piety were all unacceptable by God. The temple in Jerusalem had been robbed of its spiritual presence. In a dramatic scene in the prophecy of Ezekiel, Ezekiel claims to have witnessed "the glory of Yahweh" leaving the temple just as exiles were being taken from Jerusalem and transported to Babylon:

6. *Jerusalem's Temple Mount*, 87, 89.

Part Two: Moving Beyond Christian Folk Religion

> As I looked on ... the cherubim were standing on the south side of the house[7] when the man went in; and a cloud filled the inner court.[8] Then the glory of Yahweh rose up from the cherub to the threshold of the house; the house was filled with the cloud, and the court was full of the brightness of the glory of Yahweh ... Then the glory of Yahweh went out from the threshold of the house and stopped above the cherubim. The cherubim lifted up their wings and rose up from the earth in my sight as they went out with the wheels beside them. They stopped at the entrance of the east gate of the house of Yahweh; and the glory of the God of Israel was above them ... And the glory of Yahweh ascended from the middle of the city, and stopped on the mountain east of the city[9]. The spirit lifted me up and brought me a vision by the spirit of God into Chaldea,[10] to the exiles. Then the vision that I had seen left me. (Ezek 10:3–4, 18–19; 11:22–25).

This beautiful scene is the departure of "the glory of Yahweh" from the temple (about 586 BC), hovering over the Mount of Olives, and disappearing from sight. In Ezekiel's vision God has left the temple, Jerusalem, and the People of God, and there is no record of him returning. This is the image the people of Israel have been left with. To this day the daily prayers of the faithful at the Western Wall of the Temple Mount are for the return of "the glory of Yahweh." It is also the reason Jesus symbolically turned the tables of the temple over, throwing down the old temple, and readying it for a "new" temple, not made with hands, which Ezekiel describes towards the end of his prophecy and to which he says "the glory of Yahweh" will return (Ezek 43:2–5).

It is no coincidence that the prophet/priest Ezekiel, in the sixth century BC, is called by Yahweh "son of man" more than ninety times, and six hundred years later, Jesus, "the Son of Man," returns to the temple and symbolically tears it down, to get ready for the "new" temple. It is this "new temple" to which the "glory of Yahweh" will return in the kingdom of God/heaven. Jesus confided to his disciples that one day the beautiful temple they visited would be destroyed and "not one stone will be left here upon another; all will be thrown down" (Matt 24:2; Mark 13:2; Luke 21:6). It *did* happen, just forty years later, on July 29, AD 70, when the Tenth Legion of the Roman army obliterated Jerusalem and its temple.

7 The "house of God"–the temple.
8. ... of the temple—always a "cloud" shielding God's glory.
9. The Mount of Olives.
10. a.k.a. "Babylonia."

It was not just the renewal of the temple that his action on that first Palm Sunday symbolized, but the beginning of the renewal of the whole earth. All the earth, all its creatures, and all of humanity would start a long process of renewal. It was what Jesus had come to do, to establish God's rule on earth, the kingdom of God/heaven. The great palace and dwelling place of Yahweh would be in the "new Jerusalem"(Rev 21:22) and in the new temple not made with hands where the Almighty would reign from his throne room.

> And I heard a loud voice from the throne saying,
> "See, the home of God is among mortals.
> He will dwell with them;
> They will be his peoples,
> And God himself will be with them,
> He will wipe every tear from their eyes.
> Death will be no more;
> Mourning and crying and pain will be no more;
> For the first things have passed away." (Rev 21:3–4)

A new day and a new reality were dawning and it was not welcome news to many in Jerusalem that day.

Jesus' action in the temple did not go unnoticed. Immediately after this remarkable display of anger among the merchants in the temple, Luke (19:47) says, "The chief priests, the scribes, and the leaders of the people kept looking for a way to kill him."

The scene was set for the closing drama which played out in the next five days. Jesus had threatened the very lifeblood of the Judaism of his day. He had claimed, alluding to Daniel's prophesy in 7:13, that he was indeed the "son of man" spoken of by Daniel, that he had been sent, as God's High Priest, to overthrow the religious constabulary and sweep it clean of its corruption and illegitimate religion and establish a new order under the direction of Yahweh. All the chief priests (Sadducees), their scribal lawyers, and the aristocracy of Israel were on notice that their days were numbered.

Following the "cleansing of the temple," Jesus began to teach his disciples a "doomsday" forecast of the coming of the end of days, when the whole world will be in turmoil as God begins an overhaul of the world (Mark 13). He told of times of suffering, persecutions, sacrilege, all occurring over an unspecified time, but which any human in the last two millennia could claim described his/her own time. Thus, there has never been a period when Christians have not been sitting eagerly expecting the Second Coming (*Parousia*) of Christ to be immanent.

Part Two: Moving Beyond Christian Folk Religion

There have always been wars and rumors of wars, persecutions of the faithful, earthquakes, false prophets, and false messiahs. The "desolating sacrilege" spoken of in Mark 13:14–27 perfectly describes the erection of the god Zeus on the temple altar, and the abolition of the practice of the Jewish religion by Seleucid ruler Antiochus IV Epiphany in 167 BC. This is what is spoken of as the "abomination that desolates" in Daniel 11:31 and 12:11. Antiochus was defeated by the Hasmonean son, Judas Maccabeus (a nickname which means "the hammer), and his army of 6000 rebels, and he cleansed and rededicated the temple in December 164 BC. The Jewish holiday of Hanukkah celebrates this rededication. But this had happened almost 200 years *before* Jesus, and he certainly couldn't have meant an event which preceded him. There is, however, a "desolating sacrilege" he might very well have been speaking of. In AD 39–40, the Roman emperor, and madman, Caligula would make plans to set up his own statue in the Jewish temple and force the obstinate Jews, who demanded the right to practice their own religion as *they* saw fit, to cease their privileged religion and join the rest of the world in bowing to Roman's emperor. But the attempt failed when he was assassinated in the year 41. It may very well be the prophecy referred to in Mark 13:14–27 because it is believed the gospel was composed about the year Caligula planned the sacrilege and would have been well remembered by the main source for Mark's gospel, believed by many to be the Apostle, Peter. Mark concludes his doomsday forecast by describing Jesus' *Parousia* (Gr. for "return), or coming again, as "'the Son of Man coming in clouds' with great power and glory" (13:26, Matt 24:30; Luke 21:27).

THE CRUCIFIXION AND RESURRECTION

But this "end of days" (a.k.a. "the end of time" or "the day of the Lord") was an event far into the future. A far more important date with destiny was just days away, and of that coming event Jesus had spoken privately to his disciples on numerous occasions, but being as human as they were, they could not comprehend its significance. A short time earlier, as "they were on the road, going up to Jerusalem, and Jesus was walking ahead of them; . . . He took the twelve aside again and began to tell them what was to happen to them" (Mark 10:32–32). During this teaching session, his two youngest disciples, James and John, the sons of Zebedee, came to him and said to him:

"Teacher, we want you to do for us whatever we ask of you." And he said to them, "What is it you want me to do for you? And they said to him, "Grant us to sit, one at your right hand and one at your left, in your glory." But Jesus said to them, "You do not know what you are asking. Are you able to drink the cup that I drink, or be baptized with the baptism that I am baptized with?" They replied, "We are able." Then Jesus said to them, "The cup that I drink you will drink; and with the baptism with which I am baptized, you will be baptized; but to sit at my right hand or at my left is not mine to grant, but it is for those for whom it has been prepared."(Mark 10:35–40).

In Matthew's version of the story (20:20–23) it is the mother of James and John, traveling with the disciples, who asks the favor of Jesus for her sons, but it is believed that the Markan version is more correct, and that the two teenage boys asked the question directly. Teenagers are often presumptive enough to ask outright what they want. Here they ask for the best seats in the house, when Jesus is in his "glory," with them flanking him in the "seats," or thrones, on either side of him. What they do not understand, related to what he has just told them, is that his coming "glory" is not a reference to his return (*Parousia*), but rather his ultimate destination—the cross!

Jesus, following the direction his constant invisible companion, The Son of Man, methodically prepared for that ultimate day by daily teaching within the temple precincts, probably in the Royal Portico where he first had confronted the merchants. No doubt they were back at their jobs, and Jesus never attacked them again. But Jesus' teachings most likely took place in another part of the 600' long Portico.

I am indebted to N.T. Wright for pointing out that when Jesus said to James and John, "to sit at my right hand or at my left is not mine to grant, but it is for those for whom it has been prepared," it signaled a whole new dimension surrounding the meaning of "glory" for Jesus. Wright says of this response by Jesus:

> The significance of this in our present discussion is massive. For Mark, it is clear that the two brigands on Jesus's right and left as described in 15:27 are the ones to whom "it's been assigned already." But that means, as we might have concluded from other evidence too, that Jesus' crucifixion is the moment when he becomes king, when, as James and John say, he is "there in all [his]

glory" (10:37). That is the powerful—if deeply paradoxical—"coming of the kingdom" as spoken of in Mark 9:1.[11]

This is a phenomenal re-understanding of the cross itself, and its aftermath. If Wright is correct, and I believe he is, then I think it behooves us to look carefully at Mark 9:1, where Jesus says that "there are some standing here who will not taste death until they see that the kingdom of God has come with power" (cf. also Matt 16:28; Luke 9:27). This statement signals the time limits in which the kingdom of God will be inaugurated. It will happen within their lifetime!

What Jesus is predicting here is that the cross, rather than being an instrument of shame and defeat, when in the hands of God, becomes the instrument of displaying Jesus' greatest glory. Agony, yes; suffering, yes; death, yes; but defeat? No! It is, rather, the utter defeat of death itself, because from that moment on, as Paul says in 1 Cor 15:54–57:

> "Death has been swallowed up in victory."
> "Where, O death, is your victory?"
> "Where, O death, is your sting?"
> The sting of death is sin, and the power of sin is the law. But thanks be to God, who gives us the victory through our Lord Jesus Christ.

The cross displays the victorious Messiah, and is not "the emblem of suffering and shame" as the familiar, and beloved, hymn "The Old Rugged Cross" proclaims. It is, instead, the moment of Jesus' greatest glory, when he utters his last words, "It is finished," and breathes his last. He has completed exactly what God wanted him to do. In Gethsemane Jesus had cried out, "If it is possible, remove this cup from me," and God replied, "I cannot." From the cross Jesus had cried out the first verse of Psalm 22, "My God, my God, why have *you* abandoned me?" And God comforted him and said, "I have not, my Son, I am here suffering *with* you." Two thugs hung beside Jesus, one on each side. Pilate had offered to substitute

---

11. *How God Became King*, 227. Wright uses his own translation of the passage in this selection. I disagree with his statement that "Jesus's crucifixion is the moment when he becomes king" and would, instead, suggest that Jesus does not become king, because, as even Wright's title suggests, it is God who is king, not Jesus. Jesus is "The Son of Man," the heavenly High Priest who at that moment becomes enthroned on the "right hand of God," as described in Daniel 7:13. Wright's book was published before my article on "The Mystery of Jesus' Teaching about the Son of Man" appeared in BTB in May 2012. As of this writing I know of no disagreements of my interpretation that "Son of Man" and "High Priest" are synonymous terms.

a third thug, Barabbas, for Jesus, but the crowd demanded the crucifixion of Jesus instead. Thus, it was the innocent, dying in the place of the guilty, dying *with* the guilty. The brigands hung there in the exact spot where James and John had asked to be, but those places had already been assigned by God himself. While James and John were thinking of regal thrones, the throne on which Jesus "sat" was a cross. When Jesus asked them "Are you able to drink the cup that I drink, or be baptized with the baptism that I am baptized with?" and they said "We are able," Jesus knew they were not yet "able." James, however, was the first to "drink the cup" when he was executed by Herod Agrippa II in 44 (Acts 12:2). What happened to John, reported to be the younger brother of James, and the youngest disciple, is not known. Christian legend says that he is the only disciple never martyred and died somewhere around 100, but there is no confirmation of that.

The cross was Jesus' glory, although the world could not see it. Again we must remember what Isaiah says in 55:8–9:

> For my thoughts are not your thoughts,
> nor are your ways my ways, says Yahweh.
> For as the heavens are higher than the earth,
> so are my ways higher that your ways
> and my thoughts than your thoughts.

Paul echoed this when he wrote to the Corinthians:

> God chose what is foolish in the world to shame the wise; God chose what is weak in the world to shame the strong; God chose what is low and despised in the world, things that are not, to reduce things that are, so that no one might boast in the presence of God. (1 Cor 1:27–29)

And also in 1:18–25:

> For the message about the cross is foolishness to those who are perishing, but to us who are being saved it is the power of God. For it is written,
>
> > "I will destroy the wisdom of the wise,
> > and the discernment of the discerning I will thwart."
>
> Where is the one who is wise? Where is the scribe? Where is the debater of this age? Has not God made foolish the wisdom of the world? For since, in the wisdom of God, the world did not know God through wisdom, God decided, through the foolishness of our proclamation, to save those who believe. For Jews demand

signs and Greeks desire wisdom, but we proclaim Christ crucified, a stumbling block to Jews and foolishness to Gentiles, but to those who are called, both Jews and Greeks, Christ is the power of God and the wisdom of God. For God's foolishness is wiser than human wisdom, and God's weakness is stronger than human strength.

THE RESURRECTION, REFLECTION OF THE GLORY

On the third day following the crucifixion the definitive proof that the power and glory of the coming of the Son of Man had indeed occurred was when, on the first day of the week, while it was still dark, Jesus, Son of Man, had been raised. Only one person was the initial witness to the resurrection, and that was Mary Magdalene who was with Jesus during every crisis at the end of his earthly life.

Mary Magdalene is only mentioned twelve times in the New Testament and in all cases, except one in Luke 8:2, she is only mentioned by name as being at the foot of the cross during Jesus' crucifixion, and at his resurrection. In Luke 8:2, as well as in Matthew 27:56 and Mark 15:41, she is mentioned as one of "many women" who financially supported Jesus' ministry. We know relatively little about her, but she is so important at the end of the gospels we must spend a little time with what we do know about her.

There is no other follower of Jesus who has generated as much interest as Mary Magdalene, and much of it has come from later rumors, myths and legends, especially those found in second to third century non-canonical gospels such as the Gospel of Mary (second century) which claimed to be written *by* Mary Magdalene, however, clearly not by her. This Gnostic gospel has Matthew rebuking Peter for not believing that Mary had a special relationship with Jesus, and then telling Peter, "If the Savior made her worthy, who are you indeed to reject her? Surely the Savior knows her very well. That is why he loved her more than us."[12] Similarly, the Gnostic Gospel of Philip (also second century) says that Jesus loved Mary Magdalene "more than [all] disciples" and used to "kiss her often."[13] While such a provocative statement has caused a lot of speculation, there is absolutely no evidence from the first century

---

12. Robinson, *The Nag Hammadi Library,* 529.
13. Ibid. 148.

to substantiate such a controversial allegation, yet the musical from the 1970s *Jesus Christ Superstar* by Andrew Lloyd Weber and Tim Rice added fuel to an already burning fire of interest in the relation of Mary Magdalene to Jesus. Who can forget the most famous song from the musical when Mary sings of her feelings for Jesus?:

> I don't know how to love him, what to do, how to move him,
> I've been changed, yes, really changed.
> In these past few days when I've seen myself, I seem like someone else.

In one adult class I taught a few years ago, after mentioning Mary Magdalene, one of the students in the class asked me, "Do you think Jesus and Mary were married to each other?" Many people have speculated on that, and just a few years ago the novel by Dan Brown, *The Da Vinci Code*, sparked more interest in Mary Magdalene and Jesus. These are all based on legend, gossip, and a lot of mystery surrounding the "hidden" life of Jesus. The short answer to the question of the student is, "no, I am certain they were not married." One reason I can emphatically state I believe that is because first century Palestine was a misogynistic society. Women, for the most part, had little standing within society. In almost all cases women were only identified by their relationship with a man. There are very few women in the gospels, besides Mary Magdalene, who are not identified with a man. Most of the other women are: Mary, who is called, "the mother of Jesus," or "his mother," or "the mother of the Lord"; Joanna "the wife of Herod's steward Chuza" (Luke 8:2); "Mary the mother of James and Joseph" (Matt 27:55; Mark 15: 40; 16:1; Luke 24:10). She is also called simply "the other Mary" in Matthew (27:61 and 28:1); "Mary the wife of Clopas" (John 19:25); "the mother of the sons of Zebedee" Matthew 27:55) who is also believed to be "Salome" who, with the two Mary's brought spices for Jesus' burial. Women who are not linked by name to a man are, Suzanne, mentioned in Luke 8:2, who is never further identified and we know nothing else about her except her name. She is only mentioned as following Jesus along with Mary Magdalene and "many women." "Mary and Martha" were sisters from Bethany and along with their brother, Lazarus, were friends with Jesus. They are sometimes identified by the name of their village, Bethany, or with their brother, Lazarus, who was raised from the dead by Jesus (John 11).

An idea of how misogynistic the world of Jesus and the centuries surrounding him were is even evidenced in the canonical gospels themselves. Contrary to some popular opinions, Jesus was not a social reformer. His mission was not to establish, at that time, and egalitarian society where men and women were equal partners in ruling the affairs of the world. The world would not be ready for that for almost two millennia. No, as Jesus said himself, "Give to the emperor the things that are the emperor's, and to God the things that are God's" (Matt 22:21; Mark 12:17; Luke 20:25). He had come to inaugurate the kingdom of God, not reform society at that time. Jesus' own inner core of twelve disciples were chosen from among only male disciples, without apology. The male twelve were also told that when all things have been renewed, they will be enthroned on twelve thrones, along with the Son of Man on his throne, "judging the twelve tribes of Israel" (Matt 19:28). There is no mention of women in any leadership role, not in the gospels.

Another extreme example of the anti-feminine world in the early centuries is found in the Gnostic Gospel of Thomas (fourth century.), vs. 114, where Simon Peter speaking to Jesus about Mary Magdalene says:

> "Let Mary leave us, for women are not worthy of life." Jesus said, "I myself shall lead her in order to make her male, so that she too may become a living spirit resembling you males. For every woman who will make herself male will enter the kingdom of heaven."

Gnosticism was one of the main heresies threatening Christian orthodoxy in the first four centuries. Sayings such as these illustrate how different their values were from our values. Remember, these stories and shocking statements reflect nothing of the real sayings of Jesus, or the disciples, but they do reflect the world and values of the time. They are important, however, because they show us how high the status of Mary Magdalene had risen, even in the centuries when women were considered almost non-beings of any value.

One thing we can say we know now for a certainty is that Mary Magdalene was *not*, as is commonly thought, a reformed prostitute! There is absolutely no shred of evidence to suggest that she was. This terrible slander on her name arises from an abuse and ignorance of scripture. She is not the "woman in the city, who was a sinner" mentioned in Luke 7, who came to a Pharisee's home where Jesus was dining, and "bathed his feet with her tears", and dried them with her hair. If she had been Mary Magdalene, Luke would have introduced her by name there, but Luke introduces Mary Magdalene in 8:2 as "Mary, called Magdalene" where he also adds that she, along with "many others, provided for them out of their resources." The first time where Mary Magdalene was identified as a reformed "prostitute" was in a sermon made by the leader of the male dominated church. It was so affirmed by none other than Pope Gregory the Great in his Thirty-third Homily in 591. For almost 600 years no one ever thought of her as having been a former prostitute converted by Jesus. Just because Luke says that "seven demons had gone out" of her (8:2) does not signify that she was possessed of evil spirits of any kind. In early Christian literature "demons" could cause many kinds of sicknesses, especially mental illnesses, such as schizophrenia, paranoia, etc. Pope Gregory, who addressed his listeners only as "brothers" (no mention of women), said, "And what did these seven devils signify, if not all the vices?"[14] This is an assumption made in a male's world, where adultery was blamed on women for enticing men into lascivious acts. It was Pope Gregory who essentially invented the idea that Mary was a prostitute, who had been saved from her sinful self, by the male Jesus. From that moment on, Mary, the wealthy woman from Magdala, who, in the second century was thought to be the disciple whom Jesus loved most, was forever slandered—a "prostitute."

What we *do* know about Mary is that she was from the village called Magdala (or, more properly, Migdal) located along the southwest shore of the Sea of Galilee (Matt 15:39). We are told in all of the synoptic gospels that Jesus taught in all the synagogues of Galilee (Matt 4:23; Mark 1:39; Luke 4:15) and recently archaeologists have uncovered the floor of the synagogue in Migdal, which was decorated with beautiful mosaics. It dates from the first century and is most surely the location where he taught, and very probably, one who first heard him there was Mary. Migdal was well known as being a major center where sardines were pickled for the fishing industry. It also apparently had a large watch tower, because "Migdal" means "tower" in Aramaic. In other ancient sources it is known as Migdal Nunya (Tower of Fish).[15] We cannot know whether Mary might have acquired her "resources" from the business of pickling fish to help support Jesus' mission, but Migdal was somewhat of a resort town at the time, and wealth was not unknown there.

Regardless of how she met him, or what drew her to him, Mary accompanied Jesus to Jerusalem, and she was most likely there when he

14. Ehrman, *Peter, Paul, & Mary Magdalene*, 190.
15. Ibid., 197-8.

stormed through the temple, and there as he taught in the temple, and was surely present at his last supper, and with the disciples watching as he withdrew into the bowels of Gethsemane to pray. Mary witnessed his arrest, his conviction to be executed, and was there at the foot of the cross. While the male disciples hid in fear, and Peter denied even knowing him, Mary Magdalene was always there. She led the other women to the tomb to prepare his body for its permanent burial, and heard the declaration that Jesus was not there, he had risen. And she, and she alone, was the first to see the risen Messiah, and the first to be addressed by him as he called her by her name (John 20:11–18). There is every reason to believe that this woman, whom Jesus had cured (Mark 16:9), was perhaps the most important woman in his life near the end of his life, yet she is never again mentioned in the New Testament.

At the foot of the Mount of Olives, just to the east of Jerusalem, and its Temple Mount, is the Russian Orthodox Church of St. Mary Magdalene with its seven golden onion-shaped domes piercing the skyline. Built in 1885 by Tsar Alexander III, it is a fitting and beautifully striking tribute to one lady in Jesus' life who certainly deserves the title "Saint." She was there, not just as the first person to witness the resurrection, but surely the person who most especially was the first of his disciples to witness his "power and glory." She seemed to have constantly been the first. "The first shall be last, and the last shall be first. The twelve were first, but ended up being the last, and Mary was the last and was always there first—at the cross and resurrection.

11

A Few Parting Observations

THE SURVEY WE'VE JUST completed can be disturbing to many. You've been introduced to a new culture, new values, with new logic. These are far different from Western European values where success is measured in what we have, how important we are in social standing, and what seems to us to be "common sense." The image of Jesus seems foreign to our system of logic and what we've been brought up to believe. Things we westerners have focused on were not as important in Near Eastern theology and philosophy as they have seemed to us. The Christian Church, after being Hellenized as it moved into the Greco-Roman sphere of thinking, has taken on that thinking and has spent a lot of time debating issues of barely any concern in the original context of Holy Scripture. We see this reflected in the ancient creeds of the Church, where they plumb the depths of those things which seem of supreme importance to Greco-Roman mind—the divinity of Christ, the virgin birth, orthodox belief, our salvation ensuring our entrance into heaven, the eschaton and the final conflict on earth, and the anticipation of the Second Coming (the *Parousia*) of Christ. These are vital issues for us, but are rarely touched upon within the scriptures themselves. Ancient Israel was not fixed on what happens to them after they die. They were, however, vitally concerned with how to live lives pleasing to the creator God, Yahweh. They were concerned about their ancestral heritage as the People of God. The prophets consistently brought them back to reality by emphasizing their

Part Two: Moving Beyond Christian Folk Religion

weaknesses and what they must do to reform their lives. This also was the message of John the Baptizer who told them that his mission was to prepare "the way" for the one to follow, who would begin the renewal of all things. That's was Jesus' primary mission. His body was cleansed and purified by baptism in the running waters of the Jordan River. He faced temptation just as we face daily, and he shunned them all. He was then ready to begin the process of the renewal of all things, and ultimately to inaugurate the kingdom of God. This was accomplished on the cross and his task was complete. Then, in the resurrection he displayed to the entire world the truth that indeed, all things had begun to be new again. His physical body was whole, and immortal. It was a purely Hebrew message, but Greco-Roman thinking powerfully distorted that message.

The early church, steeped in the thinking of its culture, rather than the oriental system of logic was primarily concerned with what the relation is between the Creator God and Jesus Christ. This was important to them as spurious groups began to develop that threatened the traditional understanding of the nature of the person of Christ. Docetism, for instance, claimed that Jesus just appeared to be human and that his suffering was not real. Another variation was what became known as Nestorianism, after the teachings of Nestorius (ca 351–451), Patriarch of Constantinople, who believed that there were two separate persons in the Incarnate Christ, one Divine and one human, compared with the orthodox teaching that Christ was a single person, both God and man. The Greco-Roman mind tried to figure out the Divine Mind. Western logic sought to plumb the depths of the infinite, but that is impossible. However, it became of vital importance to the early church. It was far different than the thinking of Israel. Of primary concern for them was— are there many gods like all the nations around them believed, or one God—Yahweh? The ultimate answer they came to believe was that there was one God, and one alone, and he was the God who revealed himself to *them* and he was *their* God and theirs alone, Yahweh, God of their ancestors, who created heaven and earth. Whether this is true, or how this came about is never debated in the Hebrew Scriptures, it is simply stated as accepted truth, by the whole people of Israel. Yet the Greco-Roman mind had to determine how this could be. And so the debates raged on about *how* Jesus related to the Father, and how "really" human he was. And for three hundred years church leaders argued until a semblance of agreement was reached and finally creeds were developed to espouse the "orthodox" positions against the "heretics" who took up opposing

A Few Parting Observations

positions. Because the Apostle's Creed was not specific enough to define the nature of Christ, the Nicene Creed was formulated to specifically answer that question. Its definitive statement was issued in 325 by the Council of Nicaea. The Nicene Creed decided that Jesus is "God from God, Light from Light, true God from true God, begotten, not made, of one Being with the Father."

Perhaps the author of Psalm 2:4–8 summed up these debates when he wrote:

> He who sits in the heavens laughs;
> Yahweh has them in derision
> Then he will speak to them in his wrath,
> and terrify them in his fury saying,
> "I have set my king on Zion, my holy hill."
> I will tell of the decree of Yahweh:
> He said to me, "You are my son;
> Today I have begotten you,
> Ask of me, and I will make the nations your heritage,
> and the ends of the earth your possession.

What more do we need to know? "I have set my king on Zion, my holy hill." For Yahweh God that is that—that is the truth of the matter. Why do our Western minds have to know, "How can that be?" "You are my son," he said, "Today I have begotten you." Those are the facts, he has said, don't debate the reality.

The gospels, on the other hand, were not concerned with these issues. The problem with both of the major creeds is that neither of them addresses Jesus' primary concern, which was the establishment of the kingdom of God. There is also no mention of the mission of "the Son of Man," or the collective salvation of humanity rather than individual salvation. These are all part and parcel of a new reality, and Jesus himself introduced us to that new reality. The Prophet Isaiah tells us in 55:8–9:

> My thoughts are not your thoughts,
> nor are your ways my ways, says Yahweh.
> For as the heavens are higher than the earth,
> so are my ways higher than your ways
> and my thoughts than your thoughts.

It was into *that* world that Jesus came and ministered. His culture, values, logic, and thought processes were all Near Eastern. He was bound to the land of Israel and its people and he fit in its world of religious traditions, history, prophecy, and writings. It should not come as a shock then that his message to the twelve disciples was to go only "to the lost sheep of the house of Israel" (Matt 10:6), which he later also reiterated for himself, "I was sent only to the lost sheep of the house of Israel," (Matt 15: 24). It also should not shock the western mind that he compared a Canaanite woman and her daughter to "dogs" (Matt 15: 26; Mark 7:27). He again repeated the theme that his message was for Israel alone when he told the twelve disciples that they would one day "sit on twelve thrones, judging the twelve tribes of Israel" (Matt 19:28).

There is perhaps no better model for a first century Israelite than Jesus himself, and yet there is much in him that surprises us. He likened himself to the prophets of old (Matt 10:41; 15:57; Mark 6:4; Luke 4:24; John 4:44), as did people who came to him (Matt 14:5; 21:11, 46; Mark 6:15; Luke 1:76; 7:16; 24:19; John 4:19; 6:14; 7:40, 52; 9:17), yet in so many ways he was unlike the prophets before him. Just a quick scan or reading through the writings of the prophets and it becomes obvious that Jesus' message to his audience was different from those who preceded him. The prophets were bent on chastising the people of Israel for falling short of the expectations of Yahweh. They were flirting with Canaanite gods and goddesses, and falling away from their faith in the one and only true God of Israel. Because of this sin God was punishing them, the prophets warned, and had consigned them to two exiles, one in Assyria in the eighth century BC, and the other in the sixth century, in Babylon. None of this chastisement appears in the teachings of Jesus. He was more concerned with the excesses of the very religious, which he believed laid a burden on the common people that they were incapable of bearing (Matt 11:30; Acts 15:28). He emphasized that the Sabbath rest should not also become an additional burden, for "the sabbath was made for humankind, and not humankind for the sabbath," and then he added, "the Son of Man is even lord of the sabbath" (Mark 2:26–27). This understanding for Jesus dovetailed with his argument against the religious establishment that while Sabbath work violates the spirit of the Sabbath, doing good does not. To heal, to save a life, or to rescue an animal upon which a family relies for its living, is not work, it is loving kindness.

Jesus was not among the religious elite. He was firmly grounded in the here and now. His teaching moments were always focused on the practical, and the illustrations he used in his parables and riddles illustrated the plight of the common people around him: their lives, and their concerns. As such he distanced himself from the officials of religious

A Few Parting Observations

orthodoxy and he became their target whom they thought was not religious enough. He was scolded for not keeping the Sabbath day properly "holy," and for not choosing appropriate people with whom to associate. They chastised him for "eating with tax collectors and sinners." His healings and miracles were often interpreted by the religious authorities as indicating a pact he had with "Beelzebub" (Matt 12:24; Mark 3:22; Luke 11:15), rather than his being a man of compassion, empathy who in the process is renewing the earth where sin, sickness, scorn, and deficiency will be no more—all signs of the coming kingdom.

Perhaps one of the most startling discoveries is that Jesus was not considered a pious man. He did not pray in public, and though we are told he visited all the synagogues in the region of Galilee, we do not know if he just worshiped in them or if he taught there, or if they became meeting places where he could simply interact with the locals, and perhaps heal some of them. We only have a record of his actually taking a leadership role in one synagogue, in his home town of Nazareth, where he read from Isaiah, and then his former friends and townspeople turned on him for appearing to them to claim an authority with a wisdom and a power above that of a local boy, the "son of Joseph," and "they took offense at him" (Mark 6:1–6).

Contrary to the priests of his day, or the religious authorities, most notably the Pharisees, his religion was carried out in private, where he prayed and communicated with his Father in heaven. His most profound religious insights were often shared only with his most intimate of friends, his disciples. It is with them, and often with them alone, that he interpreted the inner meanings of the riddles he told the crowds at large, and to the crowds themselves he simply said, "He who has ears to hear, let him hear" (Matt 11:15; 13:9, 43; Mark 4:9, 23; 7:16; 8:18; Luke 14:35). His final meal, the Passover *Seder*, was a private meal with his disciples, not with any kind of assembled worshiping congregation. Indeed, he had no worshiping congregation. Crowds came, followed him and then went on with their lives. There is no indication that he ever had any kind of congregating, or worshiping community. We know of no instance, even during the Passover festival, when Jesus actually brought sacrifices to the temple, or even went to pray in the Court of Israel, which was next to the sanctuary of the temple itself.

In many ways, although he was intensely public, he was also intensely private in his religious life. This religious privacy was often the source of criticism against him by the pious authorities. They demanded to know where his authority came from, and when they asked him if he claimed to be the Messiah, he was silent. He did, however, openly claim to be "the Son of Man," yet most people had no idea what that meant. Apparently it was only the chief priests, and especially the high priest, who knew the meaning of "the Son of Man," because when called himself that, the high priest cried "Blasphemy!" and called for his death. Jesus had claimed to be the heavenly high priest, prophesied by Daniel. Caiaphas knew it, and would not countenance a usurper to his position, especially one who boldly claimed to be "heavenly." Even the leaders of the early church were baffled by "the Son of Man" claim. The Apostle Paul makes no mention of the title.

Paul wrote a lot about Jesus being the Son of God, but not one word about Jesus claiming the title of "the Son of Man," yet Jesus spoke of it more than seventy times. The title "Son of God" was only given to him by other people. It was never a self-claim. There is little wonder, therefore, that, in the first centuries of the church, debates raged over what the title "Son of God," given to him by others, meant. It is still a lively topic in adult class studies. It is worth speculating, however, how the terms "Son of God" and "Son of Man" fit in to our understanding of the Trinity, and/or the Godhead, or the Heavenly Host (Deut 4:19; 17:3; Josh 5:15; 1Kgs 22:19; 2 Kgs 23:4–5; 1 Chr 9:19; 12:22; 2 Chr14:13; 18:18; 33:3; Neh 9:6, etc.). A detailed analysis of such a complicated subject is beyond the scope of this study, but perhaps a simple diagram might be helpful. The early church, of course, studied the issue thoroughly for the better part of three centuries and arrived at the concept of "the Trinity," which is the basis of the great Creeds of the church (Apostle's Creed, Nicene Creed, and Athanasian Creed), but it is still a somewhat primitive understanding. Being a Hellenized understanding by a Gentile church it does not take into consideration a full appreciation or a full understanding of the Hebrew mind. The diagram below is my own, but may be a starting point for further dialogue:

> The Heavenly Host consists of:
> > Father God (Yahweh), who is
> > > Creator God,
> > > Heavenly Father,
> > > The one true God,
> > > King of the Universe,
> > > Everlasting, Almighty, all Powerful, and is present everywhere.

A Few Parting Observations

    Son of God (Yeshua/Jesus), enthroned at Yahweh's right hand. He is
        Yahweh's anointed Messiah,
    Son of Man: "Heavenly High Priest,"
    Savior of mankind,
    Redeemer,
    Atoner for human sins,
    Supreme judge along with Yahweh,
    And serves as an intermediary between Yahweh and humans.
Spirit of God who is
    Imbuer of Yahweh's spirit into the human heart
    Inspiration of God
Wisdom of God, who imparts into us
    The Knowledge of God,
    The Will of God,
    And is our instructor of all things spiritual.
Angelic Host who are
    The Angels of the Lord,
    Who sing God's praises,
    Who are protectors of God's creation,
    and Messengers of God.
The Redeemed of Yahweh are:
    The People of God, consisting of
        Israel's faithful,
    The underclasses of society,
        The poor,
            And all the excluded from society:
                who are the disabled,
                      the persecuted,
                      and the abused.
    And people of faith drawn in from all the nations around the world.

This is certainly a cursory attempt to understand the Godhead and his relationship with humankind. I have expanded the Godhead to include a fourth element "The Wisdom of God," which is vitally important in Hebrew thinking. The Hebrew Bible includes several books which are considered "Wisdom Literature." They are Proverbs, Job, and Ecclesiastes (a.k.a.: Qoheleth, which is the Hebrew title of Ecclesiastes and the name of the primary speaker of the book). Two other books in the Apocrypha should also be included: Sirach (a.k.a. Ecclesiasticus, or Ben Sirach) and the Wisdom of Solomon. "Wisdom" in these books is often personified as though it is a female deity, and not just a philosophy. In fact, the Greek word for Wisdom is *Sophia* and is often referred to in feminine terms:

Part Two: Moving Beyond Christian Folk Religion

"she," "her," and "mother." This is especially so in the Wisdom of Solomon: "I called on God, and the spirit of wisdom came to me. I preferred her to scepters and thrones, and I accounted wealth as nothing in comparison with her ... All good things came to me along with her" (Wis 7:7–8, 11). I'm not exactly sure how all this fits with the traditional concept of the Trinity, but I'll leave that to others far more advanced than I am to debate. God is infinite, and, as I believe someone said before me, "I could not believe in a God I could understand."

It is curious, however, that the one title Jesus *did* claim for himself, "the Son of Man," is rarely a topic of discussion within Christian churches. Related to the title "Son of God," is the common discussion over Jesus' virgin birth, yet it too, as far as we know, was never a major issue with Jesus himself. Only Matthew and Luke mention it. John says in 1:14 that "the word became flesh," but does not even broach the subject of how that occurred. Mark begins his gospel with the simple message that it is "the beginning of the good news of Jesus Christ, the Son of God," and then begins with John the Baptizer preparing the way for him. Not one word is said about Jesus' beginnings. The story of the virgin birth appears nowhere else in the New Testament, and even the Apostle Paul, who uses the title "Son of God" throughout his writings, never even hints that he was ever aware that such a miraculous birth ever took place. Paul just simply says that "Christ Jesus,

> who, though he was in the form of God,
> did not regard equality with God as something to be exploited,
> but emptied himself,
> being born in human likeness.
> And being found in human form,
> he humbled himself
> and became obedient to the point of death –
> even death on a cross. (Phil 2:5–8)

The only conclusion we can make from such massive omissions is that while several sources knew the stories of Jesus' miraculous birth, it was not widely known, and of little, if any, concern one way or another to the writers of the New Testament. But through the centuries it has been a major topic of concern within the church, highly visible in its creeds, and dogma.

The basic message of the gospels is that Jesus came onto the scene in about AD 29 as the anointed "Son of Man" who had come to establish the everlasting kingdom of God "on earth as it is in heaven" (Matt 6:10). Jesus embodied within himself the "son of man" spoken of in Daniel 7:13, as God's heavenly high priest, who was sent into the world as God's ambassador to inaugurate his kingdom. Jesus began the process of teaching the world about that kingdom, what it was like, where it is, how someone becomes a member of it, how we stay members, and what its future holds. He spoke of how that kingdom would grow, "like a mustard seed," "the smallest of all seeds, but when it has grown it is the greatest of shrubs" (Matt 13:31–32; Mark 4:30–32; Luke 13:18–19). He demonstrated that the kingdom would require a renewal of the earth, its people, its values, and its ways of life. The demonstration of that renewal was shown through healing miracles, raising the dead, exorcizing demons of mental distress and illness, and of evil spirits. Jesus told John the Baptizer's disciples to report to John about the progress of starting the kingdom, and the proof of that was that "the blind receive their sight, the lame walk, the lepers are cleansed, the deaf hear, the dead are raised, and the poor have good news brought to them" (Matt 11:5–6). It was a status report on how the kingdom was already beginning.

His parables were Jesus' primary teaching method, although often punctuated with riddles, they were outlining a description of the kingdom, its peculiar sets of values, where "the first shall be last, and the last shall be first," (Matt 19:30; 20:16; Mark 10:31; Luke 13:30) and where God's "ways are higher than your ways" (Isa 55:9). This last point he emphasized in his parable on humility and hospitality when he advised,

> When you are invited by someone to a wedding banquet, do not sit down at the place of honor, in case someone more distinguished than you has been invited . . . but when you are invited, go and sit down at the lowest place, so that when your host comes, he may say to you, "Friend, move up higher"; then you will be honored in the presence of all who sit at the table with you. For all who exalt themselves will be humbled, and those who humble themselves will be exalted. (Luke 14:7–11).

Everywhere Jesus looked he saw the disparity between the classes, and he was touched beyond anything else by the humbled of mankind. The poorest of the poor were those he treasured most. He made it clear that the poorest of the poor would not be that way in the kingdom of God. In fact, it will be exactly the opposite. That theme runs throughout his teaching and is no better illustrated in his parable of the rich man and Lazarus. Read again Jesus' parable about Lazarus, the beggar in Abraham's protection, while the rich man is in torment (Luke 16:19–31). When the rich man complained about his torment, "Abraham said, 'Child, remember that during your lifetime you received your good things, and Lazarus in like manner evil things, but now he is comforted here, and you are in agony" (v. 25). The issue here is not one of the "good" versus the "bad," but God's inherent goodness, grace, and mercy. One time a rich young man came to Jesus and asked him, "Good Teacher, what must I do to inherit eternal life," and Jesus answered him, "Why do you call me good? No one is good but God alone" (Matt 17:16–17; Mark 10:17–28). The rich man was then told that he must be willing to take all his wealth and give it to the poor, and the rich man "went away grieving" because what he *had* far exceeded what he thought would be his reward for being "good," (v. 22) and it was a price he was not willing to pay. It is for that reason Jesus concluded the story to his disciples by saying, "It will be hard for those who have wealth to enter the kingdom of God! It is easier for a camel to go through the eye of a needle than for someone who is rich to enter the kingdom of God" (vv. 24–25). The disciples were so shocked by what they heard they began to discuss among themselves about who, then, "can be saved?" (v. 26). The answer to that by Jesus comes straight from the logic of God himself, "For mortals, it is impossible, but not for God, for God all things are possible" (v. 27).

The story doesn't actually end there because Peter then queries Jesus by telling him,

> "Look, we have left everything and followed you." Jesus said, "Truly I tell you, there is no one who has left house or brothers or sisters or mother or father or children or fields, for my sake and for the sake of the good news, who will not receive a hundredfold now in this age–houses, brothers and sisters, mothers and children, and fields, with persecutions–and in the age to come eternal life. But many who are first will be last and the last will be first." (Mark 10:28–31).

This is a hard prescription for entrance into the kingdom of God. Desire for entrance requires a total denial of everything we value most, even our kith and kin, including mother and children, brothers and sisters, and even life itself through persecutions. That catalogue of heart wrenching realities was not theoretical for Jesus. When he began his ministry he walked away from his own family business as builder of houses and towns, and moved away from Nazareth to Capernaum. He gave up his family relations for the sake of his own ministry. Even when they came to him in Capernaum and called him from outside, begging him to return home, and

A Few Parting Observations

the crowd around him passed the message onto him, telling him, "Your mother and your brothers and sisters are outside asking for you." And he replied by asking this curt question, "Who are my mother and my brothers? . . . Here are my mother and my brothers! Whoever does the will of God is my brother and sister and mother" (Mark 3:33–34). His separation from his family was so complete his family went out and tried to restrain Jesus because "people were saying, 'He has gone out of his mind'" (Mark 3:21) and John says that "not even his brothers believed in him" (7:5). This is total denial of self, which he declares again elsewhere,

> If any want to become my followers, let them deny themselves and take up their cross and follow me. For those who want to save their life will lose it, and those who lose their life for my sake will find it. For what will it profit them if they gain the whole world but forfeit their life? Or what will they give in return for their life? For the Son of Man is to come with his angels in the glory of his Father, and then he will repay everyone for what has been done. Truly I tell you, there are some standing here who will not taste death before they see the Son of Man coming in his kingdom." (Matt 24– 28)

This, again, is the riddle of the ages. Save your life and you will lose it, and lose your life and you will find it. And here he links the kingdom with the cross together. That linkage is beautifully described by Wright in *How God Became King*.[1] As Wright begins the chapter, "Kingdom and Cross: *The Remaking of Meanings*," he says that "there was never a kingdom message without a cross, and Jesus's crucifixion never carried a meaning divorced from launching God's kingdom."[2]

The cross and kingdom were always foremost in Jesus' thinking. "Pick up your cross and follow me" he essentially says above to his would-be followers, and then reminds them that "there are some standing here who will not taste death before they see the Son of Man coming in his kingdom." Kingdom and cross! It is one theme, as Wright points out,[3] and Jesus moved steadily toward that end (Luke 9:51). And it was there, on the cross, where his most profound glory and victory was seen. "It is finished," he said as he died. Yes, everything was now complete. Everything he had come to do he had done. The kingdom had come as

---

1. *Op cit*, 211–49.
2. Ibid., 211.
3. Ibid., 213.

Part Two: Moving Beyond Christian Folk Religion

a "mustard seed" and was beginning to take root. He had shown that through his miracles, and through his teaching he had described it, and told how we can become members of it, and can stay members of it, and he even described how it will be in "the age to come." In many ways it is totally different from what we might have expected, but that's the way it is. The last may be first, but that's the way it is. Israel is included, but that's the way it is. It is that way because God, in his wisdom, and in his love for this world and everything in it, has decreed that that's just the way it is. It is the supreme example of God's grace, his mercy, and his loving kindness. And we too are invited to enter that kingdom, described as a great banquet hall, where the doors are flung open to all the downtrodden, the forgotten, the abused, the persecuted, and even us! That is *the* good news!

Bibliography

Allison, Dale C. Jr. 2010. "Kingdom of God." In *EDEJ* 860–61.
Beckstrom, Edward A. "The Mystery of Jesus Teaching about The Son of Man." *BTB* 2 (2012): 70–80.
Burton, Pierre. *The Comfortable Pew: A Critical Look at Christianity and the Religious Establishment in the New Age*. Philadelphia: J.P. Lippincott, 1965.
Birch, Nicholas. "7,000 Years Older than Stonehenge: The Site that Stunned Archaeologists." The *Guardian*. April 22, 2008.
Bonhoeffer, Dietrich. *The Cost of Discipleship*. Reprinted by London: SCM Press, 1948/2001.
———. *Letters and Papers from Prison*. London: SCM Press, 1953.
Burridge, Richard A. *What Are The Gospels? A Comparison with Graeco-Roman Biography*. 2nd Ed. Grand Rapids, Michigan: William B. Eerdmans Publishing Co., 2004.
Casey, Maurice. *Solution to the Son of Man Problem*. Library of New Testament Studies. New York: T&T Clark International, 2009. See also the extensive bibliography of the Son of Man literature used as primary sources by Casey, 325–38.
Charles, R.H. *The Apocrypha & Pseudepigrapha of the Old Testament*. Oxford: The Clarendon Press, 1906.
Charlesworth, James H. 1985. *The Old Testament Pseudepigrapha*. Matrix: Apocalyptic Literature and Testaments 1. Garden City, N.Y.: Doubleday.
———. Ed. *Jesus and the Dead Sea Scrolls: The Controversy Resolved*. New York: Doubleday, 1992.
Collins, John J. and Daniel C. Harlow, eds. 2010. *The Eerdmans Dictionary of Early Judaism*. Grand Rapids, Michigan: William B. Eerdmans Publishing Co.
Fletcher, Crispin H.T. 1997. "The High Priest as Divine Mediator in the Hebrew Bible: Dan 7:13 as a Test Case." *SBL Seminar Paper*. 1997. 161–75.
Ehrman, Bart D. *Lost Scriptures: Books that Did Not Make It into the New Testament*. New York: Oxford University Press. 2003.
———. *Peter, Paul, & Mary Magdalene: The Followers of Jesus in History and Legend*. New York: Oxford University Press. 2006.
Eshel, Hanan. *The Dead Sea Scrolls and the Hasmonean State*. Grand Rapids, Michigan: William B. Eerdmans Publishing Co., 2008.
Fairchild, Mark R. "Turkeys Unexcavated Synagogues: Could the worlds earliest known synagogue be buried amid rubble?" *BAR* 4 (2012): 34–41, 65.

Bibliography

Freedman, David Noel, editor. *Eerdmans Dictionary of the Bible*. Grand Rapids: Michigan: William B. Eerdmans Publishing Co. 2000.

Garcia, José Miguel. "Jesus and the Meaning of the Parables." 2008. Online at http://www.traces-cl.com/2008E/01/jesusandthe.html.

Georges, Robert A., Michael Owens Jones. *Folkloristics: An Introduction*. Bloomington, IN: Indiana University Press. 1995.

Halliday, William R. "Folklore." In *EB*. 9: 446. Chicago, 1958.

Harris, Erdman. *God's Image and Man's Imagination*. New York: Charles Scribners & Sons, 1959.

Hays, Richard B. *The Faith of Jesus Christ: The Narrative Substructure of Galatians 3:1–4:11*. Second edition, Dearborn, Michigan: William B. Eerdmans Publishing Company, 2002.

Hogan, Karina Martin. "Ezra, Fourth Book of". In *EDEJ*. 623–26.

Horn, Siegried H., revised by P. Kyle McCarter, Jr. "The Divided Monarchy: The Kingdoms of Judah and Israel." In *Ancient Israel: From Abraham to the Roman Destruction of the Temple*, 129–99. Revised & Expanded, edited by Hershel Shanks. Washington D.C.: Biblical Archaeology Society and Prentice Hall. 1999

Josephus, Flavius. *The Jewish War*. Translated by G. A. Williamson. Revised with a New Introduction, notes and Appendixes, by E. Mary Smallwood. London: Penguin Books, 1981.

Knowles, Brian. "The Hebrew Mind vs. The Western Mind." Online: www.godward.org/Hebrew Roots/hebrew_mind_vs_western_mind.

Lightfoot, J.B. 1889–1890. *The Apostolic Fathers*, Part 2, Vol. 1. 2nd Ed. London: Macmillan.

Lindars, Barbara. "Re-enter the Apocalyptic Son of Man." In *NTS*. 1975–6.

Lilley, J.P.U. "Understanding the Herem." *TB* 1 (1993): 169–77.

Magdalene, F. Rachel. "Bless, Blessing." *In EDB*. 192.

Magness, Jodi. *The Archaeology of Qumran and the Dead Sea Scrolls*. Grand Rapids, Michigan: William B. Eerdmans Publishing Company, 2002.

Mails, Thomas E. *The Mystic Warriors of the Plains*. New York: Barnes & Noble, 1991.

Mason, Steve. "Pharisees". In *EDB*. 1043–44.

Metaxas, Eric. *Bonhoeffer, Pastor, Martyr, Prophet, Spy: The Righteous Gentile vs. The Third Reich*. Nashville: Thomas Nelson, 2010.

Meyer, Ben F. *The Aims of Jesus*. London: S.C.M., 1979 reprinted with Introduction by N.T. Wright under imprint of Eugene, OR: Pickwick Publications, 2002.

Muir, John. Introduction by Bill McKibby. *The Mountains of California*. New York: The Modern Library, 2001. Originally published without the Introduction: New York: Century Co., 1894.

Murphy-O'Connor, Jerome. "Why Jesus Went Back to Galilee." *The Galilee Jesus Knew*. E-Book, *BAS*. 2008.

"Pharisees." http://en.wikipedia.org/wiki/Pharisees. 2012.

Qimron, E. and J. Strugnell. "Qumran Cave 4 V Miqsat Maase Ha-Torah." In *DJD* 10. Oxford: Clarendon Press, 1994.

Robinson, James M., General Editor. *The Nag Hammadi Library: The Definitive Translation of the Gnostic Scriptures Complete in One Volume*. San Francisco: HarperSanFrancisco. 1988.

Robinson, John A.T. *Honest to God*. Philadelphia: Westminster Press, 1963.

———. *Redating the New Testament*. Eugene, Oregon: Wipf and Stock Publishers, 2000.

Rubenstein, James. *The Cultural Landscape: An Introduction to Human Geography*. (10th Edition). New York: Prentice Hall, 2010.

Saldarini, Anthony J. *Pharisees, Scribes and Sadducees in Palestinian Society: A Sociological Approach*. Grand Rapids, Michigan: William B. Eerdmans Publishing Company, 2001.

Sanders, E. P. *Paul and Palestinian Judaism: A Comparison of Patterns of Religion*. Minneapolis: Fortress Press, 1977.

———. *Jesus and Judaism*. Minneapolis: Fortress Press, 1985.

———. *The Historical Figure of Jesus*. London: Penguin Books, 1993.

Schnelle, Udo. *Apostle Paul: His Life and Theology*. Grand Rapids, Michigan: Baker Academic, 2005. Translated by M. Eugene Boring from the German: *Paulus: Leben und Denken*. Berlin: Walter de Gruyter GmbH & Co., 2003.

Schoeps, H. J. *Paul: The Theology of the Apostle in the Light of Jewish Religious History*. Philadelphia: The Westminster Press, 1961. Translated by Harold Knight from the German and revised by the author for this English edition. Translation of *Paulus: Die Theologie des Apostels im Lichte der jüdischen Religionsgeschichte*. Tübingen: J.C.B. Mohr, 1959.

Shanks, Hershel. *Jerusalem's Temple Mount: From Solomon to the Golden Dome*. New York: The Continuum International Publishing Group Inc, 2007.

———. Ed. *Where Christianity Was Born*. Washington, D.C.: BAS. 2006.

———. Ed. *Understanding the Dead Sea Scrolls: A Reader from the Biblical Archaeology Review*. New York: Vintage Books, A Division of Random House, Inc., 1992.

———. Ed. *Ancient Israel: From Abraham to the Roman Destruction of the Temple*, Revised & Expanded. Washington D.C.: Biblical Archaeology Society and Prentice Hall. 1999.

Sheeley, Steven M. 2000. "Kingdom of God, Kingdom of Heaven". 767–68 In *EDB*.

Schiffman, Lawrence. *Reclaiming the Dead Sea Scrolls*. Philadelphia and Jerusalem: Jewish Publication Society, 1994.

Strange, James F. and Hershel Shanks, "Where Jesus Stayed in Capernaum." In *Where Christianity was Born*. Edited by Hershel Shanks. Washington, D.C.: Biblical Archaeology Society, 2006. 66–78.

Taylor, Joan E., "The Garden of Gethsemane." In *Where Christianity was Born*. 116–27.

VanderKam, James C. *The Dead Sea Scrolls Today*. Grand Rapids: Michigan, 1994.

———. and Peter Flint. *The Meaning of the Dead Sea Scrolls: Their Significance for Understanding the Bible, Judaism, Jesus and Christianity*. San Francisco: HarperSanFrancisco, 2004.

Vermes, Geza. *Jesus the Jew: A Historians Reading of the Gospels*. Minneapolis: Fortress Press, 1981.

———. *The Religion of Jesus the Jew*. Minneapolis: Fortress Press, 1993.

———. *Jesus in His Jewish Context*. Minneapolis: Fortress Press, 2003.

———. *The Complete Dead Sea Scrolls in English*. New York: Penguin Books, 2004.

———. "From Jewish to Gentile: How the Jesus Movement Became Christianity." *BAR*. 6. (2012). 53–58, 74.

Wenham, John. *Redating Matthew, Mark & Luke: A Fresh Assault on the Synoptic Problem*. Downers Grove, Illinois: InterVarsity Press, 1992.

Bibliography

Wilson, Mark. *Biblical Turkey: A Guide to the Jewish and Christian Sites of Asia Minor.* Istanbul: Ege Yayinlari, 2010.

World Christian Data Base. Center for the Study of Global Christianity, Gordon-Conwell Theological Seminary. Online: www.worldchristiandatabase.org/wcd/about/denominations.asp

Wright, N.T. *Christian Origins and the Question of God.* 3 vols. Minneapolis: Fortress Press., 1992–2003:

―――. 1992. *The New Testament and the People of God.* Vol. 1.

―――. 1996. *Jesus and the Victory of God.* Vol. 2.

―――. 2003. *The Resurrection of the Son of God.* Vol. 3.

―――. *What Saint Paul Really Said: Was Paul of Tarsus the Real Founder of Christianity?* Grand Rapids, Mich.: William B. Eerdmans Publishing Co., 1997.

―――. *Paul: In Fresh Perspective.* Minneapolis: Fortress Press, 2005.

―――. *Simply Jesus: A New Vision of Who He Was, What He Did, and Why He Matters.* New York: HarperOne, 2011.

―――. *How God Became King: The Forgotten Story of the Gospels.* New York: HarperOne, 2012.

Ancient Document Index

HEBREW BIBLE/OLD TESTAMENT

Genesis

1:28	148
1:31	52
3:5	20
8:21	92
10:10	121
11:31	54
12:1–4	146

Exodus

3:6	15, 16, 146
3:14	57
4:5	146
6:3	57
6:12	94
7	98
12:29	192
14:5–15	12
14:19	110
15:3	27
16:10	110
16:33–34	67
18:12	143
19:16	110
24:11	143
24:15	110
25:10–22	67
25:20	22, 67
26:34	67
30:6	67
31:11	68
32:3–4	60
39:1–31	111
40:3	5, 211
40:34	35, 109

Leviticus

16:2	110
17:7	21

Numbers

7:89	67
9:15	110
10:33	67
10:34–35	211
15:37–40	189
17:1–11	67
19:2	38
21:2–3	27
32:33	121

Deuteronomy

6:4	15, 60, 189
6:4–9	189
6:13	94
9:27	146
10:8	67
11:13–21	189

Ancient Document Index

Deuteronomy *(cont.)*

20:17–18	27
26:15	192
32:17	21

Joshua

6:6	67

Judges

8:21	26, 60

1 Samuel

3:3	67
4:3–4	110, 211
4:21	109
8:4–9	122
10–18	122
10:11–17	27, 122
13:7–14	124
15:28	121
24:20	121
31:1–13	124

2 Samuel

1:1–10	124
2:1–7	124
5:1–5	124
6:1–7	212
6:8–19	212
6:17	212

1 Kings

2:12	121
3:15	143
6:23–29	108
7:29	108
8:10	110
8:11	109
18:36	146
19:9–12	185

2 Kings

23:31	122
24:18	122
17	125
24–25	125

1 Chronicles, 121

10:14	121
28:5	121
29:18	146

Ezra

13:25	37, 107

Job

19:25–27	22
42:12	192

Psalms

2:4–8	227
14:1	44
22	116, 128
53:1	44
68:10	150
69:30	33, 150
82	152
107:1	39–43, 150

Isaiah

3:18–21	60
6:5	94
7:14–15	23
11:1–5	23
12:2	57
19:1	110
24:23	133
25:8	159
26:4	57
29:13–14	91
33:22	133
40:3–5	96
42:1–4	9, 202
52:7–10	133
55:8–9	219
56:7	213

Jeremiah

1:6	95

Ancient Document Index

2:26–28	59
4:2	192
7:11	213
23:51	104
52:1	122

Ezekiel

6:3–5	8–9, 13, 14, 59
8:1—10:14	108
10:3–4	214
10:18–19	125
11:16–25	125
17:24	192
40–46	101
40:1–4	101
43:18	111

Daniel

2:4b—7:28	6
4:31–32	125
7:13	107–9, 237
8–12, 108	
9:24	108
10:5	111
12:11	71

Amos

5:21–24	196

Micah

5:2–4	23
6:6–8	198

Habakkuk

2:1–2	165

Zephaniah

3:14–20	134

Zechariah

3:8	104
6:12	104
9:9	209

APOCRYPHA

Wisdom of Solomon

7:7–8	11, 232

2 Maccabees

12:40	60

PSEUDEPIGRAPHA

1 Enoch (*Similitudes of Enoch*)

37–71, 119	
38:3	113
45:3	113
47:3	107
49:2–4	103
51:1–2	113
51:3	113
55:4	113
61:8	113
69:26	113

4 Ezra

13	102
13:3–4	32, 102

NEW TESTAMENT

Matthew

3:2	84
3:3	82, 84
3:5–6	83
3:7	xv
3:11–13	132
3:14	86, 95
3:15	95
4:3	93
4:4	93
4:5–6	94

Ancient Document Index

MATTHEW (cont.)

Reference	Page
4:12	154
4:17	128
4:23	155, 223
5–7	37
5:1–11	49
5:9	175
5:10	5
5:20	196
5:43	49, 160
5:48	86
6:2–6	199
6:9	134
6:10	121, 232
6:24	192
6:33	129
7:1	131
7:2	175
7:12	175
7:14	89
7:15	143
8:5	190
8:8	28
8:11	132
8:16	143
8:38—9:1	206
9:11	114
9:18–19	23–26, 179
9:21–22	189
9:30	203–4
10:1–4	126
10:5	75
10:6	228
10:7	128
10:13	154
10:28–30	203
10:41	228
11:2–3	132
11:4–6	132
11:11	85, 157
11:15	229
11:18	90, 196
11:18–19	196
11:25	200
11:28–30	179
12:1–8	203
12:9–21	177
12:24	229
12:25	154
12:34	xv
13:9	43, 229
13:10–12	157
13:22	192
13:31–32	233
13:55	4
13:57	154
14:1–12	84
14:5	228
14:13–21	6, 202
14:16–21	6
14:36	190
15:8–9	91
15:22–28	191
15:24	132
15:26	228
15:39	223
15:57	228
16:13–20	7
16:21	207
16:24–28	116
17:5	110
17:12	112
17:16–17	234
17:22–23	207
18:4	131
19:3	174
19:14–15	16
19:23–26	48
19:27–30	113
20:17–19	112
20:18	206
20:20–23	217
20:26–27	157
21:1–11	208
21:9	209
21:12–27	213
22:1–14	135, 143
22:16	162
22:21	222
22:35	181
22:36–40	198
23:11–31	194
23:12	156
23:13–29	xvi
23:2–5	xvi
24:1–27	108

24:2	214
24:30	107, 109, 159, 206, 216
25:31–46	113
26:6–13	152
26:26	113
26:29	135
26:36–46	127
26:47	163
26:64	109
26:65	115, 180
26:67–68	180
27:32	208
27:55	221
27:56	220
27:61	221
27:62	180
28:1	221
28:19–20	186

Mark

1:1	xvi
1:3	82, 84
1:4–5	83
1:15	128
1:32	143
1:35	199
1:39	223
1:40–45	204
2:16	24, 174
2:26–27	228
2:27–28	177
3:1–6	177
3:6	162
3:16	126, 143
3:18	183
3:21	235
3:22	229
3:27	140
3:31–34	89, 154
4:9	229
4:10	157
4:19	192
4:30–32	233
4:33–34	200
4:34	179
5:21–24	35–43, 179
5:25–34	189
5:34	6
6:1–6	229
6:4	228
6:15	228
6:17–29	84
6:30–44	6, 202
7:5	235
7:6	7, xvi
7:16	229
7:27	228
8:1–10	202
8:18	229
8:27–33	7
8:34	xvii, 88
9:1	113, 218
9:2–13	127
9:9	100
9:26–27	113
10:2	174
10:15	131
10:17–28	234
10:23	131
10:24–25	48
10:31	157, 233
10:33	206–7
10:35–40	217
10:43–44	157
11:1–10	208
11:15	213
12:13	162
12:17	222
12:18	167
12:29–31	49
13:1–27	108
13:14	71, 216
13:26	107, 109, 206
14:3–9	152
14:32	200
14:43	163
14:47	201
14:62	206
15:2	114
15:27	217
15:40	221
15:41	220
16:1	221
16:9	144, 224
16:16	xvii, 47

Ancient Document Index

Luke

1:38	209
1:53	192
1:76	228
2:14	29
2:41–51	73, 173
3:1–18	83
3:4	82, 84
3:22	92
3:23	4
4:9–12	178
4:15	223
4:16–30	154
4:22	4
4:24	228
5:12–15	204
5:16	200
6:2	174
6:6–11	177
6:14–16	126
6:20–26	xv, 49, 192
6:22–23	135
6:37	131
6:38	193
7:16	228
7:28	85
7:30	181
7:33	90
7:36–50	144, 173
8:1–3	127, 200
8:14	192
8:31	207
8:33	143
8:40–42	179
9:7–9	84
9:10–17	6, 202
9:18–22	7
9:23	xvii, 88
9:26–27	113
9:51	235
9:52	42
10:9	128
10:11	128
10:21–24	200
10:25	181
10:27	198
11:15	229
11:52	156
12:22–28	141
13:4	208
13:10–17	177
13:18–19	233
13:30	151, 154, 157, 233
13:33	207
14:1–24	176
14:7–11	233
14:15–24	135
14:17	21, 23, 135, 144
14:35	229
15:1	143
16:1–9	xiv
16:19–31	xiv, 48, 151, 233
17:21	128
18:9–14	196
18:17	131
19:7	143
19:28–38	208
19:39	173, 175
20:25	222
21:5–28	108
22:32	200
23:3	114
24:7	100
24:10	221

John

1:1–2	43
1:14	232
1:23	82, 84
1:24–28	83
1:35–42	44
1:43–51	126
1:45	4
1:49	210
2:3	126
2:13–22	42
3:1–2	173
3:16	xv, 47
3:24	112
4:19	228
4:44	228
5:1–16	204
5:2–18	177
6:1–13	6, 202
6:14	228
6:15	207

6:42	4	12:2	74, 219
7:1–9	154	13:5	171
7:14–24	177	14:1	171
7:32	180	15	174
7:40–52	228	15:5	173
7:50	173	15:6	32
8:13	174	15:24	xiii
8:28	112	15:28	228
9:7–11	86, 208	17:1	10, 17, 171
9:13	174	18:10	19, 171
9:17	228	19:8	171
10:14–17	29	19:9	23, 89
11	221	22:3	173
11:1–44	178	22:4	174
11:45–55	178	23:6	136, 172
12:34	100	23:8	167
12:42	173	24:14	22, 89
13:34	198	26:5	172
14:5–6	88	26:11	174
14:6	xv		
14:22	126		
15:12	198		

Romans

1:16	134
2:9	10, 17, 133
3:28	118
5:1	35
7:7–11	22
8:35	91
9–11	35, 134
10:12	133
11:4	191
11:8	65
11:17–21	38
11:18	39
11:19–27	39
11:26	xx, 40
16:22	181

17:4	96
17:11	188
17:20–21	62
18:3	162
18:10	201
18:15	174
18:36	158
18:38	41
19:14–15	210
19:25	221
19:26	200
19:30	96
19:38–42	173
20:11–18	224
21:2	126
21:20–23	43

Acts

1:13	126, 183
2:46	32
4:32—35:11	84
5:17	163
7:56	100
8	189
9:2	89
11:26	32

1 Corinthians

1:12–13	20
1:17	159
1:25	93, 159
1:27–29	219
7:18	xiii
8:4	41
9:20	172
10:19–21	41
11:23–26	113

247

1 Corinthians (cont.)

15:9	174
15:54-55	159
16:21	181

2 Corinthians

12:7-8	181

Galatians

1:6-9	xiv
1:23	174
2:3	12, xiii
3:6	9, 147
3:28	133
6:11	181
6:12-13	xiii

Philippians

2:5-8	232
3:5-6	136, 172
4:7	xvi-xvii

Colossians

3:11	35
4:18	181

1 Thessalonians

4:13-18	52

2 Thessalonians

2:1-2	30
3:17	181

1 Timothy

5:17	187

Hebrews

1:1-3	112
2:6	100
2:17-18	112
4:14	111
5:5	10, 111
6:20	111

9:2-3	67
11:1	12
11:8	147

James

2:23	147

1 Peter

4:14	67

1 John

4:16	91

Revelation

1:7	109
1:8	43
1:11	46
1:12-16	108
1:12—3:21	113
1:13	100
3:1-2	171
4:4	111
9:7	111
11:12	110
14:14-16	100
17:4	111
18:16	111
20-22	103
21:1-6a	130
21:6	43
21:18-21	111
22:13	43

DEAD SEA SCROLLS

Blessings (1Q28b)

105, 107

Community Rule (1QS)

105, 160

Damascus Document (CD)
105, 161

EARLY CHRISTIAN WRITINGS

Barnabas, Letter of
4:6–8   37–38

Didache
1:1   37
11:1–4   37

Ignatius (*Letter to Ephesians*)
Chapter 7   98

Thomas, Gospel of
v. 114, 222

Subject Index

Apostle Paul
   Saul of Tarsus, 174, 176
   Judaizers, xvii
Apostles Creed, 19, 128
Aramaic, 4–7, 99–102, 116, 121, 157, 179, 223
Aristotle, 41
Asia Minor, 26, 32–34, 54, 58, 60–61, 145, 171–72, 208
Assyria, 55, 58, 228
Athanasian Creed, 19, 65, 230

Bonhoeffer, Dietrich, 88, 116, 137

Capernaum
   Peter's house, 155
Catholic Bible, 16
Charem, 27
Christian Folk Religion, 1, 4–30, 32, 34, 36, 38, 40, 42, 44, 46, 48, 50, 52, 54, 56, 58, 60, 62, 64, 66, 68, 70, 72, 74, 76, 79, 82, 84, 86, 88, 90, 92, 94, 96, 98, 100, 102, 104, 106, 108, 110, 112, 114, 116, 118, 120, 122, 124, 126, 128, 130, 132, 134, 136, 138, 140, 142, 144, 146, 148, 150, 152, 154, 156, 158, 162, 164, 166, 168, 170, 172, 174, 176, 178, 180, 182, 184, 186, 188, 190, 192, 194, 196, 198, 200, 202, 204, 208, 210, 212, 214, 216, 218, 220, 222, 224, 226, 228, 230, 232, 234
Common people, 16, 56, 143, 168, 170–171, 176, 228

Covenant, xiii, xix-xx, 35–39, 48–49, 67, 109–10, 115, 125, 169, 182, 185, 191–92, 211–12
Cross and Kingdom, 235

Denominations, xvii, 20, 62–64, 135, 187–88
Deuterocanonical Books, 16

Eastern Logic, 46
Einstein, Albert, 139
End of days/Time, 108, 116, 118, 132, 164, 215–16
End of the World, 25–26, 43
Epicurus, 41
Essene, 165, 183
Eucharist, 19, 37, 64, 113

First Jewish Revolt
   Sicarii, 72–73, 75, 183
   Zealots, 72, 75, 183
First shall be last and the last shall be first, 158, 192
Folk Culture, 8–10, 13
Folklore, 8–9, 12–13

Galilee, 39, 71–73, 75, 126, 154–55, 171, 178–79, 190, 202, 206, 208, 223, 229
Gentile Christian church, xvii, 36
Gnosticism, 158, 222
Göbekli Tepe, 45, 52
Greco-Roman, 40–41, 43, 60, 168–69, 225–26
Greek Philosophy, 40–41

251

Subject Index

Hasmonean, 71, 83, 161–65, 168–69, 213, 216
Healing, 6, 68, 87, 91, 96, 115, 134, 139, 145, 177–79, 190, 202–5, 233
Heaven, xiv-xvi, xix, 5, 15–16, 25–26, 29, 34–35, 47–48, 65–66, 68–69, 84–85, 91–92, 102–3, 108, 110, 113, 115–16, 120–121, 125, 128–32, 134–36, 145, 149, 156–57, 159, 167, 186–88, 190, 192–94, 196–97, 200, 202, 204, 206, 209–10, 212, 214–15, 222, 225–26, 229, 232
Hebrew Bible
  Ketuvim, 10, 18
  Nevi'im, 10, 18
  Septuagint, xiii, 16–17, 161
  Tanakh, 10, 18, 62, 169
  Torah, xiii, 5, 10, 18, 33, 62, 77, 86, 90, 102, 134, 166, 169–70, 173, 176, 181, 188
Hebrew Mind, 44, 230
Hebrew Scriptures
  Apocrypha, 16–17, 71, 125, 231
Hellenistic, xiii, 33, 161
Hellenization, 31, 33, 35, 37, 39, 41, 43, 45, 47, 49
Heresies
  Docetism, 226
  Nestorianism, 226
Holiness Code, 21, 38, 48
Holocaust, 26, 38, 61, 147–48, 194–95

Interpretation, 41, 43, 47, 66, 98, 131, 154, 161, 163–66, 175–76, 181, 218

James, brother of Jesus, 70, 74, 163
Jerusalem church, xiii, xvii, 5, 20, 31, 70, 74, 76, 163, 173–75
Jerusalem temple
  Cleansing of the temple, 71, 215
  Court of the Gentiles, 28, 44
  High Priest, 17, 56–58, 67–68, 73, 83, 108, 110–112, 114–16, 118, 163–65, 168–69, 180, 188, 207, 210, 213, 215, 218, 230–231, 233

Holy of Holies, 21, 56, 67–68, 82, 108–11, 168, 194, 210
Glory of Yahweh, 109–10, 125, 213–14
God's glory, 68, 112, 150, 214
Holy Place, 67–68, 82, 108, 110–112
House of God, 66, 169, 207, 210, 213–14
Maccabean Revolt, 71
Temple, 4, 17, 21–22, 24, 28, 31, 36, 38, 42, 44–45, 53–54, 56–57, 60, 66–71, 73–76, 81–84, 86, 93, 101, 108–12, 115, 122, 125, 136–37, 145, 150, 162–64, 168–73, 177–80, 188–90, 194, 196, 203–5, 207–17, 224, 229
Throne of God, 109, 111, 115, 194
Jesus
  Mary Magdalene, 126, 144, 155, 200, 220–224
  Messiah, 4–5, 7, 21, 23, 31, 34–35, 38, 40, 42, 48, 62, 64, 76, 88, 94, 96, 99, 103–7, 112, 114, 116, 118, 132, 135, 138, 147, 151, 154, 178, 180, 188, 210, 218, 224, 230–231
  Miracles, 65, 85, 95, 114, 128, 134, 139, 143, 158, 177–79, 204–5, 229, 233
  Piety, 90–91, 95–96, 131, 136–38, 143, 173, 181, 184–91, 193, 195–99, 201, 203, 205, 209, 213
  Prayers, 107, 187, 199–200, 202, 214
  Priest Messiah, 104–5, 107, 114, 116, 118, 210
  Quiet Piety, 96, 187, 189, 191, 193, 195, 197, 199, 201, 203, 205
  Raising the dead, 151, 179, 233
  Resurrection, xv, xxi, 21, 31, 34, 36, 38, 42, 63, 85, 96, 117, 126, 128, 155, 158–59, 167, 170, 180, 216, 220, 224, 226
  Sermon on the Mount, 37, 49, 160, 196, 199
  Son of God, xvi, xxi, 5, 9, 25, 42, 92–94, 97–99, 128, 230–232
  Virgin Birth, 225, 232
  Yeshua, 4, 38, 40, 231
Jew and Greek, 36

Subject Index

Jewish Revolt, 11, 36, 66
John the Baptist, see John the Baptizer
John the Baptizer, 7, 24–25, 82, 85, 157
Josephus, 32, 72–73, 75, 160–161, 163, 167–68, 171, 183, 208, 212

Kingdom of God/heaven, 113, 121, 128, 214–15

Logic, xiv, 33, 45–46, 85, 93, 138–40, 148, 150–151, 154, 156, 158–59, 192–93, 225–27, 234

Mary, Jesus' mother, 81, 126
Messianics, 4–5, 38–40
Muir, John, 51

Near East, 5–6, 33, 47, 54, 59, 67, 70, 101
Nicene Creed, 19, 65, 128, 227, 230

Opponents of Jesus
    Pharisees, xv-xvi, 17, 32, 73, 90, 131, 136, 143–44, 160–163, 166–76, 179–81, 183–84, 188, 193–96, 202–4, 209, 229
    Hillel the Elder, 174–75
    Sabbath, 21, 31, 161–62, 170, 174, 176–77, 184, 202–3, 208, 228–29
    Sinners, 25, 38, 103, 113, 143–44, 154, 156, 174–76, 196, 203, 229
    Shammai the Elder, 174–75
    Sadducees, 17, 160, 162–64, 166–70, 178, 180–181, 183, 188, 203, 209, 213, 215
    Sanhedrin, 115, 162, 175, 180–181
    Scribes, xv-xvi, 10, 90, 136, 144, 162–63, 176, 181–82, 188, 193–94, 196, 203, 209, 215

Parables/Riddles, xiv, 7, 77, 85, 95, 151, 157, 200, 228–29, 233
Pascal, 55
Passover, 4, 13, 31, 38, 71, 73, 86, 154, 200–201, 208–9, 229
Peasants, 72, 93, 203

People of God, xxi, 4, 21, 35, 46, 49, 61–64, 70, 115, 123, 129, 153, 191, 207, 214, 225, 231
Plato, 41, 47, 174
Pontius Pilate, 31, 41, 65, 71, 128
Poor, xiv, 3, 23, 28, 48–49, 93–94, 132, 135, 137, 141–42, 144, 148–49, 151, 153–56, 175, 191, 204, 213, 231, 233–34
Protestant Bible, 16, 18
Purification Baths
    Miqva'ot, 83, 86, 208

Qumran, 11, 83–84, 89, 105, 118, 160, 165–67

Rabbinic Movement, 17
Renewal, 43, 62, 68, 85, 87, 90–92, 95, 108, 116, 125, 127, 130, 134–35, 151, 177, 204, 215, 226, 233

Salvation, xix-xx, 24, 34, 39, 46–49, 59, 85, 87–88, 90, 96, 128, 133–35, 156, 225, 227
Second Coming of Christ
    Parousia, 206, 215–17, 225
Second Temple Period, 66
Seleucid, 70, 216
Son of Man
    Daniel 7:1368, 99–101, 113, 116, 218, 233
    God's Will, 26, 116, 129
    Heavenly High Priest, 108, 111, 114–15, 118, 169, 180, 207, 210, 213, 218, 230–231, 233
Status, xvii, 3, 19, 32, 36, 46, 49, 73, 85, 149, 153, 166–68, 196–97, 222, 233
Stoicism, 41
Synagogue, 6, 40, 61, 75, 171–73, 178–79, 202, 223, 229
Synoptics, 42, 109

Tabernacle, 21, 66, 68–69, 109, 115, 118, 211
The Way, xiv-xv, xix, 18, 24, 31, 44, 47, 55, 64, 66, 70, 73, 75, 77, 81, 84–85, 87–89, 91–92, 95–96, 105,

Subject Index

125, 132, 135, 137, 139, 146, 156, 168, 175, 186, 202, 212, 226, 232

Time and Space, xi, xvii-xviii, xxi, 5, 8, 10, 13–16, 23–25, 28–32, 34–35, 37, 40–44, 46, 51–52, 55,59, 62, 64–66, 68, 71–72, 74–75, 83–85, 88–89, 92, 94, 102, 104, 107, 116–17, 120, 123, 125, 129, 132, 134, 136–37, 140, 142–43, 152, 156, 162, 164–65, 171, 174, 176, 178, 183–84, 186–88, 191, 193, 195, 199–202, 205–6, 209–12, 215–16, 218, 220, 222–23, 225, 234

Trinity, 65, 128, 199, 230, 232

Underclasses of society, 48, 132, 138, 148–49, 151, 158, 192–93, 231

Upside down logic, 93, 151, 154, 193

Voltaire, 55

Western Mind, 44, 46, 228

Yahweh, 5, 15, 21, 23, 27–30, 44, 53, 55–63, 65–69, 71, 73, 75, 77, 82–83, 85, 90, 94–95, 101, 108–10, 112, 115, 121–25, 133–34, 136, 139, 145–50, 152, 154, 159, 185, 192, 195, 197–98, 207, 210–215, 219, 225–28, 230–231

YHWH, 56–57, 59

Zeno, 41

www.ingramcontent.com/pod-product-compliance
Lightning Source LLC
Chambersburg PA
CBHW050843230426
43667CB00012B/2121